SOCIAL IMPROVEMENT ECONOMY COST

JOHN LOK

Made with ♥ on the Notion Press Platform
www.notionpress.com

Contents

Preface

Introduction

In our societies , any kinds of products or services must need to apply demand and supply economic theory to analyze whether the kind of product or service may bc value to invent to sell or serve to their customers in consumer market, if the kind of product or service demand number is less, then it ought not to raise manufacturing number to avoid "low price " sale or if the kind of product demand number is more, then it ought raise manufacturing number to have enough number in order to raise " high price" sale to satisfy customers their needs to buy their products.However, whether your product or serive's demand number depends on supply number or your product or service's supply number depends on demand number in order to make ths sale price is reasonable high or low level and reasonable supply number valuation.

Our business society had developed long time from farming period to manufacturing period, then to service industry period, till to nowadays technology service and manufacturing period. It brings this question: Can technology or human behavior may influence economic development? Human ourselves foolish or enjoyment behavior whether which can bring economic recession? If human can forgive to do enjoyment behavior, we can help economic growth? Why do our social improvement need to spend more expenditure? I shall apply behavioral economic theory to indicate cases to attempt to explain whether our social improvement may bring what economy cost to let readers can understand.

Prologue

Contents

CHAPTER ONE

Explaining supply and demand economic theory relationship

The difference between past and nowadays economists their demand and supply economic theory explanation?

The law of supply and demand defines the relationship between the price of a given good or product and the willingness of people to either buy or sell it. Generally, as the price of a good increases, people are willing to supply more and demand less. These economists had explained economic demand and supply theory as below:

Philosopher John Locke is credited with one of the earliest written descriptions of this economic principle in his 1691 publication, Some Considerations of the Consequences of the Lowering of Interest and the Raising of the Value of Money. Locke addressed the concept of supply and demand as part of a discussion about interest rates in 17th-century England. Many merchants wanted the government to lower the cap on interest rates charged by private lenders so that people could borrow more money and thus purchase more goods. Locke argued that the free-market economy should set rates because government regulation could have unintended consequences. If the lending industry were left alone, interest rates would regulate themselves, Locke wrote: "The price of any commodity rises or falls by the proportion of the number of buyers and sellers."

Sir James Steuart's Inquiry into the Principles of Political Economy, published in 1796, was the first known printed use of the term "supply and demand." When Steuart wrote his treatise on political economy, one of his main concerns was the impact of supply and demand on laborers.

Adam Smith dealt extensively with the topic in his 1776 epic economic work, The Wealth of Nations. Often referred to as the Father of Economics, Smith explained the concept of supply and demand as an "invisible hand" that naturally guides the economy. According to Smith, the invisible hand is the automatic pricing and distribution mechanisms in the economy. Smith described a society in which bakers and butchers provide products that individuals need and want, providing a supply that meets demand and developing an economy that benefits everyone. It is important to note that Smith's ideas haven't gone without critique over the years since his ideas were first published, though. Over time, his ideas have been added to in order to represent the changing times and include concepts such as marginal utility, comparative advantage, entrepreneurship, the time-preference theory of interest, and monetary theory.

One of Marshall's most important contributions to microeconomics was his introduction of the concept of price elasticity of demand, which examines how price changes affect demand. In theory, people buy less of a particular product if the price increases, but Marshall noted that in real life, this behavior was not always true. The prices of some goods can increase without reducing demand, which means their prices are inelastic. Inelastic goods tend to include items such as medication or food that consumers deem crucial to daily life. Marshall argued that supply and demand, costs of production, and price elasticity all work together.

Nowadays economists they explain demand and supply economic theory, they have some different to past economists whose explanation as below:

How Does Supply and Demand Work? The law of supply and demand is a theory that explains the interaction between the sellers of a resource and the buyers of that resource. Generally, as price increases, people are willing to supply more and demand less and vice versa when the price falls. What does the bottom line mean. Despite the origins of the law of supply and demand beginning hundreds of years ago, it's still a topic frequently referenced and utilized today in economic theory and discussions. The theory has developed over time to accommodate recent technological and economical advancements, but the basic ideas of the theory remain largely the same.

Does demand depend on supply?

Supply and Demand Determine the Price of Goods and Quantities Produced and Consumed. Consumers may exhaust the available supply of a good by purchasing a given good or service at a high volume. This leads to an increase in demand. As demand increases, the available supply also decreases.

What does market demand depend on?

Market factors affecting demand of consumer goods. The demand for a good increases or decreases depending on several factors. This includes the product's price, perceived quality, advertising spend, consumer income, consumer confidence, and changes in taste and fashion.

Who controls the demand in supply and demand?

Supply and demand are in turn determined by technology and the conditions under which people operate. At one extreme, the market could be populated by a large number of virtually identical sellers and buyers (for example, the market for ballpoint pens).

What are the two laws of demand and supply?

The law of demand holds that the demand level for a product or a resource will decline as its price rises, and rise as the price drops. Conversely, the law of supply says higher prices boost supply of an economic good while lower ones tend to diminish it.

What factors affect demand and supply?

Price fluctuations are a strong factor affecting supply and demand. When a product gets expensive enough that the average consumer no longer feels it is worth it to buy the product, then the demand declines. This leads to cuts in production that will hopefully stabilize the product's value.

What factors affect demand and demand?

Demand may be defined as the quantity of a commodity that a consumer is able and willing to buy, at each possible price, over a given period of time. • Essential elements of demand are quantity, ability, willingness, prices, and period of time.

Which factors affect supply?

Generally, the supply of a product depends on its price and other variables such as the cost of production.

a. Price. Price can be understood as what the consumer is willing to pay to receive a good or service. ...

b. Cost of production. ...

c. Technology. ...

d. Governments' policies. ...

e. Transportation condition.

How does supply and demand work together?

It's a fundamental economic principle that when supply exceeds demand for a good or service, prices fall. When demand exceeds supply, prices tend to rise. There is an inverse relationship between the supply and prices of goods and services when demand is unchanged.

What happens to supply when demand increases?

An increase in demand, all other things unchanged, will cause the equilibrium price to rise; quantity supplied will increase. A decrease in demand will cause the equilibrium price to fall; quantity supplied will decrease.

What is the theory of demand?

Demand theory describes the way that changes in the quantity of a good or service demanded by consumers affects its price in the market, The theory states that the higher the price of a product is, all else equal, the less of it will be demanded, inferring a downward sloping demand curve.

What are the 4 basic laws of supply and demand?

1) If the supply increases and demand stays the same, the price will go down. 2) If the supply decreases and demand stays the same, the price will go up. 3) If the supply stays the same and demand increases, the price will go up. 4) If the supply stays the same and demand decreases, the price will go down.

The different types of demand are as follows:

i. Individual and Market Demand: ...

ii. Organization and Industry Demand: ...

iii. Autonomous and Derived Demand: ...

iv. Demand for Perishable and Durable Goods: ...

v. Short-term and Long-term Demand:

What creates demand for a product?

You can create demand for a unique product if you can manage to solve a persistent problem for the consumer. People are always running away from pain, and providing them with an outlet is a sure-fire way to create massive demand for your goods.

What are the 7 factors that affect supply?

The seven factors which affect the changes of supply are as follows: (i) Natural Conditions (ii) Technical Progress (iii) Change in Factor Prices (iv) Transport Improvements (v) Calamities (vi) Monopolies (vii) Fiscal Policy.

What can affect demand?

Factors Affecting Demand

Price of the Product. ...

The Consumer's Income. ...

The Price of Related Goods. ...
The Tastes and Preferences of Consumers. ...
The Consumer's Expectations. ...
The Number of Consumers in the Market.
What are the three factors affecting demand?
The demand for a product will be influenced by several factors:

Price. Usually viewed as the most important factor that affects demand.
...
Income levels. ...
Consumer tastes and preferences. ...
Competition. ...
Fashions.
What are the 4 factors of supply?
The four factors that can shift the supply curve include natural conditions, input prices, technology, and government.
What causes increase in supply?
If the cost of production is lower, the profits available at a given price will increase, and producers will produce more. With more produced at every price, the supply curve will shift to the right, meaning an increase in supply.
What causes supply changes?
A change in supply is an economic term that describes when the suppliers of a given good or service alter production or output. A change in supply can occur as a result of new technologies, such as more efficient or less expensive production processes, or a change in the number of competitors in the market.
Is supply and demand a good strategy?

When it comes to profit placement, supply and demand zones can be a great tool as well. Always place your profit target ahead of a zone so that you don't risk giving back all your profits when the open interest in that zone is filled.
How is demand created?
Demand creation is a process that fuels the revenue pipeline so the sales team can meet or exceed their quotas. In other words, it takes your big idea — the creative appeal of your brand — and turns it into sales. That sounds a lot like demand generation, which often gets confused with lead generation.
What are the two parts of demand?
Economists define demand as the quantity of a good or service that buyers are willing and able to buy at all possible prices during a certain time period.

Notice that there are two components to demand: willingness to purchase and ability to pay.

Can we control demand?

If you're willing to think and act strategically, you can easily manipulate the laws of supply and demand. It should be surprising to learn, however, that by manipulating the laws of supply and demand, you can make more profit in less time and with far fewer headaches

How do you control demand?

Here are five short-term actions to improve your demand variability management plans in this time of uncertainty:

Maintain transparent, proactive relationships with your suppliers. ...

Activate alternate sources of supply. ...

Reduce lead times. ...

Update inventory policy and planning. ...

Align supply and demand management.

What are the 8 types of demand?

There are 8 states of demand: negative demand, no demand, latent demand, falling demand, irregular demand, full demand, overfull demand and unwholesome demand.

What is Demand?

Types of Determinants of Demand. Every factor has a unique impact on demand. ...

Price of the Product. ...

The Income of the Consumers. ...

Number of Buyers in the Market. ...

Consumer's Expectations. ...

Tastes and Preferences of The Consumers. ...

Complement Goods. ...

Substitute Product.

What is theory of supply?

The law of supply is a fundamental principle of economic theory which states that, keeping other factors constant, an increase in price results in an increase in quantity supplied. In other words, there is a direct relationship between price and quantity: quantities respond in the same direction as price changes.

What are the types of supply?

There are five types of supply—market supply, short-term supply, long-term supply, joint supply, and composite supply.

Which comes first supply or demand?
Demand comes first and it's followed by the corresponding supplies. Supply and demand are both very important to economic activity. Supply is the total amount of a particular good or service available at a given time to consumers at a given price. Demand is a representation of a consumer's desire to purchase goods and services; it acts as a measurement of a consumer's willingness to purchase a specific good or service at a given price. These two economic forces influence each other; they are both important for the economy because they impact the prices of consumer goods and services within an economy and the quantities produced and consumed. Supply and demand are both keys to understanding the economy because they reflect the prices and quantities of consumer goods and services within an economy.

What are the relationship between demand and supply?
According to market economy theory, the relationship between supply and demand balances out at a point in the future; this point is called the equilibrium price.
Economists and companies analyze the relationship between supply and demand when making strategic product decisions. Both economists and companies analyze the relationship between supply and demand when making strategic product decisions. The assumption behind a market economy is that supply and demand are the best determinants for an economy's growth and health.
Consumer Behavior Influences Demand
One way that companies or economists might analyze this relationship is to create graphs that chart the equilibrium price of certain goods and services in order to determine product development and their production schedule. Consumer behavior dictates which products are produced and sold because consumers create the demand that companies attempt to meet. As a result, companies may study consumer behavior in an attempt to understand the current demand and predict future demand. It is vital that companies maintain the capacity to produce enough of a good or service that they can satisfy consumer demands.
Supply and demand are two sides of the same market coin. Generally, supply is how much of something is available or will be produced at a certain price. Demand is how much of something people want to purchase or consume at a certain price. One way to develop a more precise

relationship between the two is to consider how the price of something affects its supply and its demand. Generally when the price of a good goes up, so does the supply, since firms are willing to create more when they can sell at higher prices. But when the price of a good goes up consumers will, at the same time, generally demand less. It is the interaction of supply and demand that determines how much will be produced and consumed and at what price, converging to a state known as equilibrium.

CHAPTER TWO

Human social job change demand and supply relationship

The relationship between social change and human behavior

Human Behavioral network job brings social economic benefits

Whether human social job change it depends on social job demand more or job supply more? What does human network job mean ? Why may human network job be popular? Why human network job behavior may influence economy ?

Nowadays internet is popular to use. We can apply internet to find data , search any new things, even earn money. Why does internet may become huma network job source. For example, e-publish may be one kind of new human network job. Any authors may apply internet channel to help them to sell electronic or paper books from e-publisher web store. They may apply facebook, you tub etc. any online channel to promote themselves new books to let new readers to know whether when they may buy themselves favourable new topic books to read from electronic publisher web store.

Thus, future electronic publisher industry may help any authors to build internet network platform to help them to sell and promote ot advertise their any one new electronic or paper book topic to let global any one reader to choose to buy their any new topic books from electronic publisher web store easily and conveniently. However, it implies that electronic network platform author may be one kind of future new human network job in our societies.

How electronic network platform author job may bring economy benefit in macro economy view? A person can have few friends, contacts and still be very influential if these few
friends and contacts are themselves highly influential, e.g. one author must not need to know any one reader in global society. When they like to choose any electronic books from electronic internet network platform. They may become the author's any one topic book buyer, when they feel the author's any one topic book is fun and attract they make decision to buth the strange author whose the topic book from electronic book publisher's platform web store conventiently in short time. Although, they are strangers, they do not know themselves , but the reader can understand what it way that made Google from writing platofrm to create new creative mind and typing network job method to replace traditional hand writing book method for global authors. It will be one kind of new human network writing job.

Hence, global any one reader can apply an innovative search engine , such as google.com to find whether whom author personal new topic books are value to read from internet.

Then, the electroniuc publisher's web store may be new book store platform sale network to help the author to sell many electronic or paper books from electronic network platform
in short time. So, internet may be future new network plaform to help global any one author to create network writing job absolutely. Furthermore, internet may be popular social media
to help any one author to build goold relationship between his/her readers. It is one kind of new network, human network job. New authors do not need to buy many paper books to prepare to put in any one book shop warehouse. Their every book can print on demand to reduce out of book stock in any one book shop. They may choose to sell either electronic books or paper books both from any one book publisher web store. So, electronic network platform may be one kind of good writing channel to help human authors to create income and it can also help authors to bring new creative mind and new topic fun content books to let readers to know and buy to read from electronic publisher network platform.

Why does human behavior may be one kind of new human network job to bring global economic advantages. ALthough, it may be free income or without inocme, but the person does the network behavior, his/her behavior may be bring advantages to influence many other people's health. For this case, when a worker in a coffee shop in an airport gets a vaccination aganinst the flu, it does not only helps him or her stay healthy, but also helps the many travellers who might otherwise have been inflected if that workers caught the flu. So, the externality , the result implies the vaccination of even a part of a community conveys benefits to the whole community. For example, governments pay special attention to the vaccinations of school children, teachers, health mothers, and the elderly, categories of people particularly susceptible not only to catching, but also to transmitting a disease.

It is not accidential that governments are heavily involved with vaccination . When there are externalities, free market, fail to persuade individual incentives with society's
their the worker's decision of whether to get a vaccine ends up attracting whether other people get sick. The workers might not fully take all these other people's potential suffering into account when making her or his vaccination decision.

As Stanford University does many suggestions, understand this and tries to help them make the right decisions and so providers free flu vaccines for its staff and students.

Small pockets of unvaccinated individuals can allow a disease to gain a spread more widely well-being. For example, parent weighing the costs and benefits of a vaccine for their child is not always thinking of the consequences of that vaccination to other people. THese are markets in which subsidizing or regulating behavior can make everyone better off. Because the reason for requiring that a child be vaccinated before enrolling in school is not just to protect that child, because each child's vaccination affects others via potential contagions.

On conclusion, it seems that many traditional paper book publish business begain to change to electronic book publish business. Due, to online technology existence, it influences many readers choose to buy electronic books to read. Hence, due to readers reading demand change which is from paper book reading habit to electonic book reading habit.Then,it explains that electornic book supply number depends on electronic book reader reading demand in economic view.

Robots take our jobs behavioral and economy influences

Robot job behavior brings economy influences

Whether robot labor needs are depended on employer labor demand more or robot labor number supply more? If one day robots can replace human to do simple, even complex jobs. They will bring what influences to our global societial economy.The popular economic refrain declares that the global middle class is dying and robots will soon take our jobs, e.g. shopping center customer service jobs, library service jobs, cinema ticket sale jobs, restaurant kitchen cooker jobs, even, bus drivers, taxi drivers etc. public transport driving jobs, accountant, doctors etc. professional jobs. Whether it is beautiful or petty matter if our future societies have many human jobs can be replaced to do from robots. Businessman must may reduce to employ employees and reduce to pay salary or wage, when robots can be replaced to do their employees tasks. But, societies must bring unemployement rate rises , due to societies will have many people loss jobs when their employers choose to buy robots to serve their clients or do any office tasks or customer service or cleaning etc. tasks.

In micro economy view, employers may save money in long term, but in macro economy view, it will cause unemployment ratio rises , even crime rate rises when there are many people lose jobs in societies. These models of doom, though, fail to account for the hundreds of businesses riding the waves of change in their industries when robots may be invented to replace human to do many simple , even complex tasks in our future societies.

WE may image that one small factory needs to manufacture fishes canes to sell to supermarket, the small , cheaper stuff and higher margin parts of the fishes manufacture industry. Before, this factory needs to employe many human factory workers need to help every fresh customer makeing the perfect fishing gear, designed for performance, durability, and cost in order to achieve to manufacture every fish cane in whole fished processing manufacturing stages. Every worker needs to spend about 15 to twenty minutes to finish every fish cane , till to delivery to any supermarket to sell. If this fish canes manufacturing factory can apply manufacturing robots to help them to finish any one working tasks , every robot can only spend five minutes to finish whole fresh fish cane manufacturing process. Thus, every robot can help this factory save 10 to 15 minutes time to finsh every fish cane manufacturing process. IN fact, time is money, because when every robot can help this factory to reduce 10 to 15 minutes time to compare human worker. Then, this factory can finish about 20 fish canes in one hour if it can use robot to help it to manufacture fish canes. Otherwise, if this factory still use human workers to help it to manufacture fish canes, then it can finsh about 3 to 4 fish canes in one hour. SO, the manufacturing efficiency ensures that robots must help this fish manufacturing factory to raise fish canes number more than human workers. So, in robotic behavioral economy view, manufacturing robots must help this fish canes manufacturing factory to raise fish canes manufacturing number and deliver increasing number to supermarkets to prepare to sell every day. Robots can help this fish canes manufacturing factory bring manufacturing time saving, rising manufacturing efficiency, improving performance and reducing wages expenditure long time advantages in micro economy view. However, manufacturing robots can also bring disadvanages to society, e.g. increasing unemployment ratio, increasing crime rate,

this factory workers will lose jobs and income, they need earn social welfare from government and increasing government finance pressure in short time, even long time in macro economic view.

Stanford University graduate program in economics, Scott lecturer explained that "in demand and supply economic theory for robots supply and demand case, robots supply number increasing may influence human workers demand number decrease. It sometimes calls " the efficient frontier".

No specific human beings were mentioned in any of economics classes. As robots supply and demand in market case, They (robots) may be purely theoretical " agents" who reached to the most reasonable sale prices in order to persuade any one businessman buyer to make manufacturing robot buying decision whether robots can help him / her to bring how much saving time , saving money, saving cost, improving performance, efficiency economic benefit before he/she plans to reduce workers number when he/she decides to apply robots to replace human workers in his/her factory or office or any service department, e.g. cinema ticket sale service, shopping center customer service, shopping center cleaning , supermarket customer service etc. service or sale tasks. When robots can replace human to do any one of these tasks in any organizations. So, robots may be human worker agents who reached to prices the way robots would react to a software command. There was nothing that explained why some people thrived and others did n't or why truly brilliant, hardworking people could fail when much lazier folks succeeded." Having been admitted to the Stanford University graduate program in economics, Scott lecturer hoped to get his answers there.

How robots influence our future social changing? Using the right technology can be a boon to your business in this economy. For internet example, it is easier than ever to find well-matched customers all around the world, to stay in contact with them, and to more quickly design the products they want. If you focus solely on being cutting -edge, though you risk letting the technology

take over what should be very robust relationships with your customers , employees, and colleagues. IN nowaddays society, technoligical advances and cutomation, personal

relationships in business are more crucial than ever. I mean that robots can not replace human to serve clients to let them to feel more comfortable and passion more easily. For shoe shop case example, if the shoe shop apply one robot to serve its clients to replace human shoe salesperson to serve its shoe customers. Robots ensure that they can not persuade every shoe potential buyer to make shoe buying decision more easily when robots need to contact every shoe potential buyer. The reason is simple, because robots can not touch any one shoe buyer individual emotion very easier.

If the shoe buyer needs the robots to help him/her to choose any right shoe styles when he/she can not feel himself / herself can make the most right shoe style choice decision. The robots can not replace human shoe salesperson to make shoe style choice judgement more easily. They must need longer time to analyze whether which shoe style may be the most suitable to the shoe buyer. Otherwise, human shoe salesperson may attempt to make the most right shoe style choice decision to help any one shoe buyer to chooce the most right style shoe because he/she owns shoe style sale experience, shoe style knowledge, the most important reason is that they can feel every shoe customer individual emotion to touch whether he/she will feel comfortable or happy when they attempt to help every shoe customer to seek the most right shoe style in every shoe customer whole shoe searching processing. Othwerwise, serving robots are only one machine, they can not touch or feel every shoe customer individual emotion whether he/she feel comfortable or unhappy or happy when they need to contact them in whole shoe searching processing. Hence, I believe that some tasks robots can

not repalce human staff to do very easily. Otherwise, robots may bring disadvanatges to let any one businessman to loss his/her customers, due to robots can not touch every customer
emotion to compare human staff in service tasks more easily. Robots serving customer behaviors may cause money lose and customers number lose to the shop in micro economic view.

On conclusion, in demand and supply economic theory for robots supply and demand case, robots supply number increasing may influence human workers demand number decrease. So, it seems that robots number supply will be depended on global robots supply number more than robots demand number because when human began to accept robots to replace human to do general simple jobs in global labor market. Then, it means that global robots labor number must need to be increased in order to satisfy global businessmen workers number need. If any kinds of robot workers manufacture number is not enough to be supplied to let global future businessmen to buy, then robot supply will be shortage and they can not provide to satisfy global businessmen robots labour purchase need. So, future robot number will be depended on supply more than demand.

CHAPTER THREE

Human intellectual demand and supply behavior relationship

Intellectual human economic behaviors

What does intellectual human economic behaviors mean ? Human foolish behavior is depended on social enjoyment need more or material social supply more? I believe that when we choose or decide to do intellectual behaviors, then our societies will be influenced to bring economic growth in consequence.I shall attempt to indicate pollution case to explain how and why eithet our intellectual or foolish behaviors may bring economic growth or recession in consequence as below:

On one hand, for air pollution social case aspect example, if we only consider to buy cars to drive for working aim or holiday leisure aim. Then, our societies air will be polluted. Our health will be influenced to bad. Our car driving behaviors may cause global environment air pollution serously. In long tiem, global air pollution will bring our bodies health to be bad. Although, ourselves car driving behaviors may bring our driving travelling leisure enjoyment and comfortable feeling in short time, also we so not need to pay public transport fare often, but we need to compensate ourselves health economic intangible loss due to air pollution , when cars number increases, dirty air will cause ouselves health to become bad.

In the result, we will need to pay more medical expenditure when we are old age, due to ourselves bodies will become bad, due to we breathe global dirty air every day, due to ourselves cars pollute air in long time, e.g. 10 to 20 years, even 30 more without limited air pollution environment. So, driving cars behavior may be one kind of human foolish behavior and our foolish behavior may bring ourselves future long time medical expenditure absolutely.

One the other hand, water pollution social aspect, if we often keep much rubblish to pollute sea, oil exploration porcessing pollute ocean , ships gas pollute ocaen, then fishes will eat polluted food and drive dirty water, due to global ocean is polluted.

In fact, because human only to conside how to buy boats to carry on leisure enjoyment activities, or catch cruises to travel on the sea. Also, oil manufacturers only consider researching anywhere to find new oil exploration places to manufacture oil product, when their oil exploration processes pollute ocarn . Consequently, global fishes drink polluted warer or eat polluted food. They will have poison. SO, human will have high chance to eat poison polluted fishes, due to fishes are poison or are polluted. So, human is doing foolish activities, we only hope to find oil exploration places to pollute ocean or we only spend money to buy ticket to catch ships to travel anywhere in global ocean. All of these human foolish behaviors will bring pollution to global ocean. On consequently, we will need to compensate to eat polluted or dirty or poision fishes, ourselves bodies health will be bad. In long time, we need have high chance to pay medical expenditure when we are old. So, pollution case may be one good example to explain how and why human foolish behavior may influence ourselves future need to compensate serious medical loss.

All of these human foolish behavior will bring pollution to global ocean. On consequently, we will need to compensate to eat polluted or dirty or poison fished , ourselves bodies health will be bad. In long time, we will have high chance to pay medical expenditure, when we are old. So, pollution case may be one good example to explain how and why human ourselves intellectual or foolish behaviors may influence future long time economic loss or economic growth or recession in micro and micro economic view.

On another water pollution aspect hand, if we often keep rubbish to sea, oil exploration processing pollutes ocean and ships' gas pollute ocean, then fishes will eat polluted food and drink dirty water, due to fishes will eat polluted food and drink dirty sea water because the global ocean is polluted seriously.

In fact, because human only consider how to buy boats to carry on any leisure water activities, or catches cruises to travel on the sea. Also, oil manufacturers only consider any where to find oil exploratin places to manufacture oil products from ocean, when their pol exploration processes can plooute ocean. Consequently, global fishes drink polluted water or eat direty food. They will have poison. So, human will have high chance to eat poison fishes.

Otherwise, such as pollutin case, it can infuence inflation or deflation. Consequently, the reason indicates supply and demand theory. If air pollution is serious, then we will consider health issue, global cars demand number may be influenced to reduce, when global cars number demand will reduce, global car prices and supply number will need to change to fall down in order to attract or persuade global car consumers choose to make car purchase decision.

Hence, global car manufacture number and car price will be influenced to reduce, due to global air pollution issue. Consequently, deflation will occur because when the country citizen usually does not spend much extra saving money to buy car expensive goods. Money value will be low. Otherwise, if global cair pollution is not serious, human considers to buy cars to enjoy driving leisure lives. So, global car demand is influenced to increase , also global car price will also influenced to increase.

Consequently, gobal human will choose to buy cars to drive. Due to we accept to spend extra saving to buy expensive car goods. Car sale price and supply may be influenced to rise up. Money value is influenced to reduce. Inflation may be influenced, due to global car consumers number increases, we would not have extra money to spend easily. Car expensive goods expenditure influences our spending habit to avoid to make car purchase decision more easily. So, human intellectual or foolish activities may bring inflation or deflation consequency in possible indirectly in macro economic view.

On conclusion, above pollution case explain that how and why human intellectual or foolish economic behaviors may bring inflation or deflation consequency as wll as economic growth or recession consequency as well as any goods demand and supply increasing or decreasing consequency. It implies that human behavior may have indirect relationship to influence any goods demand and supply number to either increase or decrease result as well as any goods price will be influenced to increase or decrease in micro and macro economic view. Hence, Human foolish behavior is depended on social enjoyment need more or material social supply more because human needs to raise enjoyment feel , so we will choose to do foolish behavior, e.g. air pollution, when many people choose to buy cars to drive to replace catch public transport. So, such as car market, it depends on car demand number more than car supply number absolutely in demand and supply view.

The relationship between social change and human behavior

Why does economic changes may influence human individual behavioral change? I shall attempt to indicate shopping behavior and staying at home behavior to explain their case and effect relationsip as below:
Human behavior can be influenced by economic change or economic change can be influenced by human behavior? Why does recession may influence consumers reduce shopping desire? In social recession suitation, it is possible that many people lose jobs suddenly, due to businessmen lose many customers. They need to make decision to reduce employees number in order to continue to keep businesses. Consequently, many firms (organizations) their employees may lose jobs. When they have much time, due to lose jobs, they will feel to avoid to spend too much time and money to go to shopping often. Many losing jobs people, they will often stay at homes. So, they will reduce time to go to shopping, then non essential products won't their preferable choice purchase products. Hence, recession will change many losing jobs people their shopping or consumption desires to avoid to buy non essential products often . Usually when economic boom, many people have jobs to do because consumers number must increase when many people have jobs to do. Then, many people can accept to spend money to buy non essential products often. Many people feel spend time to go to shopping can satisfy their purchase of any kinds of new products useful psychology or desire. So, recession is one good example to explain it can influence many people do not like often to leave homes to go to shopping easily. Many people like to stay at homes, becaue they feel worry about spending too much shopping time when they leave homes. Their staying home time is one good negative shopping behavior example. So, economic change may influence human individual behavior changes , they have direct cause and efect relationship in behavioral economic view.
May human behavior influence economic change? Is it possible that human behavior may bring the country social economic change in macro economic or micro behavioral economic view ? I shall indicate publishing industry example. Do you feel that if there are many students feel learning is very important when they read many books or many of students feel interesting to read or they have reading new books in habit, then it is possible that the country will have many students like to spend time to go to any book shops to choose the books, they feel that they can help they learn new knowledge. Then the country will increase students number, they often spend time to

visit any one book shop every week. Their visiting book shops behavior which may become their habits. So, the country will increase students number, they often spend time to visit book shops. Also, it implies that visiting book shops behaviors may be their behavioral habits.

So, when the country has many students often spend time to visit book shops , their visiting book shops behaviors may help any one book shop to raise books sale chance. So, the country's student individual often visiting book shop behaviors, their habitual visiting book shops behaviors must may assist help any one book shop to increase books sale number absolutely.

Consequently, any one book shop , its books sale bumber must be influenced to increase to increase because the country will have many students like or feel need visit book shops habit in order to choose any suitable books to buy to read at home in order to raise themselves learning effort. When the country has many bok shops often have many students visit their book shops, then their books sale number may be influenced to increase. It explain why student individual visiting book shop behavior may help any one book shop sale number increases also. So, visiting shops products sale number is depended on online products supply number, if online products supply number increases, then it may cause many customers choose to buy the kind of products from online webstore. So, any shop products sale number will depend on onlint products supply number in supply and demand view.

CHAPTER FOUR

Technology or human behavior whether may influence economic growth or recession

Human Behavioral network job brings social economic benefits

What does human network job mean ? Why may human network job be popular? Why human network job behavior may influence economy ? Nowadays internet is popular to use. We can apply internet to find data , search any new things, even earn money. Why does internet may become huma network job source. For example, e-publish may be one kind of new human network job. Any authors may apply internet channel to help them to sell electronic or paper books from e-publisher web store. They may apply facebook, you tub etc. any online channel to promote themselves new books to let new readers to know whether when they may buy themselves favourable new topic books to read from electronic publisher web store.

Thus, future electronic publisher industry may help any authors to build internet network platform to help them to sell and promote ot advertise their any one new electronic or paper book topic to let global any one reader to choose to buy their any new topic books from electronic publisher web store easily and conveniently. However, it implies that electronic network platform author may be one kind of future new human network job in our societies.

How electronic network platform author job may bring economy benefit in macro economy view? A person can have few friends, contacts and still be very influential if these few
friends and contacts are themselves highly influential, e.g. one author must not need to know any one reader in global society. When they like to choose any electronic books from electronic internet network platform. They may become the author's any one topic book buyer, when they feel the author's any one topic book is fun and attract they make decision to buth the strange author whose the topic book from electronic book publisher's platform web store conventiently in short time. Although, they are strangers, they do not know themselves , but the reader can understand what it way that made Google from writing platofrm to create new creative mind and typing network job method to replace traditional hand writing book method for global authors. It will be one kind of new human network writing job.

Hence, global any one reader can apply an innovative search engine , such as google.com to find whether whom author personal new topic books are value to read from internet.
Then, the electroniuc publisher's web store may be new book store platform sale network to help the author to sell many electronic or paper books from electronic network platform
in short time. So, internet may be future new network plaform to help global any one author to create network writing job absolutely. Furthermore, internet may be popular social media
to help any one author to build goold relationship between his/her readers. It is one kind of new network, human network job. New authors do not need to buy many paper books to prepare to put in any one book shop warehouse. Their every book can print on demand to reduce out of book stock in any one book shop. They may choose to sell either electronic books or paper books both from any one book publisher web store. So, electronic network platform may be one kind of good writing channel to help human authors to create income and it can also help authors to bring new creative mind and new topic fun content books to let readers to know and buy to read from electronic publisher network platform.

Why does human behavior may be one kind of new human network job to bring global economic advantages. ALthough, it may be free income or without inocme, but the person does the network behavior, his/her behavior may be bring advantages to influence many other people's health. For this case, when a worker in a coffee shop in an airport gets a vaccination aganinst the flu, it does not only helps him or her stay healthy, but also helps the many travellers who might otherwise have been inflected if that workers caught the flu. So, the externality , the result implies the vaccination of even a part of a community conveys benefits to the whole community. For example, governments pay special attention to the vaccinations of school children, teachers, health mothers, and the elderly, categories of people particularly susceptible not only to catching, but also to transmitting a disease.

It is not accidential that governments are heavily involved with vaccination . When there are externalities, free market, fail to persuade individual incentives with society's

their the worker's decision of whether to get a vaccine ends up attracting whether other people get sick. The workers might not fully take all these other people's potential suffering into account when making her or his vaccination decision.

As Stanford University does many suggestions, understand this and tries to help them make the right decisions and so providers free flu vaccines for its staff and students.

Small pockets of unvaccinated individuals can allow a disease to gain a spread more widely well-being. For example, parent weighing the costs and benefits of a vaccine for their child is not always thinking of the consequences of that vaccination to other people. THese are markets in which subsidizing or regulating behavior can make everyone better off. Because the reason for requiring that a child be vaccinated before enrolling in school is not just to protect that child, because each child's vaccination affects others via potential contagions.

Robots take our jobs behavioral and economy influences

Robot job behavior brings economy influences

If one day robots can replace human to do simple, even complex jobs. They will bring what influences to our global societial economy.The popular economic refrain declares that the

global middle class is dying and robots will soon take our jobs, e.g. shopping center customer service jobs, library service jobs, cinema ticket sale jobs, restaurant kitchen cooker jobs,

even, bus drivers, taxi drivers etc. public transport driving jobs, accountant, doctors etc. professional jobs. Whether it is beautiful or petty matter if our future societies have many human jobs can be replaced to do from robots.

Businessman must may reduce to employ employees and reduce to pay salary or wage, when robots can be replaced to do their employees tasks. But, societies must bring unemployement rate rises , due to societies will have many people loss jobs when their employers choose to buy robots to serve their clients or do any office tasks or customer service or cleaning etc. tasks.

In micro economy view, employers may save money in long term, but in macro economy view, it will cause unemployment ratio rises , even crime rate rises when there are many people lose

jobs in societies. These models of doom, though, fail to account for the hundreds of businesses riding the waves of change in their industries when robots may be invented to replace human to do many simple , even complex tasks in our future societies.

WE may image that one small factory needs to manufacture fishes canes to sell to supermarket, the small , cheaper stuff and higher margin parts of the fishes manufacture industry. Before, this factory needs to employe many human factory workers need to help every fresh customer makeing the perfect fishing gear, designed for performance, durability, and cost in order to achieve to manufacture every fish cane in whole fished processing manufacturing stages. Every worker needs to spend about 15 to twenty minutes to finish every fish cane , till to delivery to any supermarket to sell. If this fish canes manufacturing factory can apply manufacturing robots to help them to finish any one working tasks , every robot can only spend five minutes to finish whole fresh fish cane manufacturing process. Thus, every robot can

help this factory save 10 to 15 minutes time to finsh every fish cane manufacturing process. IN fact, time is money, because when every robot can help this factory to reduce 10 to 15 minutes time to compare human worker. Then, this factory can finish about 20 fish canes in one hour if it can use robot to help it to manufacture fish canes. Otherwise, if this factory still use human workers to help it to manufacture fish canes, then it can finsh about 3 to 4 fish canes in one hour. SO, the manufacturing efficiency ensures that robots must help this fish manufacturing factory to raise fish canes number more than human workers. So, in robotic behavioral economy view, manufacturing robots must help this fish canes manufacturing factory to raise fish canes manufacturing number and deliver increasing number to supermarkets to prepare to sell every day. Robots can help this fish canes manufacturing factory bring manufacturing time saving,

rising manufacturing efficiency, improving performance and reducing wages expenditure long time advantages in micro economy view. However, manufacturing robots can also bring disadvanages to society, e.g. increasing unemployment ratio, increasing crime rate,
this factory workers will lose jobs and income, they need earn social welfare from government and increasing government finance pressure in short time, even long time in macro economic view.

Stanford University graduate program in economics, Scott lecturer explained that "in demand and supply economic theory for robots supply and demand case, robots supply number increasing may influence human workers demand number decrease. It sometimes calls " the efficient frontier".
No specific human beings were mentioned in any of economics classes. As robots supply and demand in market case, They (robots) may be purely theoretical " agents" who reached to the most reasonable sale prices in order to persuade any one businessman buyer to make manufacturing robot buying decision whether robots can help him / her to bring how much saving time , saving money, saving cost, improving performance, efficiency economic benefit before he/she plans to reduce workers number when he/ she decides to apply robots to replace human workers in his/her factory or office or any service department, e.g. cinema ticket sale service, shopping center customer service, shopping center cleaning , supermarket customer service etc. service or sale tasks. When robots can replace human to do any one of these tasks in any organizations. So, robots may be human worker agents who reached to prices the way robots would react to a software command. There was nothing that explained why some people thrived and others did n't or why truly brilliant, hardworking people could fail when much lazier folks succeeded." Having been admitted to the Stanford University graduate program in economics, Scott lecturer hoped to get his answers there.

How robots influence our future social changing? Using the right technology can be a boon to your business in this economy. For internet example, it is easier than ever to find well-matched customers all around the world, to stay in contact with them, and to more quickly design the products they want. If you focus solely on being cutting -edge, though you risk letting the technology
take over what should be very robust relationships with your customers , employees, and colleagues. IN nowaddays society, technoligical advances

and cutomation, personal
relationships in business are more crucial than ever. I mean that robots can not replace human to serve clients to let them to feel more comfortable and passion more easily. For shoe shop case example, if the shoe shop apply one robot to serve its clients to replace human shoe salesperson to serve its shoe customers. Robots ensure that they can not persuade every shoe potential buyer to make shoe buying decision more easily when robots need to contact every shoe potential buyer. The reason is simple, because robots can not touch any one shoe buyer individual emotion very easier.
If the shoe buyer needs the robots to help him/her to choose any right shoe styles when he/she can not feel himself / herself can make the most right shoe style choice decision. The robots can not replace human shoe salesperson to make shoe style choice judgement more easily. They must need longer time to analyze whether which shoe style may be the most suitable to the shoe buyer. Otherwise, human shoe salesperson may attempt to make the most right shoe style choice decision to help any one shoe buyer to chooce the most right style shoe because he/she owns shoe style sale experience, shoe style knowledge, the most important reason is that they can feel every shoe customer individual emotion to touch whether he/she will feel comfortable or happy when they attempt to help every shoe customer to seek the most right shoe style in every shoe customer whole shoe searching processing. Othwerwise, serving robots are only one machine, they can not touch or feel every shoe customer individual emotion whether he/she feel comfortable or unhappy or happy when they need to contact them in whole shoe searching processing. Hence, I believe that some tasks robots can
not repalce human staff to do very easily. Otherwise, robots may bring disadvanatges to let any one businessman to loss his/her customers, due to robots can not touch every customer
emotion to compare human staff in service tasks more easily. Robots serving customer behaviors may cause money lose and customers number lose to the shop in micro economic view.

Intellectual human economic behaviors

What does intellectual human economic behaviors mean ? I believe that when we choose or decide to do intellectual behaviors, then our societies will be influenced to bring economic growth in consequence.I shall attempt to indicate pollution case to explain how and why eithet our intellectual or foolish behaviors may bring economic growth or recession in consequence

as below:
On one hand, for air pollution social case aspect example, if we only consider to buy cars to drive for working aimr or holiday leisure aim. Then, our societies air will be polluted. Our health will be influenced to bad. Our car driving behaviors may cause global environment air pollution serously. In long tiem, global air pollution will bring our bodies health to be bad. Although, ourselves car driving behaviors may bring our driving travelling leisure enjoyment and comfortable feeling in short time, also we so not need to pay public transport fare often, but we need to compensate ourselves health economic intangible loss due to air pollution , when cars number increases, dirty air will cause ouselves health to become bad.
In the result, we will need to pay more medical expenditure when we are old age, due to ourselves bodies will become bad, due to we breathe global dirty air every day, due to ourselves cars pollute air in long time, e.g. 10 to 20 years, even 30 more without limited air pollution environment. So, driving cars behavior may be one kind of human foolish behavior and our foolish behavior may bring ourselves future long time medical expenditure absolutely.
One the other hand, water pollution social aspect, if we often keep much rubblish to pollute sea, oil exploration porcessing pollute ocean , ships gas pollute ocaen, then fishes will eat polluted food and drive dirty water, due to global ocean is polluted.
In fact, because human only to conside how to buy boats to carry on leisure enjoyment activities, or catch cruises to travel on the sea. Also, oil manufacturers only consider researching anywhere to find new oil exploration places to manufacture oil product, when their oil exploration processes pollute ocarn . Consequently, global fishes drink polluted warer or eat polluted food. They will have poison. SO, human will have high chance to eat poison polluted fishes, due to fishes are poison or are polluted. So, human is doing foolish activities, we only hope to find oil exploration places to pollute ocean or we only spend money to buy ticket to catch ships to travel anywhere in global ocean. All of these human foolish behaviors will bring pollution to global ocean. On consequently, we will need to compensate to eat polluted or dirty or poision fishes, ourselves bodies health will be bad. In long time, we need have high chance to pay medical expenditure when we are old. So, pollution case may be one good example to explain how and why human foolish behavior may influence ourselves future need to compensate serious medical loss.

All of these human foolish behavior will bring pollution to global ocean. On consequently, we will need to compensate to eat polluted or dirty or poison fished , ourselves bodies health will be bad. In long time, we will have high chance to pay medical expenditure, when we are old. So, pollution case may be one good example to explain how and why human ourselves intellectual or foolish behaviors may influence future long time economic loss or economic growth or recession in micro and micro economic view.

On another water pollution aspect hand, if we often keep rubbish to sea, oil exploration processing pollutes ocean and ships' gas pollute ocean, then fishes will eat polluted food and drink dirty water, due to fishes will eat polluted food and drink dirty sea water because the global ocean is polluted seriously.

In fact, because human only consider how to buy boats to carry on any leisure water activities, or catches cruises to travel on the sea. Also, oil manufacturers only consider any where to find oil exploratin places to manufacture oil products from ocean, when their pol exploration processes can plooute ocean. Consequently, global fishes drink polluted water or eat direty food. They will have poison. So, human will have high chance to eat poison fishes.

Otherwise, such as pollutin case, it can infuence inflation or deflation. Consequently, the reason indicates supply and demand theory. If air pollution is serious, then we will consider health issue, global cars demand number may be influenced to reduce, when global cars number demand will reduce, global car prices and supply number will need to change to fall down in order to attract or persuade global car consumers choose to make car purchase decision.

Hence, global car manufacture number and car price will be influenced to reduce, due to global air pollution issue. Consequently, deflation will occur because when the country citizen usually does not spend much extra saving money to buy car expensive goods. Money value will be low. Otherwise, if global cair pollution is not serious, human considers to buy cars to enjoy driving leisure lives. So, global car demand is influenced to increase , also global car price will also influenced to increase.

Consequently, gobal human will choose to buy cars to drive. Due to we accept to spend extra saving to buy expensive car goods. Car sale price and supply may be influenced to rise up. Money value is influenced to reduce. Inflation may be influenced, due to global car consumers number increases, we would not have extra money to spend easily. Car expensive goods expenditure influences our spending habit to avoid to make car purchase decision more easily. So, human intellectual or foolish activities may bring inflation or deflation consequency in possible indirectly in macro economic view.

On conclusion, above pollution case explain that how and why human intellectual or foolish economic behaviors may bring inflation or deflation consequency as wll as economic growth or recession consequency as well as any goods demand and supply incrcasing or decreasing consequency. It implies that human behavior may have indirect relationship to influence any goods demand and supply number to either increase or decrease result as well as any goods price will be influenced to increase or decrease in micro and macro economic view.

The relationship between social change and human behavior

Why does economic changes may influence human individual behavioral change? I shall attempt to indicate shopping behavior and staying at home behavior to explain their case and effect relationsip as below:

Human behavior can be influenced by economic change or economic change can be influenced by human behavior? Why does recession may influence consumers reduce shopping desire? In social recession suitation, it is possible that many people lose jobs suddenly, due to businessmen lose many customers. They need to make decision to reduce employees number in order to continue to keep businesses. Consequently, many firms (organizations) their employees may lose jobs. When they have much time, due to lose jobs, they will feel to avoid to spend too much time and money to go to shopping often. Many losing jobs people, they will often stay at homes. So, they will reduce time to go to shopping, then non essential products won't their preferable choice purchase products. Hence, recession will change many losing jobs people their shopping or consumption desires to avoid to buy non essential products often . Usually when economic boom, many people have jobs to do because consumers number must increase when many people have jobs to do. Then, many people can accept to spend money to buy non essential products often. Many people feel spend time to go to shopping can satisfy their purchase of any kinds of new products useful psychology or desire. So, recession is one good example to explain it can influence many people do not like often to leave homes to go to shopping easily. Many people like to stay at homes, becaue they feel worry about spending too much shopping time when they leave homes. Their staying home time is one good negative shopping behavior example. So, economic change may influence human individual behavior changes , they have direct cause and efect relationship in behavioral economic view.

May human behavior influence economic change? Is it possible that human behavior may bring the country social economic change in macro economic or micro behavioral economic view ? I shall indicate publishing industry example. Do you feel that if there are many students feel learning is very important when they read many books or many of students feel interesting to read or they have reading new books in habit, then it is possible that the country will have many students like to spend time to go to any book shops to choose the books, they feel that they can help they learn new knowledge. Then the country will increase students number, they often spend time to visit any one book shop every week. Their visiting book shops behavior which may become their habits. So, the country will increase students number, they often spend time to visit book shops. Also, it implies that visiting book shops behaviors may be their behavioral habits.

So, when the country has many students often spend time to visit book shops , their visiting book shops behaviors may help any one book shop to raise books sale chance. So, the country's student individual often visiting book shop behaviors, their habitual visiting book shops behaviors must may assist help any one book shop to increase books sale number absolutely.

Consequently, any one book shop , its books sale bumber must be influenced to increase to increase because the country will have many students like or feel need visit book shops habit in order to choose any suitable books to buy to read at home in order to raise themselves learning effort. When the country has many bok shops often have many students visit their book shops, then their books sale number may be influenced to increase. It explain why student individual visiting book shop behavior may help any one book shop sale number increases also.

How human productive behavior may influence economic development

May any country which citizen behavior assist themselves country development? It is one cause and effect economic question. I mean that if the country itself citicen can not concentrate mind or energy to choose to do one kind of industry in order to let themselves country can bring the most benefit, then whether the counry itself economy can bring the most serious economic benefit. I shall attempt to indicate these countries themselves indistry choice to explain whether these countries themselves citizen productive behavior may help themselves countries to achieve the largest economic benefits. I shall indicate as below:

New Zealand farmer individual wine productive behavior

For New Zealand country example, this country concerns itself effort is foucs on farming agricultural aspect. So, this country has many farmers concentrate on farming agricultural aspect. May New Zealanders choose to spend time to produce different kinds of wines, e.g. wine or red grape wine is for the people are eating meat, or they are eating dinner.

When these New Zealanders their behaviors choose to do farming or agriculture to grow and produce different kinds of taste of white or red grape wine drinking products job. Themselves grape agriculture behavior will influence these New Zealanders themselves, they can learn how to improve different kinds of grape wine drinking products in order to achieve every kinds of white or read grape wines taste improving aim during their white or red grape producing process.

Why can New Zealander every individual white or read grape wine producers improve their white or read grape wine taste more easily? In behavioral economic view, it can explain that why any one New Zealander white or read grape wine producer can be encouraged or excited or persuaded to concentrate nervous and energy and effort to learn how to improve their white or red grape wine products easily.

In fact, New Zealand is one agricultural food export country. It has good natural environment resource , e.g. land, seed to provide any one farmer to produce themselves any kinds of agricultrual food products, e.g. fruit, or wine food products. Because New Zealanders know themselves country has enough natural resource . So, in common, many New Zealanders choose to attempt to do farming agricultural jobs in order to export themselves any kinds of fruit or meat or wine products to overseas or sell to domestic in order to earn profit.

So, when these New Zealand farmers number has been increasing every year. This country farmers will feel themsleves competition between this New Zealand farmers themselves are serious due to they may feel New Zealanders choose to do agriculture businesses in order to export themselves different kinds of farming food to overseas or sell to local to earn profit.

Hence, when many New Zealand farmers feel that farmers number has been increasing every year. They will feel themselves competition is serious. They must need to spend much time and nervous and effort to research what method is the best how to produce the best taste of white or red grape wine products in order to let local or overseas wine buyers to choose to buy his/her producing white or read grpae products to drink.

Hence, in competition psychological view, may influence many New Zealand white or reaad wine producers had been beginning to change their learning behavior on researching what method is the best in order to produce the best quality of taste red or white wine products to sell in order to attract overseas or local white or read grape wine drinkers to choose to buy his/her wine products. Their behavior will focus on learning how to raising or improving white or read grape wine taste method more than only focus on producing a large number white or red grape wine products. They believe wine quality is more important to compare wine producing number. So, New Zealand wine producers themselves wine producers behaviors have been changing on concentrating on researching wine quality method aspect more then wine producing number aspect in behavioral economic view.

America high technological productive behavior

For America example, US is one high technological country, it owns many high technological knowledge talent inventors, e.g. computer science inventors. Hence, US must attract many diferent countries owning high technological computer inventors choose to go to US to develop their computer science profession career. Also, it seems that when many computer science inventors or professions choose to go to US to develop themselves computer science new career. In behavioral economic view, due to their leaving themselves countries choice, which may bring influence themselve country job behaviors need to be changed. They must need to adapt US new live. Because they will forgive their past computer science job. These computer science professionals need to spend time to adapt US new lives. They " past computer science job behaviors" will need to be changed to their new US any computer employer's new computer science job model.

Because their traditional computer science jobs needed to be forgot in their themselves countries. They will feel their old computer science job knowledge and behavior needed to change in order to let their US any one new of computer company employer feels satisfactory to accept their new working behavior in any one US computer organization.

So, on the other hand, many US computer company employer will feel that they must need time to accept any one new overseas computer science professions their working behaviors, their working attitude daily, because these foreign comouter science professional, their past computer working behaviors and working attitude must be different to US domestic computer science professions.

In behavioral economic view, these overseas computer science professions, their working behaviors and attitude must be needed to change in order to adapt any one US new computer company itself domestic or local computer science professional stafs themselves daily working behaviors and attitude because these overseas and local computer science professionals must need to team work together.

In behavioral economic view, it is only one way that foreign computer science professionals must need to change themselves past country traditiona daily working behaviors and attitude in order to cooperate with these US local computer science professionals in teams more easily.

Consequently, if these foreign compute science professionals can change their past working behaviors and attitude to let any one US local computer science professional feels to cooperate with them easily in short time. Then, the US computer company itself whole computer professional teams themselves efficiencies will be influenced to raised or improved by the changing past working attitude and working behaviors of these foreign computer science professionals. So, in behavioral economic view, only if US any one computer company hopes itself computer teams themselves efficiency can be raised or improved when it decides to employ foreign computer science professionals and US domestic computer science professionals. They need to work in teams together. They must need to let these foreign computer science professionals to know how to change their working behaviors and attitude to let their domestic computer science professionals feel easy to work together. Then, the US computer company itself whole team efficiency must be rasied or improved easily in short time.

- China share market investing behavior

For China share market example, economic development depends on financial market. Because if many Chinese have interest to invest to carry on shares buying and selling activities in orde to learn how to earn shares interest and share profit when the China shareholder can make decision to sell himself/herself shares in the the high price, then he/she can earn money when he/she can sell the China company's shares in the high sale share price position.

If China has many Chinese like to spend time to carry on investing shares activities. Themselves shares buying and selling behaviors will influence China has many companies can increase fund from many Chinese

shareholders in order to have enough money to expand or develop themselves businesses in China in long term.
Consequently, when China can have many Chinese like to attempt to carry on buying and selling shares investing behaviors in China share market. Themselves buying and selling shares behaviors can help many Chinese companies have effort to increase enough money or capital in order to continue to do their businesses in long term absolutely. So, it explains why when many Chinese become shareholders , they can assist China will have many companies continue to develop their businesses if many Chinese like to carry on shares buying and selling investing behaviors in long time in China financial investment market nowadays in behavioral economic view.

Why has any individual country have many people invest share behavior which can influence the country's macro consumption desire?
I shall apply shares market buying and selling investment behavior to explaiin why shares investment behavior which may impact the country's overal consumption desire as below:
In behavioral economic view, I assume that when the coutry has many people have interest to attempt to carry on shares buying and selling investment behavior, then their frequent shares buying and selling behaviors which may bring negactive consumption desire or shopping desire of these shares investors their consumer behavior.
The reason is simple, when the country has many share buyers number suddenly been increasing rapidly. Consequently, these large group share investors must need to spend much time to research any kinds of company shares variations, whether when their share prices will rise up of fall down in order to achieve buying the company's shares in the lowest price and selling the company's shares in the highest price level in order to earn profit.
Basic on this reason, they must need to spend much extra time to research share prices changing behavior every day, e.g. one working person will wait to leave his/her job, after he/she can spend time to gather data to research the day's share price changing behavior after dinner. So, the working person's right time may be his/her share price market research behavior. Before he/she may spend his/her night time to go to shopping after dinner, but nowadays, he/she will fogive to do his/her shopping behavior before dinner or after dinner at hight sometime. He/she will make decision to spend much night time to turn on computer to click on share market website to research his/her share purchase choice to investigate whether

his/her share price whether it rises up or falls down at the moment in order to make his/her share buying or selling decision at ever night time.
I mean the when the country has many people are share investors, their shares investment behavioral spenging time which will influence many shops lose customers at might often because the country will have many people feel need to spend night time to turn on computer or watch television to investigate share price variation. So, the country will have many people / share investors choosc to stay at home in order to carry on share price variation investigation behavior, they need to listen share market update news from radios or watch the share market update news from computer or TV at home every night. Consequenly, they must reduce times to leave themselves homes at night. So, their shopping behavior also will be reduced. Because these share investors feel need to spend time to investigate share price variation news at homes which can bring economic benefits (high opportunity benefits) when they choose to forgive to leave homes to go to shopping times (opportunity cost) every night.
On conclusion, it seems that when the country has many people are share investors, then their share price investigating behavior may bring negative shopping emotion at night. Consequently, the country's any one shop may lose many customers from this share investor consumer group in behavioral economic view. Hence, when the country's share investors number had been increasing rapidly, it will influence any shops lose many customers from this share investing customer group at night frequenly in short time, even long time in behavioral economic view, because their shopping desires or shopping emotion will be brought negative feeling when they make decisions to spend much time to listen radios or watch TV or computers share price update nes at night. Hence, share market will bring negative impact to influence consumer shopping desire or negative shopping emotion in behavioral economic view.

Can technology influence human shopping behavioral change?
Nowadays, technological development has reached mature stage, whether technological mature stage may bring positive or negative shopping emotion influence to global consumers. I shall aplly internet inventin or ecommerce shopping channel tool to explain whether internet technology can bring postive or negative influence to global consumer behavior in behavioral economic view.
Internet is a good technological tool, it brings e-commerce business chance.

In fact, commonly, global has have many businessmen choose to use internet channel to carry on their products transactions between global online-buyers and their electronic websites. So, global many shoppers had begun to feel online shopping is more convenient to compare visiting shops shopping. Their shopping behaviors have been changed from internet technological tool. Global has many shoppers choose to buy any products from any overseas or local businessmen their web stores. They only need to spend time to find any businessmen their webstores to choose the most suitable products to pay visa to buy from their webstores. at homes. So, in general, global had have may shoppers had changed their shopping behaviors from visiting shops to visiting webstores at homes often.

So, it seems that internet technological tool had influenced global many shops disappear, but internet webstores will be replaced their actual shops on streets. Some of businessmen either they choose webstores to replace shops or choose websotes and shops both or still keep shops only. Hence, internet tool influences global businessmen have three kinds of products sale channels to let globa local and overseas consumers to choose how to buy their products.

However, in fact, many of global shoppers, youngers and olders had begun to accept to buy any products from webstores. They feel to spend time to leave homes to visit shops , their shopping behaviors will be wasted time to not essential part to their daily lives. Hence, since internet technological invention, it had changed many consumers their traditional visiting shops shopping habit to change to buying products from webstores channel.

However, on the one hand, internet creates webstores ecommerce shopping channel to let global many consumers do not need to leave homes to go to shopping. It brings negative visiting shops shopping emotion to global general consumers nowadays. But on the other hand, it also brings positive visiting internet webstores shopping emotion to global general consumer nowadays. So, it seems that global many consumers feel that they often do not need to spend much time to go out shopping. Many global consumers feel convenient and enjoy to choose any products to buy from different internet webstores, when the online buyer chooses the most suitable product, he she only needs to pay visa card to buy the product from the online seller's webstore conveniently at home.

Hence, online shopping can bring economic benefit to online buyers, e.g. avoiding walking time or spending transport fare to visit the shop to go to shopping, shortening or reducing shopping time to do another important matter.

On conclusion, global many consumers began feel online shopping can bring more economic benefits on shortening shopping time, avoiding transport fare spending aspect. So, online shopping will be popular shopping behavior for future long time. It may encourage global many shoppers can make rapid shopping decision in short time in order to carry on any products buying transaction to global any one online shopper in short time easily in behavioral economic view. So, global many businessmen had begun to build themselves one attraction webstore in order to persuade different countries consumers to choose to click themselves webstores from internet channel to buy any kinds of products in short time easily.

So, internet technology had changed consumers traditional shopping behaviors to build positive online shopping emotion as well as raise online sellers' any products sale chance easily in behavioral economic view.

Why and how human behavior may influence the country's economic growth or recession?

When one country has many people choose to do the same matter for one period, whether their behavior may influence the country's pvera; economic growth or recession . I shall attempt to indicate cases toexplain their relationship as below:

For flowing rubblish behavioral case example, do you feel that when the country has many people often flow rubblish on the streets, instead of their flowing rubblish behavior may bring streets dirty? But, their flowing rubblish behavior may explain that this country has people may have enough money to buy food to ear, or enough cloths to wear, enough bottles of water to drink, even they may have enough money to buy new television, radio, refrigeraters , washing machines, desktops or laptops electronic home products from old to new to use in order to satisfy their living needs. So, when they flow old electronic home products, their flowing old home electronic products behaviors may seem that they have enough money to buy other new home electronic products to replace old home electronic products to use at homes.

However, it seems thaat this country ought have many people have jobs to do. So, many of them, they can easy to make purchase decison to flow any old home electronic products and buy any new home electronic products to use . Because this country has many people have jobs to do. So, they can often not use old home electonic products to become rubblishs to flow on streets after they had bought any kinds of new home electronic homes.

In fact, it also implies that this country's economy grows rapidly. So, many businesses can glow up rapdly. When they expanded their businesses, they must need to increase employees number in order to let they help themselves to raise productivity or serve their clients absolutely. So, when the country has many businesses can grow up, it seems that its economy must be better or it is improved to compare past. Due to many different kinds of home electronic products had been often bought to use by this country people in this period. So, this country's any streets can be observed that expensive electronic home products were flowed on streets anywhere. then, this country will have many electronic home products sellers can sell their home electronic products very easily. When this country has many people can find any kinds of jobs to do easily. So, due to unemploymen rate had been decreasing.

In behavioral economic view, as this many electronic home products rubblish country case, we can observe this country may have many people have jobs to do. So, consumption number has been increased long time. So, cheap food, or expensive home electronic products may be rubblish on any streets. This country's people , their flowing rubblish behaviors may be explained that many of people have enough jobs to do, so they have ability to buy any good taste food to eat or buy any kinds of expensive electronic home products to use. So, this country's economy may be improved for this long period. So, in behavioral economic view, when this country can have many electronic home products rubblishs are flowed on anywherer in streets frequently. It seems that this country will have many people have jobs to do, so it causes they often change old home electronic products or replaced them easily, when they have enough income to spend to buy any kinds of new home electronic products to use at homes easily. Moreover, their flowing old electronic home products behaviors also indicate that this country has many people their salaries may be increased in possible from their emplyers. When this country can have many different kinds of home electornic products are sold. It means that this country's electronic home products needs or demand had been increasing, due to many people have jobs to do and income increases to excite their living of needs also improve. Consequently, this country may seem have better economic improvement. We can observe from this country's electronic home products rubblish increasing income in theis period.

On conclusion, this country ought experience economic growth at this period. So, " flowing expensive electronic home rubblish increasing number

" may seem that this country's economic growth is rapidly in this period, due to many people have jobs to do as well as salaries increase in this period.

Technology how impacts human behavior changing?

Technology how influences human behavior to bring changing? For example, online share purchase and sale transaction from smart phone brings share investor can do share buying or selling transation in any where and any time conveniently, non manual driving auto vehicle, bring car owner feels comfortable and spends free time to do other matter, e.g. reading, listening mucis in himself or herself car freely. electrical energy vehicle can help car owner to reduce air polluton and it can brings the drivers do not feel drive long time in any journeys in order to avoid air pollution for environmental protection responsible car drivers in our societies. Thus, they will drive long time in any journeys when they can drive electronic energy cars to replace oil energy cars.

However, online technology can also bring consumers can choose to stay at homes to buy any things from seller individual online webstore conveniently. Such as online technology can bring shoppers do not need to spend much time to visit shops to buy any things. They can choose any kinds of products from any online sellers individual online webstores conveniently at homes. Online technology excite busy consumers can make purchase decision easily as well as it can help online sellers sell any kinds of products from internet easily.

In behavioral economic view, technology can change human behavior to be improved, it can let human feels comfortable, more free time ro use, rapid making any decisions, such as apply smart phones to make share purchase or sale transaction decision, online shopping decision, even travelling any where decision in short time, when the traveller finds the most cheap hotel accommodation room price and air ticket price frm any travel agent online tourism webstore, then the potential travel customer can follow the online hotel accommodation price and air ticket price data to make decision when to buy the air ticket from the airline travel agent or make decision when to prebook which hotel accommodation room to go to the country to travel from online travel agent tourism webstores. So, technology can encourage global any country travelers to make anywhere to trvel rapidly. If the traveler can find the country's general hotel rooms and airline tickets prices had been decreasing more sightly. The traveler may make travel decision to choose the country to travel in short time, then he/she can prebook the country;s any hotel room and airline ticket to pay by visa fraom the country's any hotel and airline travel agent webstores., before one week, even one month or more easily. Hence, online technology can also encourage traveler individual frequent travel times to be increased, due to global travelers can find any hotel rooms and airline tickets prices from internet conveniently at homes. They do not need to spend time to visit any airline travel agent to enquire travel choice country's hotel rooms prices and airline ticket prices. They can compare global travel of countries choices ' all hotels rooms and airline agents air tickets prices to make prebook airline seat and hotel room decision before one week, one month even six months early.

On conclusion, online technology can encourage global travelers can make travelling any where and when traveling time desicions easily. It can excite tourism industry develops in long time. Also, such as electricity cars invention can encourage environment protection car owners do car purchase decision easily, because they can choose to drive electronic energy cars to replace oil energy cars in order to avoid air pollution occurs easily. So, electronic cars can increase electronic car purchasrs number, due to many of environmental protection attitude of car owners can choose to drive electricity cars to bring air cleans, even non -manual driving cars can encourage lazy driving and free time driving car owners to choose to buy non-manual (artificial intelligent) cars to drive , because they can spend much free time to read, listen music or do any matters in themselves cars, they do not need to drive cars, robotic (AI) auto driving machine is such one non-manual driver to help them to drive themselves cars confidently. So, non-manual driving cars can attract lazy and enjoying free time driving car owners to choose to buy to replace traditional manual cars to drive easily. Moreover, online share transaction can help any share investors to make share buying and selling decision in short time easily. When they can apply smart phones technological tool to carry on share buying and selling activities easily. They can observe any share rising or falling price suitation from smart phones in any where any any time easily. So, smart phone technology can help global any shareholders to make share purchase and sale transaction easily. So, technology can encourage human makes decision in short time rapidly.

How and why employees behaviors may influence economy development?

In behavioral economy view,I believe the country's any organizational employees behavior may bring indirect relationship to influence the country's long term economic development. I shall indicate past manufacture industry social development period to explain their relationship. For many countries' past business activities had belonged to manufacturing industry, such as US, UK past before 1980 year, it focused on steel manufacturing and steel manufacturing related machine products. So, US, Uk developed countries manufacturing industries may be past main country's economic income sources. I assume US , UK past had one million number different kinds of industries. They ought had about seven houndred thousand number organizational businesses were belonged to manufactured industry. They may include:

Steel manufacturing and steel related machine manufacturing, e.g. vehicle manufacturing, home appliances, e.g. washing machine, television, radio, refrigerate cooler, heater, air condition etc. different kinds of different kinds of steel -related manufacturing machine, they were manufactured from US, UK steel machine manufacturers. So, US, Uk the other three hundred thousand number industry may be general service industry, e.g. hotel service, restaurent, cinema, public transport service, tourism lesiure , wine bar, supermarket etc. different kinds of non-manufacturing industries business organizations were operated in UK, US past before 1980 year.

So, in UK, US developed countries industry development history, they ought have high percentage of businesses belonged to steel related manufacturing machine and steel products. Also, in the past before 1980 year, US, Uk business employers , they employed many workers are manufacturing workers. They needed to spend long time to work in factories. They were skillful workers, and they are trained to manufacturing cars, washing machine, television, heater, etc. even steel itself different kinds of steel related products to prepare to deliver to their shops to sell to US, Uk local or overseas clients.

So, I believe that past UK, US ought employ many employees, they belonged to skillful manufacturing workers, manufacture increasing steel machine or steel related machine number of products rapidly daily. So, if UK, US had had many of these manufacturing factories owned high skillful workers, then their manufacturing steel-related machine or steel both kinds of products number must be influenced to raise rapidly. Consequently, their steel machine manufacturing products would been exported to overseas or would been sold to local both markets , they may be influenced to raise sale number. They (these manufacturing workers) needed to be trained to know how to manufactur these different kinds of machine products in the efficient teams and they ought to be trained to raise their efficiencies in order to shorten time to manufacturing many kinds of steel related manufacturing machine or steel itself products rapidly. So , if their efficiencies and manufacturing performance was improved, these US, UK any one manufacturing worker and their teams ought achieve raising productivities significantly.

Hence, when past UK, US manufacturing industry development period, if these two countries‘ any manufacturing factories could have many manufacturing workers could be trained to be skillful and proficient manufacturing workers. Then, in past every day to these factories workers, they ought help their steel or steel related manufacturing employers to raise any kinds of machine or steel products number in every team. So, when past in the manufacturing industry development, US, UK could have many factories' manufacturing workers themselves steel or steel related machine products manufacturing skill could be trained to to improve to any kinds of these machine or steel manufacuring products quality as well as their products number could be influenced to raise by themselves skillful improvement significantly every day.

Then, what would be influenced to occur to past UK, US manufacturing industry period? In behavioral economic view, when these two manufacturing industry developed countries, such as UK, US , if they had many factories workers can be trained to improve their skill in order to achieve any kinds of steel or steel-related machine products quality could be improved as well as products manufacturing number could be also increased absolutely.

In consequence, past UK and US both countries ought increase themselves any kinds of steel and steel related machine products number to be supplied to themselves local shops to let local clients to choose any one kind of machine manufacturing products to buy easily as well as they could also export to supply overseas any countries to buy their different kinds of steel or steel related machine products to let overseas steel or steel related manufacturing machine product buyers, they can have many of these different kinds of these steel or steel-related different kinds of manufacturing machine from UK and UK these both countries easily to compare other countries.

On conclusion, I believe that past US, and UK macro manufacturing industry income GDP would increase significantly. So, they would have good economic growth performance because when many of these manufacturing workers themselves manufacturing effort could be improved. So, it explained when employees manufacturing abilities can influence economic growth indirectly.

Robots invention whether they can help organizations to raise efficiencies or inefficiencies?

In behavioral economic view, in any organizations, when the organization hopes its worker teams can raise efficiencies , the organization may choose to increase more workers number and/or it can provide training to improve these workets themselves skills in order to raise their efficiencies. For one warehouse example, when the warehouse increases many goods , they are needed to delivered these goods from the shelves to the delivering destination locations. If this warehouse supervisors feel these workers themselves goods delivery speeds are slow, which is possible due to this warehouse's workers number is not enough. So, this warehouse supervisor ought increase workers number in order to increase their goods delivery speed in order to deliver goods from the shelves to every indicated goods delivery destination in order to let any one lorry driver can transport the right kinds of goods and ensure the accurate goods number to transport to any one client home rapidly.

However, if this warehouse supervisor planed to buy several warehouse goods delivery robots to assist these warehouse workers to find the right kinds of goods from shelves and then deliver to the right destination location in the warehouse. So, these warehouse orkers can concentrate on counting the accurate goods number and ensuring the right kinds of goods in order to prepare to let lorry drivers to transport these goods to these goods of buyers themselvers homes rapidly. Consequently, in the first step, robots can concentrate on finding th right goods from shelves and delivers them to the right goods transportation of location destination. Then, in the second step, these warehouse workers can concentrate on counting the accurate goods number and ensuring the right kinds of goods in order to prepare to put them to the lorry. Consequently, when warehouse robots and warehouse workers can cooperate to work together, the most important, robots, can deal on finding the right kinds of goods and deal on delivering the accurate number of goods of job duty as well as these warehouse workers can only concentrte on counting the right kinds of goods number in order to avoid it has none any mistake of wrong kinds of goods and inaccurate goods of delivery number to be transported to the lorry and to deliver to any one buyer's home.

So, it seems that warehouse robots ought help any one warehouse worker to raise himself efficiency and avoid goods delivery of mistake occurrence easily as well as their help to warehouse workers that can let any one goods buyer feels their goods can be delivered to their homes rapidly. Moreover, warehouse robots can also help these warehouse workers to raise efficiencies because warehouse robots can help them to shorten goods delivery time between any one shelf and any one goods delivery destination of location in the warehuse because robots may help them to find the right kinds of goods from the right shelf in the short time. So, any one worker does not need to spend long time to seek anywhere is the right shelf location for the kind of goods when the kind of goods are needed to deliver to the buyer's home from lorry. Warehouse robots can help them to do this aspect of " finding the goods from the right shelf in short time job duty". So, any one warehouse worker only needed tospend less time to do the counting of any right kind of goods number and ensuring the right kind of goods job duty. Consequently, this warehouse 's any one worker, his any one kind of goods delivery time may be reduced, because robots' assistance and they may have more confidence to avoid mistake to deliver the wrong number of goods and/or the wrong kind of goods to any one goods buyer's home.

On conclusion, it seems that warehouse robots ought may help any one warehouse worker to raise efficiency for any one team in the warehouse as well as the warehouse any one supervisor does not need to spend much time to observe any one worker individual performance for " goods delivery job duty aspect" because their goods delivery job duty that had been replaced to do by these several warehouse robots. Robots can achieve the more accurate of right kinds of goods and the right number of goods delviery job performance to compare any one of human warehouse worker themselves right kinds of goods of delivery and right number of goods of delivery job performance. So, when robots can participate to cooperate with this warehouse's any one worker to do their goods of delivery job duty in this warehouse every day. Then, robots can raies any one of supervisor individual confidence in order to let they do not need to spend time to observe any one of worker individual whose goods of delivery job performane. They can concentrate on supervising any one worker whose goods transport to lorry in the final step in order to avoid to deliver wrong goods number and / or wrong kind of goods to any one goods buyer's home every day. Consequently, this warehouse's overall teams of their delviery of goods performance many be improved by robotss' participatin to goods of delivery task as well as this warehouse's oveall teams themselves efficiencies may be influenced to raise by robots' goods of delivery task participation.

Why social behavior may influence organizational strategy needs to be changed ?

Why any organizations need to know whether nowadays social behaivor how has been changing in order to implement the kind of the most right strategy to achieve the profit aim pursue in possible. I shall indicate nowadays ecommerce or online, customer shopping behavior to explain above question concerns they ought have close relationship between social behavior and organizational strategic choice or organizational behavioral changing need.

On nowadays ecommerce business, or online shopping model, this kind of shopping model in global many young and old age consumers like to apply internet tool to choose any country sellers website stores in order to stay at home to buy any kinds of products from themselves webstores in global societies.

In fact, online shopping model had been popular for long time above to twenty years. Most of global sellers will make decision to design themselves webstores in order to attract global many online buyers to choose to buy their products from themselves webstores. So, it seems that social consumers purchase behaviors had been changed to online shopping from internet invention.

Hence, social consumers purchase behavioral changes may influence any organizations' strategies need to be changed from visiting shops purchase strategy model to online purchase strategy model, if the seller still concentrate on concentrate on considerate how to design itelf , but neglects to considerate how to design itself webstore, e.g. how to design attract product photos to put on itself webstore, how to arrange sale price information location to be putted on webstore and visa card payment location on itself webstore in order to let any one online buyer can feel very easier to buy itself any kinds of products from itself webstore. Then, its potential online buyers will be influenced to increase number when they can find this online seller itself any kinds of products photes and every kinds of product sale price information and visa card payment channel locations easily from itself webstore.

So, it implies that nowadays any one seller ought need to design one webstore to let any one online overseas and domestic consumers can have chance to click itself webstore to choose any one kind of product to buy conveniently when he/she does not hope to leave him/her home to go to shop, because nowadays social shopping behaviors had been influenced to change when internet invention, them it gives another online purchase method to replace visiting shops purchase method to global any one buyer in nowadays societies.

So, if nowadays any one seller still concentrate on how to design itself shop display in order to put any kinds of product on shelf in order to let any one visiting shop customer to find the kind of product to buy, but it neglects to change to choose to pursue another new technological shopping method, such as webstore purchase method in order to implement effective strategy to design the most right webstore as well as in order to attract global overseas and local consumers to find itself webstore easily from website and find its any one kind of product phots and sale price and visa card payment button in order to choose to buy itself any kinds of products in the short time. Consequently I believe that the seller will lose many customers from overseas and local when its other same or similar product sellers choose to design themselves webstores in order to let global any one product buyer can buy themselves any one kind of product when they can pay visa card to buy their products from them webstores conveniently when they stay at home habitly. Then, the seller will lose many global potential customers in long time.

On conclusion, in behavioral economic view, any consumer behavioral social changing, which will influence any in order to avoid customers number loses significantly . In future time, organizations need to make rapid decision in order to implement the most reasonable and the most useful strategy in order to avoid global potential customers number reduces or lose them in long time. So, social behavioral changing environment ought influence any global organizations need to decide how to change themselves strategies in order to avoid customers loses significantly in future time.

How and why human behavior may influence economic growth or recession?

May ourselves daily behaviors influence our global societial continue economic growth or recession? Do they have cause and effect close relationship between human behaviors and global economic growth or recession? I shall apply behavioral economic theory to analyze and explain whether ourselves daily behaviors and our global societial economic growth or recession which have close cause and effect relationship as below:

Every country itself economic development must depend on any business activities, otherwise, any kinds of business activities must need ourselves business activities or behaviors in order to achieve any business activities as well as achieve the country's overall economic development in macro view. However, any country's overall business activites or behaviors which must depend on any kinds of individual businessmen, themselves employees daily working behavior or activity or performance in order to help them to attract or increase many clients number to acieve " earning profit" aim. So, it seems that any individual business, itself overall every department individual working behavior is one main factor to influence the company's overall business performance.

For agricultural fruit and meat food farming industry example, such as New Zealand is a farming main target industry country. It had had many New Zealanders were daily themselves own farming businesses for many years. Their farming businesses include growing fruit, sheep, cow, pig pork, meat etc. food sale business. If the New Zealand farmer owned a large size farming land, then he will choose either growing fruit or feeding sheeps, pigs, cows to be meat to to transport to New Zealand supermarkets to help them to sell to their farmers meet to New Zealanders in order to earn profit. Thus, if the New Zealand farmer owned large size of farming lands, then he needs to employ many farming employees (farming workers) to help him to carry on farming business daily tasks, e.g. picking up friuts, feeding pigs, cows, sheeps to eat food daily. These daily farming jobs are very important to influence this New Zealand farmer's meats or fruits sale number whether they can be easy or diffcult to sell in New Zealand supermarkets , if these farming workers can own encough farming knowledge or skill to know how to pick up fruits method and make judgement to know whether it is right time to pick up the kind of fruits from the trees , as well as know how feed this pigs, sheeps, cows to eat food in order to let they are better health. Consequently, their farming behaviors which can let these animals can provide the best taste and enough meat from these animals to let New Zealander to buy to eat from New Zealand any one supermarket. Even these New Zealand farming workers can know whether the kinds of fruits, e.g. oranges, apples, gapes etc. fruits whether they ought be picked up from the trees at the right time. Consequently, they can make judgement to decide to pick up any kinds of the best taste fruits to let any one New Zealander to buy to eat from any one supermarket in New Zealand. Otherwise, if they do not make judegement to know whether the kind of fruit ought not be picked up because they still need longer time to continue grow up to increase fruit size and better taste from the trees in order to let any one fruit buyer can feel better taste when they eat this kind of fruit later. If they can buy this kind of fruit to eat later, then this New Zealand farmer's his fruit buyers can buy the best taste of this kind of fruit to eat from an yone supermarket in New Zealand. Consequently, many New Zealand supermarkets will choose to buy any kinds of fruits from this farmer fruit supplier when they feel this farmer's fruits can provide more better taste fruits to compare other farmers' fruits.

Thus, due to New Zealand is one farming main income source country. It's any kinds of fruits and meats need to be export to overseas to sell , instead of local sale. It's GDP percent is very high to whole country 's overall income source. So, any one New Zealand farmer individual and any one farming worker individual working behavior will influence its economy whether it is influenced to grow or recession possible. Moreover, it also seems that farming workers' farming knowledge and skill will influence themselves farming daily activities to achieve the aim of the number of increase or decrease to any kinds of fruits whether they are better taste or the number of increase of decrease to any kinds of meats whether they are better taste to supply to any one New Zealand fruit or meat buyers to eat from any one New Zealand supermarket. So, it implies that any one New Zealand farming worker individual farming behavior may influence any kinds of fruits or any kinds of meat taste because they are transported to any one supermarket to sell in New Zealand.

Consequently, if New Zealans had many farmers can teach god farming knowledge and skill to let their any one farming workers know how to decide judgement to decide when it is right time to pick up any kinds of fruits from trees , or how to grow them on soil in order to let they can grow rapidly. Then, many different kinds of fruits can be provided to let any one New Zealanders can eat the best taste of fruits when their fruits are supplied to any one New Zealand supermarkets. Even, if they knew how to feed foods to pigs, cows, sheeps to eat daily. Then they can be more health and they can provide the best taste of meats to let any one New Zealanders can buy their meats from any one New Zealand supermarkets. Moreover, their fruits and meats can be transported to overseas to let any one country fruits or meats buyers can choose any kinds of New Zealand meats and fruits to buy to eat from themselves countries supermarkets. Then, many overseas fruit and meat buyers will perfer to choose New Zealand any kinds of fruits or meats to buy to compare other countries fruits or meats to buy when they go to any one local supermarkets.

On conclusion, it seems that New Zealand farming workers themselves farming behavior may influence their farming employers any kinds of fruits or meats sale number and incomc because their farming task behaviors must influence whether their fruits or meats taste are the better taste or worse taste to compare their other local farmers (the farmer competitors) whose fruits or meats taste. If tthe farmer's any one farming worker can be trained to learn how to know to feed animals skill and when is the most right time to pick up any kinds of fruits from trees or how to grow them on the soil methods. Due to these farming worker individual farming behavior may influence his different finds of fruits and meats sale number to be increase or decrease, so these any one New Zealand farmer must need to depend on any one farming worker whose farming working methods, if their farming working behaviors can be the best to influence any kinds of fruits to grow rapid or any kinds of pigs, cows, sheeps animals grow up rapidly , then their sale number may be increase significantly and their taste can be improved to let any New Zealand or overseas meat or fruit buyer to buy to eat to feel from any one New Zealand or overseas supermarkets, then New Zealand's agriculture industry must be influenced to increase. In the world, any one fruit or meat buyer must choose to buy New Zealand's fruit and meat to eat in prefer to compare other countries' fruits and meats. So, New Zealand's GDP may be influenced to raise from any one New Zealand farming worker individual farming working behaviors.

Reasons why human behavior may influence economic recession or growth?

Can ourselves daily behaviors or activies influence ourselves countries' economic growth or recession? I shall attempt to explain the reasons why they have direct or indirect relationship between human behavior and economy growth or recession as below:

I shall indicate environment pollition case to attempt to explain above question. Our societies had been experiencing servious environment pollution challenge. However, environment pollution , such as air pollution is caused by air planes and vehicles emission by air planes and vehicles emission as well as water pollution is caused by plastic rubblish, or dirty water or oil or gas chemical material, these both kinds of pollution ought may bring economic recession and this both kinds of pollution are caused by human ourselves daily foolish activities.

I believe human behavior and economy and pollution which have cause and effect relationship. I shall analyze this environment pollution case to explain why they have case and effect relationship between human foolish behavior and environment pollution and economic recession as below:

When global societies had many people like to buy cars to drive to bring emission to fresh air on the roads as well as many manufacturing factories will bring emission to pollute fresh air in their manufacturing processes. Factories and cars will bring air pollution , due to factories need to pollute fresh air in order to manufacture many products and car owners need to drive their cars to go to offices or leisure places. Their cars will also bring emisson to pollute fresh air. On consequence, car owners themselves frequent driving behaviors and factory workers themselves frequent manufacturing behaviors may bring environment pollution. Technology or human behavior whether may influence economic growth or recession. Moreover, air planes also brings emission to pollute air when they are flying in sky. Also, when ships bring oil pollution or sea plastic rubblishs bring pollution to global oceans.

In fact, manufactuers and cars owners, such as factories workers manufacturing behaviours ans car owners driving behaviors and pilots driving air planes flying behaviors and ships transport behaviors, which may cause plastic rubblish, oil or gas emission to sky or sea or on the road to cause ocean and air pollution is serious. However, human ourselves need to buy cars to drive to satisfy ourselves driving leisure or enjoyment, travelers need to catch air planes to travel to enjoy leisure needs, factories workers need help factories to manufacture many products to sell to customers to satisfy their using needs. oil exploration needs to find lands to explore new oil lands.

All of these business and leisure activites may bring serious air and water pollution. However, due to serious air and water pollution will bring earth warming challenge , such as some countries temperature will be influences to rise up to 40 degree or higher br earth warming. However, earth warming is caused by air and ocean pollution. Pollution must be caused by human ourselves, driving cars leisure and factories manufacturing business activities. Hence, if human decided to continue to do these foolish behaviors, we only pursue to manufacture different kinds of industrial products or drive cars to enjoy leisure aims, but we also neglect ourselves behaviors may bring environment pollution. Then, earth warming or earth temperature will be influenced to rise up absolutely in long term. Moreover, if our future earth will be influenced to bring serious high temperature effect by human ourselves these foolish behaviors.

On consequencey, warth warming will bring serious economic losses in possible because when ourselves earth temperature had been influenced to rise up to 40 degree or high. Ourselves health will be caused poor, due to we will feel difficult breath, we must need often tried and hard to work, due to our nervous and health will be influenced to poor by pollution and earth warming effect. Also, we need to pay more money to see doctors when we had long life. Then, our societies will lose may strong labors to help manufacturers to work, e.g. factories will reduce workers number to help manufacturers to produce more different kinds of products, due to workers health is general poor. Due to lacking enough workers to manufacture products, our societies will begin to reduce enough supply number of products to sell to global consumers to satisfy their use needs.

On conclusion, in behaviroal economic view, our societies will lose many labors due to their bodies are not health by air and water pollution. Global economic and business activities will be influenced to worse by global workers reducing number reason. So, economic recession will begin to occur in possible when pollution reaches the serious level.

CHAPTER FIVE

Robots Reduce Human Workers Competitive Value

Although, (AI) technology will be popular to applied to different jobs, but it still needs social acceptance to replace some human jobs. Today, it is increasingly common for people to use robots in various situations at home and in retail stores, hotels and hospitals. Robots are classified into several types based on their functionality (service and utility robots or those designed to communicate with humans) and appearance (humanoid robots or mechanical robots). The types of robot to which every country attaches particular important in the advance of robotics, reflects the sense of values and preferences of its population . Thus, (AI) will be applied to replace human to do these above different kinds of job nature. For example, U.S. has the highest level of robot utilization at home and an retail stores with its people being the most enthusiastic about the future use of robots. Otherwise, Germany shows a strong tendency to consider robots for industrial purposes, and its people feel strong to the presence of robots in their households. Japanese accepts to apply" human aid robot" that can communicate with humans and they have a high level of familiarity with robots.

Hence, it implied those three countries have accept (AI) to replace human to do any these kinds of job duty and it will influence these three countries‘ workers lose their old occupations and who will unemployed absolutely, due to many (AI) robots replace them to do their job duties in the future. Also, US will have many retail service workers or retail warehouse workers are unemployed. Germany will have many manufacturing industry's workers are unemployed. Japanese will have many communication industry workers are unemployed, such as telephone service, shopping center services etc. different kind of service industry's service staffs . It will cause these kind of workers' competitive abilities are lost in themselves countries' jobs that require such skills include software developers, court judges, nurses, high school teachers, dentists and university lecturers, these occupations are still difficult to be replaced by (AI) robots.

Are robots taking our jobs or making them? In fact, our societies will have unemployment challenges, even (AI) technology has not created before. However, after (AI) robots invention, some of human jobs will be replaced and it can raise many low skillful and low knowledge level worker unemployment number. However, I think that high productivity driven by increasingly powerful IT -enabled machines is the causes of global labor market problems and accelerating technological change will only make those problems worse.

IT technology brings this question: Are robots killing human's jobs or benefiting human's jobs? I suppose that there is a limited amount of labor to be done. The implication is that technology can create unemployment by displacing workers, such as (AI) invention, because the more efficiently worker work (using machines or (AI) robots), the loss work there is for workers to do. Even, any new jobs will be better done by machines or (AI) robots, and unemployment will still skyrocket. How do we know that humans will always be better at some work, or more importantly, enough work, than machines or (AI) robots, e.g. human drivers drive more safe or careful to compare (AI) robot drivers. But, the challenge is that it is not ensure that (AI) robots drivers must not drive careless to cause the chance of accident occurrences more than human drivers. However, technological change can be beneficial to innovation, automation and increasing productivity for businesses.

Consequently , it may seem machines can hurt wages and job for low skillful, less educated workers. Also, high educated workers are likely as less educated workers to find themselves displaced and devalued, and more education may create as many problems as it solves. Thus, in negative influence, automation effects on particular jobs shift workers to other jobs that are equally or more desirable. Workers may be highly compensated for possessing human capital that is specialized to a labor market. If technological advance is very rapid, such as (AI) invention, causing a large and very rapid drop in demand in a large labor market, the economy may not be able to absorb the sudden surplus of labor in a short period of timer when (AI) robots are popular to replace some workers to do some occupations in global societies.

For example, self-driving vehicles threaten to send truck drivers to the unemployment office. Computer programs can now write journalistic accounts of sporting events and stock price movement. There are even computers that can grade essay revolutionize some part of teaching jobs. Hence, (AI) robots will have possible to replace human brain to do any judgement, argument, and mind job duties. It implies some occupations which need human' mind will be threaten by (AI) robots, e.g. author, accountant, nurse, engineer. Thus, (AI) robots will have possible to replace some professional and high educated workers' jobs in the future.

But, technology can create new nature of jobs in possible. For example, a 60 minutes program indicated technology is putting new categories of jobs in the sites (sic) of automation, the 60% of the workforce that makes its living gathering and analyzing information. Also, recession: technology kills middle -class jobs that overall technology is eliminating for more jobs than it is creating by (AI) technology. Hence, human's brain work may be assisted by 60% of (AI) gathering and analyzing information for some occupation , e.g. space scientists, ocean scientists, earth scientists etc.

However, I believe the (AI) invention and human job competition may influence global productivity change. Productivity is economic output per unit of input, the unit of on input can be labor hours(labor productivity), but if (AI) robots replace human job, then the unit of input may be (AI) machine hours (AI) robot productivity or all production factors including labors, machines and energy (total factor of productivity). Producing more output with less input can take several forms.

The traditional notion of productivity is a form reorganizing production and/or using better or more technology to produce more output per worker hour. But when (AI) robots invention, the form can be reorganizing production and/or using better or more (AI) robots to produce more output per (AI) robot hour. Hence, if the firm apply (AI) robots to produce its products. Then , productivity improvements in the firm may result in less workers employment, due to (AI) robots replace more worker number to achieve more productivity improvement, it has economic benefits (less factor of production) , but more production in long term.

Thus, (AI) robots can help any firm to achieve productivity improvement in long term, for example, if unproductve farmers move to the city and start working for high-tech. manufacturers. The shift effect can be more dynamic and disruptive as low-productivity industries lose out in the marketplace to high -productivity industries and the compositional mix of the economy changes. Thus, in the long term (AI) robots can also be beneficial to high productivity industries to bring the mix of economy positive changes.

Moreover, automation will also produce some new jobs in firms that sell the new robot or other labor-saving technology. This means that, in general, there will be shift in the economy in the direction of higher-skill and higher wage jobs. Even if the (AI) robot invention country, US becomes a leader in (AI) robots producing productivity-enhancing technology, it will experience a growth in jobs serving foreign (AI) robots product buyers. Hence, (AI) robots can also create (AI) salespeople, (AI) manufacturing workers , (AI) inventors, scientists, (AI) software designer etc. occupations, when if all society does is move workers from insurance firms, restaurants and car factories to robot factories, productivity will have remained the same to create job needs for insurance, restaurant and car manufacturing worker service occupations for (AI) software designer, (AI) service robots manufacturer, (AI) service robot seller etc. related (AI) service robot product occupation created in (AI) robot technology job market. Hence, (AI) invention also create new (AI) technology job chance. (AI) impacts management job market.

In future, organization management will be changed from (AI) introduction. Division of labor will change and collaboration among humans and machines will increase. Companies will have to adapt their training, performance and talent acquisition strategies to account for a new found emphasis on work that hinges on human
judgement and skills, including experimentation and colloboration.

How (AI) impacts any organizational administrative management work? (AI) 's greatest impact will be on administrative coordination and control tasks, such as scheduling, resource allocation and reporting, (AI)-driven will place a higher premium on what we call " judgement work", the application of human experience and expertise to critical business decisions and practices when information available is insufficient to suggest a successful course of action. This kind of work will require new skills and mindsets; replacing people with machines is not goal in itself. When, artificial intelligence enables cost-cutting automation of routine work, it also empowers value -adding augmentation of human capabilities.

Thus, administrative and routine tasks, such as scheduling, allocation of resources, and reporting, will within intelligent machines, responsibilities that have long been reserved for humans. For instance, a typical store manager or a lead nurse at a nursing home must constantly juggle shift schedules, accounting for staff members' absense owing to illness, vaction, time or sudden departures. Many of these tasks will be automated by (AI). Imagine (AI) writing management monthly reports, it is not a distant dream. Leading news providers and Wall street banks are now using (AI) report generators to write news and analytical reports by drawing on quantitative data. The associated press, for example, expanded its quarterly earnings reporting from approximately 300 companies to nearly 3,000 with the help of (AI) powered software robots, freeing up journalists to conduct more investigative and interpretive reporting. For another example, Jobalime, a job-placement site, uses intelligent voile analysis algorithms to evaluate job applicants. The algorithm assesses paralinguistic elements of speech, such as tone and inflection, products which emotions a specific voice will elicit, and identifies the type of work at which an applicant will likely excel. In the future , (AI) machines can be applied to assist some kind of office administrative jobs duties. It's attractive to office managers to achieve more accurate judgment to do any administrative matters when who can be assisted from (AI) machines. Thus, managers need to spend time to learn how to apply (AI) machine to assist them to do more accurate judgement, and better informed choices. (AI) robots can be applied to improve the speed quality and cost of available products and services, instead of applying on productivity improvement and administrative improvement aspects. Thus, they may also displace large numbers of workers. This, possibility challenges the traditional benefits model of trying health care and retirement savings to jobs.

In an economy that employs dramatically fewer workers to deliver benefits to displaced workers. For example, the worldwide number of industrial robots has increased rapidly over the past few years. The fall prices of robots, which can operate all day without interruption, make them cost- competitive with human workers. In special consideration, in the service sector, computer algorithums can execute stock trades in a fraction of a second, much faster than any human. As those technologies become cheaper, more capable, and more widespread, they will find even more applicants in an economy.

Consequently, (AI) technology brings unemployed number increasing many businesses continued automating their operations rather than hiring additional workers. A trend among technology companies that receive massive valuations with relatively few workers. For example, in 2014 year Google was valued at $370 billion with only 55,000 employees, a tenth the size of AT & T's workforce in the 1960 year. Hence, if automation technologies like robots and artificial intelligence make jobs less secure in the future, there needs to be a way to deliver benefits outside of employment " flexi security" or flexible security is one idea for providing healthcare, education and housing assistance whether or not someone is formally employed.

In conclusion, (AI) and robots technology will raise unemployment to some occupations when (AI) replaces same industries' workers job duties in our societies in the future, but it also create new jobs to raise employment in any related (AI) robots and automated machine products in (AI) manufacturing. (AI) design, (AI) sale self-related industry, when (AI) replaces same industries' workers' job duties.

(AI) journalism, media publishing, digital communication technology trend

How to apply (AI) technology in digital communication journalism media, publishing industry? Some scientists indicate future (AI) and digital technology may consist such as: voice driven assistants, emerge. For example, Amazon e book publish applying digital technology and (AI) auto printing technology to sell e books to let readers to listen any e book content by (AI) voice driven speaker when they turn on computer to read e book contents; capable phones start to unlock the possibilities of 3D image of mobile story telling. New smart wearables include ear buds that handle instant translation and glasses that talk and hear. China and India will become a key focus for digital growth with innovations around payment online identity, and artificial intelligence. Thus, future (AI) technology can be applied to 3D image mobile story telling, online payment method to dealt online transaction publishing industry.

Thus, future (AI) technology can be applied to online e book publishing industry to make sound books to let readers feel more attractive . Such as Amazon publish has published sound e books to attract readers to choose to read any its books from online. Also, (AI) technology can also be applied to communication industry. For example, some online pure-play news, opinion and entertainment websites. It is a digital communication media, e.g. online journalism blog (AI) technology can be applied to visual storytellers to let online book readers to enjoy to listen to watch and send any online electronic book contents more attractive. Thus, future (AI) technology will be popular to assist any electronic book publishers to publish visual and sound talking storybook to let readers who can watch motive image and listen and read words from e books more attractive.

Thus, (AI) technology can be applied to internet ecommerce publishing or media industry to help any electronic book publishers to publish sound, image motion electronic book to attract global readers to read, even (AI) technology can be applied to digital entertainment industry, e.g. electronic 3D image virtual video games, computer games. It can be also applied to education industry, e.g. the first true digital native generation and are the native speakers of the digital language of computers to let student to learn different languages or translate words to compare to classroom learning more easily. It can be also applied to communication industry, e.g. (AI) mobile phone. Hence, it seems (AI) technology can be applied to publishing, communication, education , entertainment etc. different industries in the future. (AI) technology will be one kind of tool to satisfy human's daily life needs in the future and these industries has one characteristics is that they need to apply internet to operate to operate to do online business.

Thus, it has three trends of (AI) technology and internet technology need to be linked to achieve one kind of attractive technological business to satisfy client's needs. These three trends as below: All consumer trends involve the internet. It will be many consumer's online habits, shopping, working, socializing, watching TV, studying, travelling, listening. Thus, (AI) music, eating and exercising are just a few examples. This is happening because human usually use mobile broadband or Wi-Fi, rather than cables. Thus, (AI) technology will be applied to mobile to satisfy client's need absolutely.

The mobile phone can be more popular to be used more than computer or laptop tools. The reasons are because women dive the smartphone market by defining mass-market use. But as the speed of technology adoption increases mass market use becomes much quicker then before. Successful new technological products and services , such a (AI) mobile phone products now reach the mass market in popular use. It means that the time period when early adopters influence others is shorter than before. Also, since new products and services increasingly use the internet mass markets are not only faster , but are also more important than ever to consumer themselves. Most internet services become more valuable to individuals when many use them. Thus, it causes why (AI) mobile phone will be popular to be used.

Since, new products and services increasingly use the internet, in the future several trends focus on (AI) smart phone users. Consumers' familiarity with using smartphone apps. Essentially, the technologies will bring other related (AI) and internet service needs, e.g. sound and image emotion e book needs, (AI) mobile communication needs, e-virtual games or e-3D image virtual games etc. entertainment activities needs with such a large part of the world's population now online, it is clear that there is strength in numbers.

Thus, (AI) imagines , if future any (AI) and internet related services or products new technology is easy to use and inexpensive, when the latest products reach the mass market almost as quickly as they reach the early adopters and industry experts. I believe that any (AI) and internet related products or services must be popular to accept to consume for entertainment or useful aim. For example, with major players including Apply, Facebook and Google had invested (AI) technology to develop their businesses. (AI) technology has the potential to disrupt everything in the coming years, from the lives of connected consumers to every industry (AI) will be an alternative route for brands to reach consumers with convincing and relevant messages. Digital technology will assist of the future, then it can improve technology to bring this effect, such as sophisticated software machine learning and speech recognition effective. Hence, Google, Facebook , Yahoo web site service companies can apply (AI) technology to help other companies to advertise their businesses, such as travel, retail, and education etc. industries more attractive. (AI) technology can be applied to internet company to be aware and familiar enough to drive among mainstream consumers, it can create online experience to travel, retail , education and other entertainment needs to online consumers to seek their entertainment needs more easily. Hence, in the future (AI) technology and internet related entertainment service needs will be raised in this (AI) and online consumption market.

- (AI) healthcare service industry development

In the future, (AI) medical internet technology tool can be applied to assist individual's health at the center of their focus, e.g. smartwatch compatible mobile app. patients can let personalized reminders for taking their medication snap pictures of their prescriptions to expedite refills, and scan their insurance card. So that, store clerks are prepared with up-to-date patients' information . (AI) owned health operated technological clinics can help patients to receive treatment for minor illnesses, flu shots, cholesterol screenings and more than a dozen other medical services, all of which can be patients who can't make it to a physical location. (AI) healthcare services organizations can provide various telemedicine services. So, patients can receive care via phone or video chat.

For example, one London-based intelligent Brewing company has developed an (AI) system to continuously collect and incorporate customer feedback, which the system itself uses to brew ne various of the company's beers. Thus, the beer clients can give feedback to talk to the algorithm (AI) machine, whenever or anywhere who're drinking the beer. It is such any healthcare services organizations can apply (AI) machine to collect patient's feedback to talk to the algorithum (AI) machine whenever or anywhere who're eating any medicines. So doctors can know every patient's health conditions any time. If the patients feel uncomfortable, the doctor can know from (AI) machine notification to decide whether the patient needs to eat another new medicine or keep to eat same medicine is better. Hence, (AI) medial internet technological body check report machine will be proper to be needed to serve any hospitals' patients in the future.

However , it brings this question. How can (AI) medical internet technological body check report machine apply to hospital more efficient? The essential new medicine co-workers for the health service digital age health service leaders need apply (AI) medical report machines and artificial intelligence to the newest recruits to the workforce bringing new skills to help health service staffs do new jobs and reinventing what's possible, building the health service workforce for today's digital health service demands for patients. Thus, technology-driven health service model innovation from the health service organization outside in and providing digital health service ecosystems for patients to use the (AI) health service equipment will be popular to be accepted to be used.

● I Robot and internet things future machine
men invention

Nowadays, there are some company, which apply internet and (AI) I Robot technology to do any similar human job nature. For fishing industry example, one company, known for creating the Roomba, I Robot is now working with marine conservationists to launch an ocean-patrolling intelligent robot to hunt and manage invasive species, protecting native populations. And evolved industries like precision agriculture are ramping of our increasing population. Area of practice that once seemed impossible to digitize are fundamentally changing because of the impacts of (AI), internet of things capabilities and big data analytics, which have many potentially positive impactions for society.

For textile industry example, automation is nothing new, it has shaped the workplace to replace human jobs to boost productivity in the textile industry. Textile machines have had a generally positive impact over gears, creating value and allowing textile workers to take up more rewarding age will likely continue to create opportunities and lead to new textile industries, companies and textile occupations. It may also compensate for a demographically driven slowdown in the growth of the textile workforce. The future impact of textile (AI) and automatic and internet link is somewhat uncertain. It seems textile industry will be trend to accept (AI) textile workers and internet of thing to replace traditional manual textile workers to produce any shirts, cloths etc. wearing products in factories popularly, during the (AI) textile machine and internet thing technology can be invented to reach the mature stage in the future.

For factory worker transportation job example, they have also expanded their influence, migrating from the factory floor to the service sector and taking the place of humans in a range of activities from financial transactions to transport route optimization. Further (AI) machines and robots are increasingly programmed to learn, meaning they improve with time and undertake cognitive activities. Hence, (AI) machines and internet technology enable automation of work activities to raise factory workers‘ efficient and performances, also factories can reduce manual worker numbers, due to (AI) machine workers' assistance.

Future, (AI) robotics technologies and internet technique have these different kinds of characteristics: For soft robotics example, it is non-rigid robots construct with soft and deformable materials that can manipulate items of varying size, shape and weight with a single device. For swarm robotics, it coordinated multi-robot systems often involving large numbers of mostly physical robots. For touch/factile robotic example, it robotic body pails (often biologically inspired hands) with capability to sense, touch , dexterity robots example, serpentine robots with many internal degrees of freedom to threat through tightly packed spaces for humanoid robots example, robots physical is similar to human being often bi-pedal that investigate variety capable of performing human tasks , including movement across terrains, object recognition, speech sensing etc. For autonomous cars and trucks example, it is capable of operating with a human pilot, e.g. the unarmed general atomics Predator XPUAV with roughly half the wingspan of a Boeing 737 can fly autonomously for up to 35 hours from take-off to landing, for unmanned aerial vehicles example, flying vehicles capable of operating without a human pilot, the unarmed general atomics predator -XPUAV , with roughly half the wingspan of a Boing 737, and fly autonomously for up to 35 hours from take off to landing, for (AI) chat bots example, (AI) systems designed to simulate conversation with human users, particularly those integrated into massaging apps.

In Dec. 2015. the general service administration of the US Govt. described how it used a chat bot named Mrs. Landingham (a character from the television show the west wing) to help onboard new employees. Finally, for robotic process automation example, class of software robots that replicates the actions of a human being interacting with the user interfaces of both software systems. Enables the automation of many back-office work flows without requiring expensive IT integration . Hence, future (AI) robot machine men will have different functions to be applied to different industries to use in possible.

Statistics Denmark shows that (AI) automation potential robots will influence few jobs are completely automatable , but close to half consists of 40% automatable tasks: It showed example occupations include share of automated, such as brewing machine operators are more than 80%, logging equipment operators are more than 50%, roofers , stock tasks clerks, travel agent are more than 50%, farmers , nursing assistants are more than 30%, physicians, teachers , managers are more than 10%.

For example, humans perform a wide variety of tasks from planting corn to examine spreadsheets, meeting clients and lifting crates in a store. Each of these actions requires a combination of innate or acquired capabilities, internet technique assistance, ranging from social perceptiveness to fine motor skills and natural language understanding. To understand and map automation feasibility by existing technology. Mc Kinsey has developed a framework of 18 technical capabilities that can substitute tasks performed by humans. The capabilities are grouped in five categories: sensory, cognitive, language, social and emotional and physical. So, it seems (AI) robot machine men and internet technique will have possible combination to invent to own human's emotion , language, learning, task skill abilities.

Mckinsey global institute analysis also showed current technologies have achieved different levels of human performance across 18 capabilities include: sensory perception, autonomously infer and integrate complex input using sensors, cognitive capabilities reorganizing known patterns/ categories supervised learnings, generating novel, logical reasoning/ problem solving, optimization and planning, creative, information retrieval, coordination with multiple agents, output articulation/presentation, national language processing, social and emotional capabilities-natural language understanding, social and emotion sense, reasoning output, physical capabilities-fine motor skills, navigation mobility. Hence, it seems (AI) robots and internet technological will combine to invent to own human' some skills to replace human to do some kind of tasks in possible.

In conclusion, future (AI) robot and internet will be needed to link to cooperate together to raise human's work efficiency in popular.

How artificial intelligence replaces human job possibility

What is the risk of automation for jobs to replace human job? In recent years, there has been a revival of concerns that automation and digitalization night after all result in jobless future. As I argue, this might lead to an overestimation of job (AI) automate , as occupations labelled as high-risk occupations often still contain a substantial share of tasks that are hard to automate.

For example, when the share of (AI) automatable jobs is 6% in Korea, the corresponding share is 12% in Australia. Differences between countries may reflect general differences in workplace organization, differences in previous investments into (AI) automation technologies as well as differences in the education of workers across countries. I also discover that (AI) automation and digitalization are unlikely to destroy large numbers of jobs. But, however, low qualified labors are likely to raise costs as the (AI) automate of their jobs is higher compared to highly qualified workers.

In fact, (AI) technology will influence some new technology to replace some human's job, such as driverless car, the largely autonomous smart factory , service robots or 3D printing. These technologies are driven by advances in computing power, robotics and artificial intelligence and ultimately redefine what type of human capabilities machines are able to do.

Hence, question brings whether (AI) invention will influence general human jobs to be replaced by (AI) autonomous jobs? Whether will the potential foe automation with actual employment loss? In particular, the technical possibility to use (AI) machines rather tasks need not mean that the substitution of humans by machines actually takes place.

Whether (AI) technology replaces human's some job, it is beneficial to our society or not. Instead, machines are increasingly capable of performing non-routine cognitive tasks, such as driving or legal writing . In particular, advances in the field of machine learning (ML), e.g. computational statistics and visions, data mining, artificial intelligences allow for automating cognitive task, when the use of (ML) in mobile robotics (MR) also allows for automating certain manual tasks. So, it seems, (AI) technology can replace some labor job, e.g. warehouse transportation, even mind's job, e.g. legal writing, driving in possible.

For example, if (AI) automatic non-manual driving can reduce hurt or death risk, it is beneficial to our society, or (AI) automatic robots can more any heavy things (products) in warehouse safely. Then, it can reduce the warehouse labor's bodies hour risk, it is beneficial to the workers. Even, if (AI) robot can write any legal documents, no any word errors in short time. It is beneficial to the law companies , but it also bring unemployment chance, due to these jobs can be replaced by (AI) robots to do in the future. Hence, it will cause some occupation to be disappeared, due to (AI) robots can do our these kinds of jobs in the future.

Frey & Osborne (2013) reported these kinds of occupations will be replaced by (AI) robots in possible. They include computer, engineering, financial, management, legal , art and medium, community service, education, healthcare practitioners and technical service, sales and related, office and administrative support, farming, fishing and forestry, construction and extraction, installation, maintenance, and repair , production, transportation and material moving. It seems our future some professional occupations will have possible to the replaced by (AI) robots to replace, instead of labor jobs. Hence, (AI) robots technology will have much trend to replace high knowledge or low knowledge skillful labors in the future.

In conclusion, it implies that only using information on task-usage at the individual level leads to significantly lower estimates of jobs " at risk", some workers in occupations with according to high automate nevertheless often perform tasks with are hard to automate. Why can (AI) replace human to do some kinds of jobs? (AI) artificial intelligence refers to the ability of a computer or a computer enable robotic system to process information and produce outcomes in a manner similar to the thought process of humans in learning, decision making and solving problem. By extension, the goal of (AI) systems is to develop systems to capable of tasking complex problems in ways similar to human's logic and reasons who feel in our future. Hence, it means future (AI) robots has effort to replace human to do any jobs in possible.

(AI) directions for future non-manual
control road vehicles market

Future road vehicle products and technologies must meet social, economic and environmental protection and driving safety goals , and satisfying market requirements for mobility, accident reducing, performance, cost desirability. Thus, (AI) auto-non manual control vehicles need to be followed this direction to invent. To satisfy future driver's safety of needs, enhanced vehicle speed desired functional performance of road transportation system, required and desired technological response, including research needs. It is long term up to 20 years vision, for (AI) auto non-manual research. Thus, (AI) auto non manual vehicle manufacturers need often to revise their (AI) vehicles functions to raise to improve their system performance and driving industry driver's needs, e.g. private drivers need or public transportation driver's need or business client's need. Hence, future (AI) transportation will need have individual driving consumer and business driving consumer both targets.

Thus, future (AI) automation manual control vehicles need to deliver high impact technology solutions to meet social , economic and environmental and safe goals. Engine needs to be improved efficiency , performance, drivability, reliability, durability and speed-to-market together with reduced emissions and cost; hybrid, electric and alternatively fuel (AI) non manual control vehicle technology development, leading to new fuel and power systems, such as hydrogen, fuel cells and batteries, which satisfy future social, economic and environmental and safe goals. Software, sensors, electronics and telematics technology development are needed to be lead to improve vehicle performance, control and adaptability, intelligent , mobility and security, structure and materials technology development, leading to improved safety, performance and leading to flexibility with reduced cost and environmental pollution to achieve the (AI) non manual drivers to feel (AI) vehicle performance, auto control and adaptability is better to compare traditional manual driving vehicles.

In fact, in traditional manual driving market, Japan and USA had had over 80% of world car production by six major global groups. In the future, it is possible only USA can dominate (AI) non manual auto driving vehicle manufacturing market if Japan had no effort to manufacture any (AI) auto non manual control vehicles. So, it means that it is only Japan is USA potential (AI) auto non manual control vehicle manufacturing competitors. Also, it means that it is only USA has effort to export (AI) auto non manual control vehicles to global (AI) auto non manual control vehicle market.

Thus, in long term, (AI) non manual control vehicle product market development, USA (AI) vehicle manufacturers will have these requirement to win new technological competition to traditional manual control vehicle. The requirements include: low cost fuel, low carbon, fuel cell and telematics technologies, the technological roadmap function, such as detailed consideration clear provision of other important areas to the drivers. When the (AI) non manual auto drivers are sitting in the non manual control auto vehicle. Although, who does not need to drive, but who need to know how to go to anywhere by electric road map show clearly. So, the driver won't lose direction and he/she can know the (AI) non manual control vehicles is driving to anywhere in any time, even when who is sleeping.

In the future, the (AI) non manual control vehicles need to be invented to satisfy any business , transportation clients' needs, instead of individual clients needs, e.g. cans, trucks, buses, emergency and utility vehicles, trains, trams etc. Hence, technological road mapping is one important tool to help any business, transportation (AI) non manual control vehicle clients. Technological roadmap is a technique that is used in industry to support strategic planning for (AI) non manual driving vehicles in the future. Electronic road maps generally take the form of multi-layered time based charts, linking technology developments to future (AI) non manual control vehicle market requirements.

Technology road mapping is a flexible technique and the roadmap architecture and process for developing the roadmap most generally be customized to meeting the particular aims. Why technology roadmap will be popular to (AI_ non manual control vehicles. It's advantages include: It is a technology solutions and options that can enable the performance targets to be achieved engine hybrid, electric and alternatively fueled vehicles, software, sensors electronics and telematics, structures and materials design and manufacturing process. It is road transport system performance measures and targets tool, in response to the trends and get (AI) non manual control vehicle drivers to get society, economy, environment protection, low cost driving benefits, also it can help any transportation clients to know how to go to anywhere clearly. Hence, technological road map will be one good tool to assist (AI) non manual control auto vehicle to develop future road driving market.

Reference(source)

Frey & Osborne (2013), The future of employment: How susceptible are jobs to computerization? University of Oxford.

Mckinsey Global Institute Analysis

Statistics Denmark, Global automation impact model, Makinsey analysis

(AI) development second stage

(AI) -driven automation industry development

(AI) -driven automation industry will create wealth and expand economy growth to any countries, but it will be accompanied by changed in the skills that workers need to learn. One of main ways that technology increases productivity is by decreasing the number of labor hours needed to create a unit of output. It implies (AI) technology will influence low educated and low skillful labor number to be decreased (reduction employment number).

In contrast, technological change tended to work in a different direction throughout the nowadays. The advance of computer and the internet raised the relative productivity of higher skilled workers. So, routine-intensive occupations that focused on predictable tasks disappearance, such as switch board, operators, filming checkers, travel agents and assembling line workers etc. were particularly replaced by new technologies.

However, today, it may be challenging to predict exactly which jobs will be most immediately affected by (AI) driven-automation. The reason is because (AI) is not a single technology, but rather a collection of technologies that are felt unevenly through the economy to influence job changing both negatively and positively. In positively view point, (AI) driven-automation will make many workers more productive and increase demand for certain skills. Consequently, new jobs are likely to be directly create in areas , such as the development and supervision of (AI) as well as indirectly created in a range of areas throughout the economy as higher incomes lead to expanded demand. Otherwise, in negatively view point, many traditional human needed (demand) skillful jobs will be threatened by automation are highly concentrated among lower-paid, lower-skilled and less -educated workers. It means automation will cause pressure on demand for this group, pressure and employment, if (AI) can replace the low skilled and less educated workers' jobs. Thus, (AI) will have negative influence to impact on the labor market.

(AI) capabilities will enable automation of some tasks that have long required human labor. Why can (AI) replace some simple human jobs? For example, advances in robotics are expanding machines' abilities to interact with and sharp the physical world. Combined , (AI) and robotics will give rise to smarter machines that can perform more sophisticated functions than ever before and brings more advantages that humans have exercised. This will permit automation of many tasks now performed by human workers and could change the shape of the labor market and human activity.

How (AI) influences labor market

Today, it may be challenging to predict exactly which jobs will be most immediately affected by (AI)-driven automation. Because (AI) is not a single technology, but rather a collection of technologies that are applied to specific tasks.

Some specific predictions are possible based on the current (AI) technology. For example, driving jobs and house cleaning jobs, bank counter service jobs, telephone enquiry service operators. Restaurant cooking jobs, simple accounting record service jobs etc. that require relatively less education to perform. Advancements in computer vision and related technologies have made the feasibility of fully appear more likely, potentially displacing some workers in driving-dominant professions. Seemingly similar robot, for which the operational tasks is less specific of navigating to a specific destination when following a set of given rules and preserving safety.

In the future, the effects of (AI) on the labor market in the decade ahead will continue the trend toward skill-biased change that computerization and communication innovations have driven in recent decades. Thus, some human driving occupation will be disappeared or replaced by (AI) automation driven. For example, bus drivers, light truck or delivery services drivers, heavy and tractor-trailer truck drivers, school drivers, tax drivers, travel bus drivers.

However, (AI) technology could enable some workers to focus time on other job responsibilities, boosting their productivity, and actually raised

wage growth among those still holding the reshaped jobs. For example, salespeople, who currently spend a considerable amount of time driving could find themselves able to do other work when a car drives them from place to place, or inspectors and appraisers could fill out paperwork, when their car drives itself. This (AI) -driven technology should make these workers more productive, with (AI) -driven technology serving as a complement, not a substitute. New jobs will also likely be created, both in existing occupations cheaper transportation costs with lower prices and increase demand for products and all the related occupations, such as service and fulfillment, and in new occupations not currently foreseeable.
What kind of jobs will be created by (AI) technology? Predicting future job growth is extremely difficult, due to it depends on technologies or substitute for existing today as well as they may complement or substitute for existing human skills and jobs. However, (AI) will also lead to substantial indirect job creation to the degree it raises productivity and wages, it may also lead to higher consumption that would support additional jobs from high-end draft production to restaurant and retail. The future(AI) " augmented intelligence", the technology's role is as assisting and expanding the productivity of individuals rather than replacing human work. Thus, based on the biased-technical change framework, demand for labor will likely increase the most in the areas where humans complement (AI) automation technologies. For example, (AI) technology , such as IBM's Watson may improve early detection of some cancers or other illnesses, but a human healthcare professional is needed to work with patients to understand and translate patients' symptoms, inform patients of treatment options, and guide patients through treatment plans. Shipping companies may also partner workers who pick up and deliver products over the last feet with (AI) enabled autonomous vehicles that move workers efficiently from site to site. In such cases, (AI) augments what a human is able to do and allows individuals to either be move effective in their specially task or to operate on a larger scale. Thus, it seems (AI) technology will also create new jobs, raise productivities and workers‘ efficiencies.

Redefining management in the workforce of artificial intelligence

In the future, due to artificial intelligence influences to some kind of human jobs nature. So, the kind of human jobs of management methods will also need to change to adapt the artificial intelligence technology input to their organizations. It will cause challenges for every executive and manager if who won't have effort to manage their teams how to apply artificial intelligence technology to work efficiently and easily. For example, division of labor will change among humans and machines will increase. Thus, companies will have to adapt their training performance and talent strategies how to emphasize on work that how to make human judgment and skills and experimentation. Thus, (IA)'s greatest impact will be on administrative coordination and control tasks, such as scheduling , resource allocation.

In fact, mangers will encounter this challenges: How to apply human experience and expertise to judge critical business decisions and practices when the information available is insufficient to suggest a successful course of action? Due to this kind of work will require new skills and mindsets. I shall indicate these change management methods to adapt (AI) technology. Such as: administration and routine tasks, scheduling , allocation of resources and reporting will fall within the intelligence machines, responsibilities that have long been reserved for humans. For example, a typical store manager or a lead nurse at a nursing home most constantly arrange shift schedules, accounting for staff members' absences owing to illness, vacation time or sudden departures.

Thus, the managers need to learn how to arrange new division of labor within the organizations after (AI) technology had been implemented to the organization. Artificial intelligence is currently influencing into once considered exclusive to humans: assessing and acting on human emotions and personality traits. The influences to managers need to change their strategies to adapt (AI) technology implements include such as below:

Firstly, managers need to spend the bulk of their time on coordination and control tasks from intelligent system implements. Their time spending on these major three aspects from impact of intelligent system: coordinate and control, solve problems and collaborate and people and community , strategy and innovation three aspects. Thus (AI) will influence managers need to change their judgment method to teach whose teams how to adapt the (AI) system operations in any organizations.

Secondly, (AI) will influence top, middle and low level management needs to change to adapt the (AI) technology operations to any owned (AI) technology organizations in the future. Intelligent machines must be trained in context. Just like humans , on-the-job training is a requirement for such machines because they typically arrive with only very general capabilities. To get the most from (AI), managers at all levels must participate in the instructional experience and in the learning process and provides managers' familiarity with such systems on these aspects, e.g. How the system works and generate advice, how the system has a proven track record , how the system provides convincing explanations , how the system can make simple rule- based decisions.

Thirdly, managers need to learn how to make judgment more accurate (AI) systems assistance. Although (AI) will invariably take on more routine work and even augment human decision-making, it won't judgment work, the application of human experience and expertise to critical business decisions when the information available is insufficient to suggest a successful course of action or reliable enough to suggest an obvious course of action. For a sense of the nature of judgment work, consider big data marketing and sales analytics. Such analytics often provide insights that can inform promotional campaigns, including predicting which promotions will generate desired sales brand further into the future, marketing executives need use judgment, combining analytics with their own and others' insight and experience.

The application of experience and expertise to critical business decisions and practice represents the real value of human judgment. But, when artificial intelligent machines are implemented to any organizations to assist the low, middle and top level management to make any business judgment. These forms of judgment work that managers can gather data interpretation, idea development more absolute from (AI) machine assistance. Thus, why these level management executives need to learn how to apply (AI) machines to help them to make any business judgment more accurate.

How (AI) influences organizational change

Consequently creative and social intelligence will be in even greater demand as (AI) makes in management and the workforce. This development will represent a long term trend in labor markets , one characterized by intensifying demand and reward for social skills with a growing desire for creative capabilities, managers will seek to fashion of ideas and hypotheses from inside and outside of the enterprise to shape solutions to their most pressing business problems. Thus, (AI) will influence overall organizational team members who have chance to participate any decision to make more accurate business judgment.

Many managers mistakenly view judgment work as only an individual discipline, failing to appreciate that it can also involve decide interpersonal and organizational practices. In more complex settings, judgment is typically a collective outcome of individuals' and teams' diverse perspectives, insights and experiences. And often , the resulting choices are better informed than decisions that an individual would have arrived at on his or her own.

Thus, when any organizations apply (AI) technology to assist managers to gather data and ideas to make any judgment. In these cases, organizations can create the conditions for effective collective judgment by establishing structures , such as " shadow advisory boards" that prompt managers and employees to source and synthesize multiple perspectives. Thus, a traditional organization (firm) might freshen its thinking is t put together a shadow advisory board, comprised of young, digital people who can apply (AI) machine assistance to make judgment work more accurate whether related to people development, problem-solving or strategizing and innovating for considerable degrees of creative and social intelligence.

Thus, on the one hand, (AI) technology machine augmentation and automation can give these advantages to human (organization managers) , e.g. developing people and community, solving problems and collaborating, coordinating and controlling work, shaping strategy and leading innovation. Besides, on the other hand, the next generation managers need have these individual attitude to treat intelligent machines to be as colleagues.

When, judgment is a human skill, intelligent machines can accelerate human learning that supports it, assisting in data -driven simulations, scenarios and search and discovery activities. Focuses on judgment work, some decisions require insight beyond what data can tell them. This is the sweet sport for human judgment, the application of experience and expertise to critical business decisions and practices. Thus, managers will also need to find ways to learn how to use digital (AI) technologies to tap into the knowledge and judgment of partners, customer external stakeholders and role models in other industries after the (AI) machine had been implemented to the organization.

Future works change:
Automation, employment
and productivity

Human future " micro to macro" industry trends will be affected business strategy and public policy by (AI) technology. In the future (AI) technology will influence those six themes: productivity and growth, natural resources, labor markets, the evolution of global financial markets, the economic impact of technology and innovation and urbanization. However, (AI) technology will bring economic benefits of tackling gender inequality, a new global competition, Chinese innovation and digital globalization.

Nowadays, advances in robotics artificial intelligence, and machine learning are in a new age of automation, as machines match or outperform human performance in a development to any countries. For example, automation of activities can enable businesses to improve performance by reducing errors and improving quality and speed, and in some cases achieving outcomes that go beyond human capabilities. For example, some research indicated automation could raise productivity growth globally by 0.8 to 1.4 % annually; more than 2,000 work activities across 800 occupations. When less than 5% of all occupations can be automated using demonstrated technologies about 60% of all occupations have at least 30% of constituent activities that could be automated. Many occupations will change that will be automated away: Activities most susceptible to automation involve physical activities, in highly structured and predictable environments, as well as the collection and processing of data. They are most prevalent in manufacturing , accommodation and food service and retail trade and include some middle-skill jobs. For example, such as natural language processing is a key factor. Beyond technical feasibility, the cost of technology competition with labor including skills and supply and demand dynamics, performance benefits including and beyond labor cost savings, and social and regulatory acceptance will be affected by (AI) automation technology. Thus, (AI) automation will impact to influence global employment in those aspects as below:

Firstly, assuming that people are displaced by automation will find other employment. The anticipated shift in the activities in the labor force is of a similar order as the long-term shift away from agriculture and decreases in manufacturing share of employment. Both of manufacturing and agriculture industries which would be accompanied by the creation of new types of work not foreseen at the time.

Secondly, for business, the performance benefits of automation are relatively clear. Thus, the businessmen have opportunities for their micro economies to benefits from the productivity growth potential and macro economies to benefit to encourage continued progress and innovation , investment and market incentives. At the same time, employers must innovate policies to help workers and institutions adapt to the impact on employment.

This will likely include rethinking education and training, income support and safety nets , as well as support for those dislocated, when employees need to leave themselves homes to move to other cities to learn new (AI) automation works. Thus, individuals in the workplace will need to engage move comprehensively with machines as part of their everyday activities, and acquire new skills that will be in demand in the new automation age. Consequently , the scale of shifts in the labor force over many decades that automation technologies can be a similar order to the long -term technology -enables shifts in the developed countries‘ workforces away from agriculture in the 21 th century. Those shifts did not result in long-term mass unemployment because they were accompanied by the creation of new types of work not foreseen at the time. However, human will still be needed in the workforce when the total productivity gains are caused by (AI) technology.

What occupations will be influenced by (AI) technology.

In the future, scientists predict that these occupations will be influenced by (AI) technology mostly. They include : retail salespeople, food and beverage service workers, language or translation teachers, health practitioners. Since these work activities have a more relevant occupations are made up of a range of activities with different potential for (AI) automation . For example, a retail salesperson will spend more time interacting with customers, stocking shelves , or ringing up sales. Each of these activities is distinct and requires different capabilities to perform successfully.

Thus, these job activities have similar simple control characteristics. Simple activities include greet customers, answer questions about products and services, clean and maintain work areas, demonstrate product feature process sales and transactions. All these activities can have similar simple activities in order to (AI) machines can be learn how to do these activities from (AI) technology . For example, the capability perception includes sensory perception, cognitive capabilities, such as retrieving automation, recognizing known patterns(supervised learning), logical reasoning problem solving.

Thus, (AI) machine is such human, which has feeling and emotion, such as social and emotional sensing, judgement reasoning methods, natural language understanding and physical capabilities, such as mobility , navigation, gross motor skill, fine motor skills. It seems that the future, (AI) human invents machines which will have these human characteristics to do human similar behavioral job duties more easily and efficiently. It implies these above human occupations will be replaced by (AI) human invention machines in the future. Due to (AI) creation, it is possible to cause unemployment number of these above workers will increase because (AI) machines can do their similar job behavioral activities.

Consequently, employers won't need to employ many of these skillful labor. Otherwise, they can buy less number (AI) machines to attempt to do whose job activities more easily and efficiently. So, it seems (AI) machines will have more high work performance to replace these occupation workers' work performance. Finally, these occupation worker unemployment number will only increase when the (AI) machines had been invented to achieve to do their work behavioral activities absolutely success in the future.

Whether (A) technology machine labor will replace human worker more or assist human worker more

There is no single agreed definition of a robot how outcome of a task that is completed without human intervention. When some definitions require the task to be completed by a physical machine moves and respond to its environment, other definitions use the term robot in connection with tasks completed by software , without physical embodiment.

However, to answer the question : Whether (AI) technology machine labor will replace human worker more or assist human worker more. I shall indicate some examples to let readers to judge whether (AI) technology can create new jobs or reduce old jobs.

Firstly, I shall explain what (AI) function is. (AI) is a service robot that performs useful tasks for humans or equipment excluding industrial automation application . Thus, the classification of a robot into industrial robot or service robot is done according to its intended application. It is also a personal service robot or a service robot for personal used for a non commercial task, usually by lay persons . Examples are domestic servant robot, and pet exercising robot. It is also a professional service robot or a service robot for professional used for a commercial task, usually operated by a properly trained operator. Examples, are cleaning robot for public places, delivery robot in offices or hospitals, fire-fighting robot, rehabilitation robot and surgery robot in hospitals. Thus, these functions will be future (AI) application to our daily life necessaries or business necessaries.

However, some authors agree (AI) will bring negative outcomes of automation, due to raise competiveness, reduce human job nature. Otherwise, other authors argue (AI) will bring positive outcomes of automation, due to raise productivities, job creation, assist humans work.

On the positive outcome hand, robots can increase productivity . This is particularly important for small-to medium sized businesses both are in developed and developing countries economies. It also enables large companies to increase their competitiveness through faster product development and delivery. Increased use of robot is also enabling companies in high cost countries to re shore, or bring back to their domestic base parts of the supply chain that will have previously outsourced to sources of cheaper labor. Currently , the greater threat to employment is not a automation, but an inability to remain competitive. Automation has led overall to an increase in labor demand and positive impact on wages. The reason is that the middle-income/middle-skilled jobs have reduced as a proportion of overall contribution to employment and earnings leading to fears of increasing income inequality, the skills range within the middle income bracket is large. Thus, robots are driving an increase in demand for workers at the higher -skilled and with a positive impact on wages. This issue is how to enable middle-income earners in the lower-income range to unskilled or retain. Finally, the (AI) positive impact supporter who argue the future will be robots and humans can work together.

However, on the negative outcome hand, robots can substitute labor activities, but don't replace jobs. They believe that less than 10% of jobs are fully automatable. Increasingly , robots are used to complement and augment labor activities, the net impact on jobs and the quality of work is positive. Automation can provide the opportunity for humans to focus on higher-skilled, higher-quality and higher-paid tasks. Robots can improve productivity when they are applied to tasks that which perform more efficiently and to a higher and more consistent level of quality than humans. For example, increased productivity is enabling some firms, such as Whirlpool, Caterpillar and Ford Motors company in the US restructure their supply chains, bringing back parts of the manufacturing process to the country of origin. Thus, productivity gains due to robotics and automation are important not just at the company level, but also for build industry and nation competitiveness.

I suppose that productivity can be raised. What are the impacts of robots on employment? Firstly, the main focus of development has been on personal entertainment, which does not drive worker productivity (manufacturing production). When the internet (information and communication technology (ICT)) innovation. This is borne and by findings that manufacturing productivity, which has been driven by innovations in automation rather than consumer technologies, has government strongly than productivity in the services sectors of the economy in most nature economies. It seems (AI) automation will create many jobs in internet communication entertainment game industry. For example, many young people like to use internet to play any electronic games from computer or mobile at home or outside home conveniently. Thus, (AI) automation will increase demand to be invented to any new entertainment game from internet channel. It will need to employ many (AI) entertainment game inventors to create many automation entertainment games. Thus, (AI) automation in internet entertainment game industry will need human (AI) entertainment game inventors to invent the knowledge-based capital of (AI) automation entertainment games. The (AI) entertainment game inventors will need own research and development skills, form specific skills, organizational know-how skills, databased knowledge, design and various forms of intellectual property to do these (AI) automation entertainment game invention occupations in the future.

International Federation Of Robotics(2016) indicated that China will be as a major robotics manufacturer and user of robots, benefiting from jobs created by robot manufacturing and productivity gains from robot use. Chins had sold of robots to any one single market every year since 2017 year. The Chinese government has included a focus on robotics in its 10 year strategy. In order to achieve its target of a robot density of 150 units per 10, 000 workers by 2020 year. Thus, Chinese companies will have to install around 650,000 new industrial robots between 2016 to 2020 year, 2.5 times more than installed globally in 2015 year.

Hence, China (AI) manufacturing industry will need to employ many workers . It implies (AI) manufacturing industry will create many new occupations in China. Also, ministry of economy, trade and industry (2015) also showed that Japan currently has the largest stock of industrial robots in operations, primarily in the automation industry. Driven by a rapidly aging population and low productivity rates, the Japanese government has sights on a 20-fold increase in the use of robots in the non-manufacturing sector and a three-fold growth rate of labor productivity in the service sector both by 2020 year. Thus, it also implies Japan will need many robots to be provide to service industry. Due to robots will provide to serve any businessmen's clients. Thus, it is possible that the service workers won't be dismissed as well as it is depended on the serving job nature to decide whether Japan's service workers can still serve to their employer when the service (AI) robots are applied to whose employers.

Consequently, it seems that (AI) can create employment, Ministry of economy, trade and industry (2015) showed that such as China will develop the major (AI) automation manufacturing industry. The (AI) employers will need to employ many workers to manufacture any these different kinds of (AI) robots to satisfy China or overseas individual or business buyers needs. But, (AI) can also cause unemployment to the low skillful service workers. Such as if Japan some service businesses choose to buy any (AI) service robots to replace their service staffs to serve their clients. It is possible that the service staffs will be dismissed, due to (AI) robots can do such as their same service job duties to achieve better service performance. Thus, today, it is increasingly common for people to use robots in various situations at home and in retail stores, hotels and hospitals these service industries. Robots are classified into server types based on their functionality (service and utility robots or those designed to communicate with humans) and appearance (humanoid robots or mechanical robots). The type of robot, to which each country allocated particular importance in the advance of robotics, reflects the sense of values and preferences of its population. Thus, if the country has high population needs to use robots, then they will influence either more new jobs creation or more old job loss in the country's (AI) manufacturing or (AI) service industries both. For example, Japan respondents often associate the term " robot " with humanoid robots that can communicate with human and they have a high level of familiarity with robot. The US has the highest level of robot utilization at home and in retail stores with its people being the most enthusiastic about the future use of robots. Germany shows a strong tendency to consider robots for industrial purposes and its people feel strong effort to the presence of robots in their households.

In conclusion, to judge whether how (AI) will influence the country's employment to be better or worse. It will depend on the country home buyers (users) or business buyers (users) how to use (AI) for their daily needs. If the country , such as US retail stores need to use (AI) , it will have possible to reduce some or many retail service workers. Even, if the country , such as Japan has many home users need to use (AI) , it will not influence the employment market. Otherwise, it will raise (AI) salespeople numbers. Even, if the country, such as Germany and China will have many (AI) manufacturers, then it will create many (AI) manufacturing occupations for these (AI) manufactory workers.

Consequently, (AI) robots manufacturing and service needs will have positive or negative impact to any country's employment. It will depend on the (AI) service provision and service workers' job nature as well as the manufacturing workers of (AI) knowledge level to decide their employment chance in their country's employment market.

What does artificial intelligence(AI) development stage mean

- What (AI) function is?

Some scientists explain that artificial intelligence means which is an expert system, computer software that embodies a portion of the specialized knowledge of a human portion in a specific, narrow domain, owns decision making ability of human expert. The (AI)technology is based on the premise that what makes a person an expert is years of experience that enables who recognizes certain patterns in a problem as being similar to pattern. For example, in the future artificial intelligence system can be applied to control air traffic, design to computer configuration, medical diagnosis, instruction/training, speech/interpretation, monitoring to (nuclear plant), planning to mission, factory scheduling, prediction weather, repairing telephone, automatic driving etc. different industries.

Artificial intelligence characteristics include: creative, adaptive , common sense, fact processing, quick replication, broad focus permanent and consistent skill. Otherwise, traditional computer expert system disadvantage includes perishable, unpredictable, slow reproduction, expensive, slow reproduction, slow processing lacks inspiration, needs instruction, narrow focus only machine knowledge. So, artificial intelligence is a branch of computer science devoted to creating computer to influence software and hardware to attempt to create human intelligence or human intelligent behavior. It is learning from experience, responds flexibility in situation that are, new or not anticipated.

Thus, (AI) can be learnt programmed knowledge to solve problems, using reasoning in solving problem, understanding and inferring facts and rules, recognizing the relative importance of different elements in a situation. In summary, artificial intelligence is concerned with two basic ideas mainly: The first idea, it involves studying the thought processes of humans to understand what intelligence is; the second idea, it deals with representing thought processes using companies to create artificially intelligent entities for testing the theories of intelligence.

- Can (AI) impact human job nature?

Human need concern this question: Will artificial intelligence (AI) reduce some human jobs in order to instead of replacing machines to do? Due to artificial intelligence is the ability of machines to do thing, that people would require intelligence. For example, artificial intelligence machine man driving(self-driver), it (AI) machine man driving research is an attempt to discover and describe aspects of human intelligence that can be simulated by driving machine functions. Alternatively, (AI) mathematical research may be another viewed as an attempt to develop a mathematical theory function to describe the abilities and actions of things (natural or man-made) exhibiting intelligent behavior and server as a design of intelligent calculation machine function.

Why do humans need artificial intelligence machines to instead of traditional human service job? For example, can artificial intelligence machine man (self-driving) driver drive to replace human driver? I shall compare the differences between humans and computers : The characteristics of humans are good at recognizing various things, either seen before or not, recognizing the relationship patterns between things. Human thinking is common sense reasoning, combining all types of sensory input, acting appropriately in novel situations, learning new things and changing behavior patterns, making decisions , even when given incomplete information, working with noisy, incomplete information gathering behaviors . However, characteristics of computers are good at: The tasks humans do naturally are extremely difficult for a computer program as intelligent, which must be able to do the same kind of tack as humans do naturally.

Hence, (AI) is an combination of many different success and technologies: Linguistics - computational and socio, philosophy-logic, philosophy of mind and of language, electronical engineering -image and speech processing, pattern recognition, robotics, machine learning, neural networks, optimization scheduling, management information system and decision making. So, it is possible that (AI) can impact human job nature to instead of human working behavior in the future.

● How can human society job nature to be changed to artificial intelligent society?

From the first intelligent perspective reason view point, artificial intelligence is making machines " intelligent" acting as humans expect people to act. Artificial intelligence has ability to distinguish computer responses from human responses, it owns knowledge to solve expert problem. From another research perspective reason view point, artificial intelligence is the study of how to make computers do things which, at the moment, people do better (Rich & Knight, 1991, p.3).

(AI) researchers are native in a variety of domains, e.g. formal tasks (mathematics, games), tasks (perception, robotics, natural language, common sense reasoning), expert tasks (financial analysis, medical diagnostics, engineering, scientific analysis and other areas).

From the second business perspective reason view point, (AI) is a set of many powerful tools, and methodologies for using those tools to solve business problems. From a programming perspective reason view point, (AI) includes the study of symbolic programming problem solving and search .

From the third human technological perspective reason view point, today's computer can do many well-defined tasks, for example, arithmetic operations, are much faster and more accurate than human beings. However, the computers' interaction with their environment is not very sophisticated yet. How can human test whether a computer has reached the general intelligence level of a human being? Can a computer convince a human interrogator that it is a human? But before thinking of such advanced kinds of machines, human will start developing our own extremely simple " intelligent" machines.

So, it is possible that human society job nature will to be changed to artificial intelligent society when (AI) technology is developed to the mature stage in the future.

● Why does human need artificial intelligence machines?

One of major division in (AI) is between humans who think (AI) is the only serious way of finding out how we (human) work and human who want companies to do very smart things, independently of how we (human) work. This is the important distinction between cognitive scientists vs engineers. One of another major division in (AI) is between symbolic (AI), which represents information through symbols and their relationships. Specific Algorithms are used to process these symbols to solve problems or deduce new knowledge and connectionist. So (AI) , which represents information in network. Biological processes underlying learning, task performance and problem solving are imitated from human mind behaviors.

Thus, it is possible that artificial intelligence machines can do the better judgicious behavior to compare human.

● How does artificial intelligence influence future working changing in automation employment and productivity aspects?

In the automation changing influence aspect, as companies increasingly use robots on production lines or algorithms to optimize their logistics manage inventory, any carry out other core business functions. Technological advances are creating a new automation age in which ever-smarter and more flexible machines will be deployed on an ever larger scale in the marketplace. However, researching artificial intelligence with how influences human working nature. We need to answer these questions: How will automation transform the workplace? What will the implications for employment? And what is likely to be its impact both on productivity in the global economy and on employment?

Advances in robotics, artificial intelligence, and machine learning are growing in a new age of automation as machines match or outperform human performance in a range of work activities, including ones requiring cognitive capabilities. What factors are determined the changing in workplace adoption by artificial intelligence innovation? What advantages are automation? Automation of activities can be enabled businesses to improve performance by reducing errors and improving quality and speed, and achieving outcomes that go beyond human capabilities.

Some scientists indicated based on their scenario modeling. They estimated automation could raise producing growth globally by 0.8 to 1.4 percent annually. Almost, the activities people are paid almost $16 trillion in wages to do in global economy have the potential to be automated by adopting currently demonstrated technology. According to their analysis of more than 2,000 work activities across 800 occupations. When less than 5% of all occupations have of least 30% of activities that could be automated. They also indicated that technical economic and social factors will determine automation. Continued technical progress, for example, in areas such as natural language processing is a key factor beyond technical feasibility , the cost of technology, competition with labor including skills, and supply and demand dynamics, performance benefits including and beyond labor cost

savings and social and regulatory acceptance will affect (alter) the scope of automation.
Other some scientists also indicate U.S. country for example, the anticipate shift in the activities in labor force of a similar order of magnitude as the long term sight away from agriculture and decreases in manufacturing. Share of employment in the United States both which were achieved. So, those factors can influence why artificial intelligence technology needs. So, it is possible that future agriculture and manufacturing both industries will apply (AI) technology manufacturer-kind of job nature to raise productivity instead of farmers, fruit picking workers, farming transportation labours as well as factory manufacturing workers and supervisors etc. human-kind of job nature.

- Is artificial intelligence possible to replace labor ?

Not just intelligence, but also debating, if machines are capable of having a conscious minds. Artificial intelligence has those characteristics as below:
On functionalism aspect, artificial intelligence inputs mental states, sensory inputs, (beliefs, desires being in pain feeling) and behavioral outputs. Since mental states are identified by a functional role, which are thoughts to be manifested in various systems. Even, perhaps computers which are physical devices with electronic substrate that inform computations on inputs to give outputs similar to brains which are artificial intelligence composed of part any intrinsic relationship to each other. Thus, artificial intelligence activities is not the whole itself, but into parts or on external influence on the parts.
On dualism aspect, artificial intelligence is a set of views about the relationship between mind are matter. On materialism aspect, it builds the only thing that exists is matter, including consciousness.
On biological naturalism aspect, it is similar a human brain than feels pains makes mental situation. So, artificial intelligence is similar biologist which might to be excited to human labor work.
Hence, it seems artificial intelligence can change (alter) or replace human labor work of nature in possible in the future.

- Can (AI) technology replace human labour nature of work?

On technological innovation reason view point, the history development of artificial intelligence studying the intelligence is one of most ancient scientific discipline. The history development of artificial intelligence what aims to achieve human use to sense, learn remember and think, logic probability, decision making and calculation develop from mathematics, instead of replacement human labor functions.

Artificial intelligence history development aim is the scientific analysis of skills in connection and practice with the appearance of computers from 1950 year beginning. The artificial intelligence (AI) can deal with the ultimate challenges. How can (either biological or electronic) mind sense, understand and manipulate a world that is much simple and more complex than itself? And what if would human like to construct something with such capabilities?

The general-purpose software of the early period of (AI) were only able to solve simple tasks effectively and failed when which should be used in a wider range or an more difficult tasks. One of the sources of difficulty was that early software had very few or mix knowledge about the problems which handled, and activities successes by simply syntactic manipulation. Moreover, the other difficulty was that many problems that were tried to solve by the (AI) were untreatable.

The early (AI) software whether trying step sequences based on the basic facts about the problem that should be solved, experimented with different combinations till which found a solution. From the end the 1960 year, developing the so-called expert systems were emphasized. These systems had (sue-based) knowledge base about the field which handled. Till to the beginning of the 1970 year, (Prolog) the logical programming language was born, which was built in the computation realization of a version of the resolution calculus. (Prolog) is a remarkably prevalent tool in developing expert systems (on medical, judiciary and other scopes), but natural language parsers were implemented in this language. Then, in 1981 s, the Japanese announced the fifth generation computer system project, a 10 years plan to build an intelligent computer system that use the (Prolog) language as a machine code. Nowadays, (AI) can be applied any industries, such as car manufacturing industry can use (AI) technological machine-men manufacture car, instead of replacing human labors in factory. Even, in the future, using (AI) machine-men drivers can drive any private cars or public transportation tools, instead of replacing human drivers, e.g. bus, train, tram, ferry etc. Also in the future, machine-men can replace housewives to serve families to do housekeeping clean job , e.g. cleaning toilets, bathrooms, kitchens, even cooking functions at home. So (AI) machine-man can reduce housewives works at home. Moreover, (AI) machine man can take care old people , when who are living at homes or elder care centers.

So, it seems artificial intelligence (AI) will be possible developed to manufacture a new generation machine-man to assist (serve) families to do any simply cleaning or cooking jobs at homes. Moreover, the overall demand of (AI) general social needs will also rise, such as security, driving transportation tools, restaurant cleaning, elder centers care service etc. So, it seems that individual or families or social needs of (AI) will be increase in the future. Thus, it will influence macro economy growth (GDP) if there are large house family consumer group and hotel or bus or taxis or ferry etc. different business consumer group demand any artificial intelligence machine numbers increasing. Then, the artificial intelligence products and material manufacturers must need to buy many artificaial intelligence materials to produce any kinds of artificial intelligence machines to prepare to satisfy consumer individual needs. Consequently, macro economy will grow to the owned artificial intelligence development countries, e.g. US, China, UK.

- Why can artificial intelligence satisfy human needs?

First, On machine-man satisfactory demand aspect view point, it makes computers that think, it is the automation of activities. We associate with human thinking: like decision making, learning. It is the act of creating machine that perform function that require intelligence when performed by people. It is the study of mental faculties through the use of computational models. It is the study of computations that make it possible to perceive, reason and act. It is a branch of computer science that is concerned with the automation of intelligent behavior. It is anything in computing service that human don't yet know how to do property.

Second, on thought aspect artificial intelligence means systems thank think like humans, systems that think rationally.

Third, on behavioral aspect, artificial intelligence systems that act like human and that systems act rationally. However, the basic objective of (AI) is to represent human's thought processes in computation . These machines are supposed to exhibit behavior that. It is performed by a human being, would be considered intelligent. However, some authors feel (AI) has disadvantages, such as it is not creative, it is excited in the use of sensory devices, it can't make use of a very wide context of experiences and it does not use common sense.

For speech recognition and understanding function needs example, (AI) can be applied in speech recognition and understanding function, which (AI) speech or voice recognition is a data input method. For example, the computer recognizes and understands one (or a few) word commands. Speech understanding on the other hand is the computer's ability to understanding a spoken language. That is , the computer understands the meaning of sentences, an paragraphs through (AI).

So, (AI) can be attempted to learn human language how to speak. It is similar to translate human language skill, instead of actual human speaking skill. Also, (AI) can assist handicap learning or language student how to listen different languages by machine-man sounds from computers more accurately.

So, it seems that it (AI) can replace human language teachers speaking function and can change teaching language nature of job in language speaking and listening education industry.

● Is artificial intelligence one good choice for human future technological benefit?

Nowadays, new technology development is popular. However, artificial intelligence is one kind of new technology choice among different technologies innovation. So it brings this question: Is artificial intelligence technology value to invest? To answer this question. I shall indicate some other new technology developments to compare (AI) technology development to judge which has urgent needs to achieve human expectation nowadays.

For example, why is green peace interested in new technologies? New technologies features prominently in our ongoing campaigns against genetic modified crops and number power. However, which are also an integral part of our solutions to environmental challenges, including renewable energy technologies, such as solar, wind and wave (water) power energy as well as waste treatment technologies, such as mechanical, biological treatment.

It seems humans need concern how to apply (AI) technology to solve environment pollution challenges in our future. So, environment protective, agriculture, natural energy technology will be popular demand to attempt to apply (AI) technology to solve their challenges or apply (AI) to assist to develop their industry.

How AI development stage to influence economy growth

How can artificial intelligence technology influence economy?

Advances in artificial intelligence (AI) technology and related fields have opened up new markets and new opportunities progress in critical areas, such as health, education, energy, economic development, social welfare and the environment pollution.

(AI) automation will continue to create wealth and expand the global economy development in the future. However, when many will benefits that growth won't be costless and will be accompanied by changes in the skills, that workers need to increase productivity in the economy and structural changes in the economy. So, in the skills that workers need to succeed in the economy and structural changes.

I shall indicate why aggressive policy action will be needed to help Americans who are disadvantaged by these changes , due to (AI) technology is caused. For automation industry change example, artificial intelligence (AI) capabilities will enable automation of some tasks that have long required human labor. These artificial intelligence technology introduction can increase new opportunities for individuals. The economy and society, but (AI) has also the potential to disrupt be current livelihoods of many Americans. However, (AI) leads to unemployment and increase in inequality over the long run depends not only on the (AI) technology itself, but also on the institutions and policies that are changed.

Thus, it is possible that (AI) technology will raise some countries unemployment number if the employer apply (AI) technology workers to work instead of human labor in their factories, but it can also raise productivities for these employers.

- Can (AI) influence global economy growth?

Technological progress is main driver of growth of GDP per capita, allowing output to increase faster than labor and capital . However, technology can increase productivity, but also decrease the number of labor hours needed to create a unit of output. So (AI) causes unequal to labor wage decreases, even reduces the number of labor to manufacture, e.g. artificial intelligence technology of automation car manufacturing industry; clothing manufacturing industry; plane manufacturing etc. high technology of artificial intelligence manufacturing method. But (AI) should be potential environment benefit, although it raises unemployment ratio. Moreover, it can rise production , due to many skilled craft were replaced by the combination of machines and lower-skilled labor. The result of (AI) technology introduction , it causes output per hour risen when inequality declined, driving up average living standards, but the labor of some high-skill workers was no longer as valuable in the market. Otherwise, if (AI) technology is continue developed to be success. Some routine intensive occupations will be loss, which focused on predictable, e.g. easily programmable tasks, such as switchboard operators, filing clerks, travel agents, and assembly line workers would be particularly replaced by new (AI) technology. However, at the same time, (AI) technology development will bring these benefits: improvement in education (training (AI) technology scientists) , due to (AI) manufacturing technology needs are raising to businesses and institutional changes, such as the reduction in unionization and raising in the minimum wage to the (AI) manufacturing technology skilled labor in factories.

Because (AI) technology is not a single technology, but rather a collection of technologies that are applied to specific tasks, the effects of (AI) will be felt unevenly though the economy. It will bring some tasks will be most easily automated than others , and some jobs will be affected more than others, both negatively and positively. Finally, new jobs are likely to be directly created in areas , such as the development and supervision of (AI) as well as indirectly created in a range areas though out the economy as higher incomes lead to expanded demand.

However, if (AI) technology could dominate global labor markets. If labor productivity increases, do not influence into wage increases, then the large economic gains brought about by (AI) technology could be increased wealth inequality, due to employers can reduce production cost, but workers (labors) wages will not be increased, even will be decreased. Hence, it seems the (AI) technology will bring disadvantages to labor market to cause unemployment or reduce wages in possible, although it can reduce employer individual salary (wage) expenditure and it can raise productivity.

- How can artificial intelligence impact global economy growth?

Artificial intelligence (AI) technology is a branch of computer science that aims to create intelligent machines that work and react like humans. So, (AI) is a technology that appears to impact (influence) human preference by learning, understanding complex contents, enhancing humans in executing both routine and non-routine tasks. In the future, (AI) technology that can be virtual personal assistant, as well as it may exist, such as robots with human-like processing capabilities.

How can (AI) technology impact global economy growth over the next 10 years? During this time period, (AI) technology is predicted to have wide-ranging applications including: Machine learning that automates analytical model building by using algorithms that allow machines to operate without

human assistance.
In global education aspect, potential applications include predicting cause-and-effect relationships from biological data, identifying new drugs, self-driving cars, and protecting against fraud, improved natural language processing that allows computers to continue to better analysis, understand and generate language to interface with humans using natural human languages. For example, transcribing notes dictated by physicians, automatically drafting articles and translating text and speech. So (AI) technology can be applied to education aspect to improve humans' knowledge level.
In visual art aspect, (AI) machine vision that allows computers to identify objects, scenes and activities in images. Current applications of (AI) machine vision include providing objective descriptions for the blind seeing(visual) needs.
We except the economic effects of (AI) technology to include both direct GDP growth from sectors that develop or manufacture. (AI) technology and indirect GDP growth through increased productivity in existing sectors that employ some form of (AI). If (AI) technology is an increasingly critical component of more products, it will become an integral part of many people's lives. Thus, (AI)'s ability to influence economic activity, rather than the economic or development status of the region. (AI) has the potential to impact income classes and to bring significant gains to both developed and developing countries. For example, (AI) has the potential to optimize good production around the world by analyzing agricultural regions and identifying what is necessary to improve crop yields.
In estimating the future economic effects by (AI) technology innovation, it is important to note that it is challenging to accurately predict which applications of (AI) will ultimately be commercially successful. In micro level economic influence, we need to apply methodologies to estimate the economic effects of investment in firms developing (AI) technology since investment levels in a technology are a telling sign of the future potential of that (AI) technology.

● How can (AI) influence GDP of high income countries in the next ten years?

How (AI)'s development may affect the global economy over the next ten years. In fact, (AI) technology has the potential to affect business across the global in a wide range of industries in ways only a number of technologies have done in the parts. For example, (AI) technology's expected to be a useful tool for enhancing human capabilities and in some instances replacing functions, such as driving a car, adoption of broadband internet, mobile telephone, industrial robotic automation have served to enhance human capabilities.

However, significant public debate has focused on projections of (AI) technology's effect on the labor force. However, large companies prefer to invest in (AI) technological industry. For example, face book's (AI) research lab., google machine intelligence lab. and micro soft machine learning and artificial intelligence research division are all making advances in (AI) technology and investing in the industry's top talent. Additionally, between 2010 year and 2015 year, nearly $5 billion in venture capital funding invested in firms across the global developing and employing (AI) technology (Facebook (AI) Research).

- How can artificial intelligence impact on workplace?

Modern information technologies and the labor economy growth of machines is powered by artificial intelligence have already strongly influenced the world of work in the 21 ST century. Computers, algorithms and software simplify every tasks and it is impossible to image how most of our life could be managed without them. How can be the information economy characterized by exponential growth replaces the most production industry based on economy of scales? What will the future world of work look like and how long will it take to get? Will the future world of work be a world where humans spend less time earning their livelihood? Alternatively, are mass unemployment, mass poverty and social distortions also possible scenario for the future, where robots, artificial intelligence systems play an increasingly central role? These questions concern how artificial intelligence further development . Can influence labor economy growth on workplace ? When the labor market has widespread impact on intelligence property, information technology, product liability, competition and labor and employment laws.

How (AI) technology impacts on labor workplace.

The future influence any organizations how labor economies use of (AI) can be analyzed, such as deep machine learning is based on a set of model high level data. Unlike human workers, the machines are connected the whole time in workplace. If one machine makes a mistake, all autonomous systems will keep this in mind and will avoid the same mistake the next time.

Over the long run intelligent machines will win against every human expert.

Production robots have been replacing employees because of the (AI) technology. They work more precisely than humans and cost loss. Creative solutions like 3D printers and the self learning ability of these production robots will replace human workers, the automatic data recording and data processing, traditional back office activities are no longer in demand. Autonomous software will collect necessary information and will send it to the employee who needs it. Additionally, dematerialization leads to the phenomenon that traditional physical products are becoming software. For example, CD or DVDs are being replaced by streaming services. The replacement of traditional event ticket, e-travel ticket service products or hard cash will be the next step, due to the possibility of payment by smartphone. So, (AI) technology will impact human's daily life consumption behaviors in the future. For another example, transportation tools, such as boats and ferries and private vehicles will use sensors and navigating without human input. Taxi and truck drivers will become obsolete, the stock store applies to stock managers and postal carriers of the delivery is distributed by (AI) machine delivery method.

What is the relationship between (AI) and (CRM)?

● Can (AI) technology impact on customer relationship management (CRM) ?

Nowadays , (AI) is a technology almost as old as the computer industry itself, it is similar with the advent of personal assistants function to businesses and personal promotion channel, such as (Amazon's Alexa, Apple's Siri, Google's Assistant) image recognition (face book), personalized recommendations (Netflix , Amazon). Those innovations have been driven by a increase in processing power, lower cost hardware, and the exploding creation and availability of data. It seems, (AI) technology can impact global customer service management method.

How to forecast economic impact modeling to (AI) will affect global economy? Can human forecast business revenue growth and job creation (or destruction) based on (AI) applied to customer relationship management (CRM) activities? In addition to the economic impact on (AI) or (CRM) which can include an estimate of the economic impact attributable to sales forces customer base. What can economic benefits be brought to (CRM) from (AI) technology?

Artificial intelligence(AI) comprises a set of technologies that use natural language processing, machine learning, knowledge graphs, and other tools to answer questions, discover insights and provide recommendations. Computer systems can use (AI) hypothesize and formulate possible answers based on available evidence can be trained through the ingestion of vast amounts of content, and automatically adapt and learn from (AI) self mistakes and failures.

So, any business organizations (customer service departments) can provide efficient and effective customer relationship management of excellent customer service quality if which applied (AI) technology system. The different type of (AI) systems include: (AI) system platforms, machine learning (AI) based data preparation and enrichment tools, machine vision/ image recognition, voice speech recognition, text analysis and natural language processing, bots , e.g. face book website and virtual digital assistance solutions, social media pattern analysis , sentiment analysis, advanced numerical analysis (e.g. IOT streaming , machine logs), supporting technologies, knowledge base dialog management, Q&A processing etc. different (AI) technology system customer relationship management (CRM) tools.

(AI) (CRM) of activity can include these categories, such as: corporate marketing, marketing operation, field marketing, customer support, digital commerce, customer analytics, customer influenced product or service design, product or service pricing, finance information, presentation, customer billing, inventory , logistics and fulfilment support, partner management etc. different CRM tools.

(AI) technology of CRM has been carrying on plan different stages to achieve CRM personal assistant tool for businesses. The stages are such as, in the beginning stage of (AI) projects in place, implement now, pilot phase next year in the final stage of (AI) customer relationship management tools are foreseeable future. So, this CRM technology has been improved to plan in different stages every year to prepare to achieve full capacity of CRM service quality for businesses to use in the future.

Hence, how to develop an estimate prediction of the economic impact (AI) technologies could have CRM activities, which depends on gathering macroeconomic information on business revenue and the basic marketing of business revenue and the basic markup of business expenses by major functions (customer support, marketing and sales , production etc.)

An economic impact model that can gather data together and forecast the results how (AI) artificial intelligence technology brings (CRM) customer relationship management benefits to businesses, e.g. surveys investigation includes IT spending by sample countries, GDP and population estimates and forecasts, revenue per employee and ratios of IT spend to GDP. Surveys (questionnaire questions) of forecast results are influenced by (AI) impact can include: results are projected from surveys and rely on estimates are made by respondents on the expected financial improvements in categories of (AI) –assisted customer relationship management activities. The forecast assumes that these estimates are correct; financial estimates are based on estimates of "first year" improvement from full (AI) implementation; forecasts are from planning to implement any artificial intelligence of customer relationship management (CRM) projects, the improvement forecast is of categories of activity , e.g. corporate marketing , digital commerce, and customer analytics. They are not estimates of ROI for the (AI) software. They rely on conservative estimates to which each of these entities might affect company revenue, expenses or productivity. They also rely on estimates of the penetration of software in customer relationship management activities . Net new jobs created are based on the ratio of new revenue to jobs required to support that revenue . They can assume that 50% of the net new revenue will support increases in labor and the rest will go for capital and other operating expenses that may replace jobs lost to automation.

In the future, some of the ways in micro economic benefits to any organizations. (AI) technology is expected to impact CRM activities include: Spending up sales cycles, improving lead generation and qualification solving customer support problems faster (raising service quality), helping companies improve brand campaigns and recognition, lowering costs of support calls when increasing resolution rates, lowering the cost of recruiting employees and partners, increasing revenue from optimized product marketing, optimizing price, distribution logistics and preventing loss through fraud detection. So, micro economic benefits view point, it seems that (AI) CRM technology can raise any companies economic benefits for care term.

Artificial intelligence enables machines or the in-build software to behave like human beings which allows these decisions and act. The advent of (AI) is leading , talking, making decisions and act. The advent of (AI) is leading to new technologies advances and transforming the economic and employment opportunities for humans in a positive way. (AI) related technologies can facilitate our live. For example, industrial robotics, robotic medical assistants, smart games, financial forecasting software, big data analysis, algorithms in health and bioinformatics, pilotless cargo places, drone ambulances and general purpose and workplace robots and others. (Disruptors technologies: Advances that will transform life, business and the global economy).

Artificial intelligence also known as computational intelligence is defined as " the human –like intelligence exhibited by machines or software. It is theorized that intelligence of humans can be described and intelligence machines or software can simulate it. These machines software can be reasonable , learn, perceive and process information, like human mind and thus facilitate human life. They can think and act for us. So, artificial intelligence is an interdisciplinary field of study including computer science, neuroscience, psychology, linguistics and philosophy.

However, (AI) research and developments have economically impacted many industries, such as robotics, telecommunications, computer applications , health, finance, heavy manufacturing, transportation, aviation, e-service and e-commerce, military , music and movie, toys and games entertainment etc. industries.

In fact, many ideas, systems and technologies have been developing in the world of (AI) technology. However, which are net called or considered (AI) products, rather which are mentioned with their specific names, such as smart graphics, machine learning, e-commerce etc. (i.e. this is called (AI) effect).

- How can (AI) technology influence digital economy?

Nowadays, (AI) related industrial applications will replace most human power in fields, including call centers, customer services and air cargo transportation. (AI) technologies also help weather forecasting based on repeated rainfall pattern (data) recognition, through robotics (i.e. floor cleaning, moving lawns etc.) transporting people and products with unmanned vehicles, sending space unmanned smart shuttles, developing robotic arms, predicting market values in stock exchanges by internet, making homes safer, helping elderly and disabled using robotic servants etc.

Among the (AI) related technologies , there are a few that significance for the impact on society and especially on digital economy . (AI) is particularly influential in machine learning. Such as robotics, transportation, finance, health and bioinformatics, e-commerce , e-games, big online data gathering and internet-of-things. For example, machine e-learning is based in bioinformatics and robots that can learn new skills for better caregiving in healthcare. What is machine e-learning? Machines can e-learn from e-data gathering, coming up generalizations and making decisions to act in certain ways from internet.

There are important applications , such as e-machine perception, electronic online natural language learning processing, online search engines, online bioinformatics, online brain –computer interface, online game playing, online robot locomotion, online advertising, online computations finances, online health monitoring, online DNA classification and decision making, online in chemistry –cheminformatics . So, online machine learning can positively impact productivity and it can enhance information and analytical system from (AI) online channel.

What is robotics? Robotics is one of the most strongly influenced fields in (AI). For example, heavy manufacturing industries, robots and used and man power is replaced for effectiveness, precision, and accuracy, especially in respective or dangerous tasks, including welding, assembling , picking and placing .

So, robots can acquire new skills or adapt the changing dynamic environment. Also, artificial intelligence can be applied in developing transportation. For example, automated vehicles, driver assistance systems , safety systems, collision avoidance systems and public transportation. Moreover, (AI) technology has proven to produce some of the best tools to predict stock market fluctuations from internet data gathering method. It's predictions are based on ever-evolving predictions algorithms and systems learn new models and make connections between historical data and new data to measure stock market trading more accurate from internet data gathering channel.

In health field, especially in health data processing , analysis, decision making support and medical diagnosis. So, online data can show which patients will need what treatment and what alternative drugs could be used more accurate from (AI) online data gathering method. Bioinformatics is an interdisciplinary field combining statistics, (AI) online technology can help in discovering data patterns and modeling through the application of machine learning, artificial neural networks and genetic algorithms. For example, further (AI) technology development of human genome project of online data sequences.

Online shopping can be facilitated by virtual assistants developed through (AI) technology and these assistants can offer the best advice. (AI) online purchase coming after every product image recommendations and personalization bring important revenue to shopping online sites, like Amazon . Smart computer graphics and games, artificial intelligence is useful in smarter computer, graphics, scene modeling , scene rendering processes in order to create, for example, effective human –robot interactions , online machine learning, online strategic games techniques etc. online computer related (AI) software.

So, online big data analysis and big data does have a critical need in the world of online intelligence machines and software in our future. In other words, (AI) offers online technology to enable online big data analysis to provide industrial organizations with valuable information for effective decision making in short time. For example, what IBM's Watson achieved: this machine used 200 million of structured and unstructured content with a special technology of hypothesis generation, massive evidence gathering, analysis and scoring from internet channel.

Finally, (AI) online technology another related internet invention (internet of things) (IOT) is the network of machines or objects connected through internet. These connected objects can sense their internal and external environment, communicate with each other, can send critical data and finally can make decisions to act or correct their environment from (AI) online technology. For example, factories can monitor and automatically change production processes, hospitals can monitor and regulate the health conditions of their patients , schools can collect data from facilities and cars can send data to car makers from (AI) online technology.

Partner predicts that (IOT) market will create about trillion amount value by 2020 year. Although machines collect big data from their environment, whether which gain an insight or learn from these online data largely depends on the (AI) online machine learning principals and (AI) online technology. In 2013, Mckinsey estimated that disruptive technologies closely related with potential economic impact in 2025 year between $7.1 to $13.1 trillion amount (automation of knowledge work, advanced robotics, autonomous or near-autonomous vehicles).

What is the relationship between
(AI) and global digital economy development ?

● Could work activities in China be automated
making in the nation with the world's largest automation potential?

Can (AI) technology influence China economy? Could China workers be affected and jobs made up of routine work activities and predictable? Will programmable tasks be particularly impact to China employment market ? When impact on labor market is likely to be gradual at the aggregate level, it can be sudden and dramatic at the level of specific work activities, rending some job obsolete fairly. Overall (AI) technology will raise digital skills when reducing demand for medium incomer inequality for China workers. It seems (AI) technology's effect on productivity could be crucial to China's future economic growth as the population ages are increasing.

In China, some biggest technological companies driving significant investments in research and development. Moreover, China is one of the leading global (AI) technology development county. However, China will need to focus on building its innovation capacity. For example, United States and United Kingdom are currently producing more influential (AI) technological research. However, if China planed to achieve (AI) technology success, it's traditional industries will need to develop technical know-how –to and overcoming implementation costs prepare to develop (AI) . When (AI) technology is introduced into China society, China government needs to raise concerning ethical, legal, technological security etc. business questions. Also, surrounding issues include privacy, discrimination, legal liability and regulation. It aims to encourage overseas investors to choose to invest (AI) technological industry to raise GDP growth and manufacturing industries income growth for long term in China. If China encouraged overseas (AI) technology investment in its country. It is possible to influence China employment market to be changed. Because (AI) technology will impact to influence China people daily life. Due to (AI) technology is introduced to China society, many rich people will prefer to spend to buy any high (AI) technological products for entertainment or learning or machine man driving etc. daily necessity activities. Then it will raise GDP growth and will raise (AI) manufacturers or related-(AI) technological manufacturers profit. It is beneficial to China because it can become one high knowledgeable and (AI) technological economical society. But it will bring bad influences to raise unemployment chance for the low skillful labor. In labor economy aspect influence , how (AI) technology can influence China low skillful labor unemployment ratio raising. The raising low skill labor unemployment reason is because China low skillful human labors are argued or are replaced by (AI) technology creating new challenges to introduce to influence China society of simply human manufacturing job nature to be changed to be high (AI) technology manufacturing job nature in any China factories. Moreover, when (AI) technology introduction to China, it will cause other related social challenges in China. The varied (AI) related challenges, including the difficulty of creating safe and reliable hardware for sensing and affecting (transportation and education), the challenges of gaining public trust, a low resource comities and public safety and security, the challenges of overcoming fears or marginalizing humans in China employment and workplace and the risk of diminishing interpersonal trust because the low skillful labors won't believe any China employers will give chance to employ them , due to (AI) technology will replace their skills and man manufacturing of productivity is much less to compare to (AI) technology manufacturing method.

- How does (AI) technology influence

the future of employment change?

Are future nature of jobs changed to computerization from (AI) technology? Where are the probability of computing occupations from (AI) technology influence? What is expected impacts of future computing on labor market from (AI) technology influence? John Maynard Keynes's frequently cited prediction of widespread technological unemployment " du to our discovery of means of economic the use of labor outrunning the pace of which we can find new used of labor" (Keynes, 1933, p.3).

In the future, (AI) technology will impact some nature of occupations to change computing. This chance will also influence some countries' economic change. For example, some factory human labors hand routine manufacturing tasks will be changed to computerization of routine manufacturing tasks by (AI) technological machine men hand manufacturing method. it will cause a structured shift in the labor market, with workers reallocating their labor supply from middle-income manufacturing to low-income service occupations.

Arguably, this is because the manual tasks of service occupations are less computerization, as who require a higher degree of flexibility and physical adaptability. So, (AI) technology will influence the human hand labor skillful occupation nature of task cheaper , such as vehicle manufacturing , ship manufacturing, computer manufacturing, steel manufacturing, television, radio etc. home electronic products of heavy machine industry change. Due to (AI) technology machine man will be proper to be used to manufacturing these electronic products when the (AI) technology innovation can develop to the mature stage. Then, any countries manufacturers will choose to use (AI) technology machine man, instead of human hand production.

Supposing the future prices of computing are fallen, seriously, problem solving skills are becoming relatively productive, explaining the substantial employment growth in manufacturing occupations, involving cognitive tasks where skilled labor has a comparative advantage, as well as the increase education needs for (AI) technology computing of machine man subject study.

Prediction of education needs for (AI) technology student numbers will increase, due to manufacturing industry needs many (AI) technology students in future employment market. Another (AI) technology influence if the future (AI) technological innovation, e.g. machine man manufacturing or machine man service industries will both increase demand, then with more sophistic software technologies will be disrupted labor markets by marketing workers redundant.

For publishing industry, what is striking about the case in paper book publishing industry will be unpopular? Due to the electronic book publishing industry will be popular, e.g. Amazon publish . (AI) technology can influence paper book manufacturing method which is replaced by machine man electronic book manufacturing method as well as it will cause the computerization is no longer confined to routine manufacturing tasks. Due to (AI) machine man manufacturing technology will be proper to be used to manufacture any products in short time efficiently and effectively , e.g. electronic book products. In the future, if it is fact to occur this case, such as (AI) technological machine man manufacturing method will be adopted (applied) to manufacture electronic books or any products in possible. (AI) technology will cause many manufacturing workers are unemployed. It is beneficial to employers, who can reduce to spend much wages expenditure to employ manufacturing workers, but it will cause many manufacturing workers loss jobs and reduce income to support whose families lives. It will cause social challenges, e.g. increasing stealing crimes if the manufacturing workers had not other skills to find other jobs to do easily. So, manufacturers need to concern over technological unemployment which will be hardly future phenomenon if who decided to dismiss all manufacturing workers, due to (AI) technology machine men replace to them.

If (AI) technology can be innovated to produce any kinds of machine man to serve any service or manufacturing industries successfully. Then, it will bring these questions: Can future that workers be influenced to be automation employment and productivity by (AI) technology influence? Does it impact to influence the (AI) technology countries' productivity and growth and natural resources development and labor markets and evolution of global financial markets and economic impact of technology and innovation and urbanization etc. issues? How will automation transform the workplace? What will be the implication for employment? What is likely to be its impact both on productivity in the global economy and on employment?

In fact, automatic of activities can enable businesses to improve performance by reducing errors chance and improving quality and speed, and same cases achieving outcomes that go beyond human capabilities. Some economists indicate (AI) technology would give a needed boost to economic growth and prosperity have of the working age population in many countries. Based on the scenario modeling, they estimate automation could raise productivity growth globally by 0.8 to 1.4 % annually. They also indicated that almost half the activities people are almost $1.6 trillion in wages to do in the global economy have the potential to be automated adapting current demonstrates technology, according to their analysis of more than 2,000 work activities across 800 occupations. When less than 5% of all occupations can be automated entirely using demonstrated technology, about 60% of all occupations have at least 30% of worker made activities, that would be automated. More occupation will change to be automated. They also indicated for business performance benefits of automation are relatively clear, but the issues are more complicated by policy making to attract foreign investors. Beyond technical feasibility, the cost of technology, competition labor will include skills and supply and demand dynamics, performance benefits and beyond labor cost savings and social and regulatory acceptance will affect the automation. Their predictions suggest that half of today work activities could be automated by 2055 year, but this could happen 10 to 20 years earlier or latter depending on the various factors in addition to their wider economic condition.

Some scientists suggest (AI) technology is finally starting to deliver real-life business benefits. Computer power is growing significantly , algorithms are becoming more sophisticated and perhaps most important of all, the world is generating vast quantities of the fuel that powers (AI) technology data billions of gigabytes of it every day. Also, online firms are digital natives, such as Google online search service company is investing on (AI) technology. For new though most of the news if coming from the suppliers of (AI) technologies. And many new users are only in the experimental phase. Few products are on the market or are likely to arrive these soon to drive immediate and widespread adoption. As a result, analysts believe (AI) technology's potential will give true economic benefit in the future. (AI) industry will introduce to suppliers and users to raise economic potential of (AI) technology.

In the future, (AI) technology systems can solve business problems. Some scientists categorized those into five technology systems that are key areas of (AI) technology development: robotics and autonomous vehicles, computer vision language virtual agents and machine learning , which is based on algorithms that learn from data without replying on rules-based programming in order to draw conclusions or direct an action.

Such as computer vision and language includes natural language processing, analytics, speech recognition technology, some are about learning from information, such as about machine learning and others are related to acting on information, such as robotics, autonomous vehicles and virtual agents, which are computer programs that can converse with humans. Machine learning and a subfield called deep learning are artificial intelligence applications.

● Can artificial intelligence impact
global economy growth?

Artificial intelligence (AI) is a term first defined in 1956 year. It is a branch of computer science that aims to create intelligent machines that work and react like humans. In contrast today, 60 years later, (AI) is characterized by a number of applications, including computers playing games against humans and understanding human languages, virtual personal assistants, and robotics which involve computers seeing , hearing and reacting to sensory stimuli. In the future, technologists predict for (AI) technology ranging from (AI) being used as a tool to aid relatively simple processes for robots with human like mental capabilities, who expect (AI) technology can emulate human performance by learning, coming to mind its own conclusions, understanding complex content, engaging in dialog with people, enhancing human cognitive performance or replacing humans in executing both routine and non-routine tasks. In existing industry, (AI) technology is used , such as targeted advertising and virtual used personal assistant as well as the (AI) technology that my exist in the future, such as robots with human vehicle processing capabilities.

The range of (AI) technology's progress in the future will determine the economic impact future of (AI) technology on the global economy with more limited advances and applications (i.e. weak (AI) only) corresponding to more limited economic impacts and more substantial progress, i.e. strong (AI) technology is corresponding to more significant economic impact.

(AI) technology learning that automates analytical model, including predicting cause-and-effect relationship from biological data, identifying new drugs, self-driving cars and protecting against fraud etc. functions. Also (AI) learning can improve natural language processing that allows computers to continue to better analyze, understand and generate language to interface with human using the natural human language, virtual personal assistant, helps users by providing scheduling appointment, reminds organizing personal finance and finding providers of various services, machine vision allows (AI) machine man to identify object, scenes and activities in detect pedestrians and bicyclists.

We expect the economic effects of (AI) technology to include both direct GDP growth from sectors that develop or manufacture (AI) technology and indirect GDP growth through increased productivity in existing sectors that employ some from of (AI) technology. If (AI) producing sectors could grow, then it could lead to increase revenues and employment of (AI) technological professionals within these existing firms as well as the potential creation of entirely new economic activities to any countries' societies productivity improvement in existing sectors could be realized through faster and move efficient processes and decision making as well as increased (AI) technological knowledge and access to information available in societies easily.

In the future, if (AI) technology is an increasingly critical component of more products, it will become an integral part of necessary products of many people's lives. The extent of (AI)'s economy effort is also likely to vary from region to region, thought variation may be more dependent on the predominate economic activity of a region and the (AI) ability can influence economic activity, rather then the economic or developmental status of the regions. (AI) technology can move accessibility and can use source development to do international business between one country and another country.

So (AI) technology has the potential to give benefits to different income chooses and to bring significant gains to both developed and developing countries. For agricultural technology, (AI) has the potential to optimize food production around the world by analyzing agricultural regions and identifying what is necessary to improve crop yield. In total, (AI) technology gives greater economic impact to any countries agricultural regions if which implemented (AI) technology to grow crop , fruit etc. food production in the farms.

Investment in (AI) technology is such as capital investment to any countries' public or private enterprises. So, it will have large economic impact to the future . If the (AI) technology is reasonable invested to the different needs aspect by the public or private enterprises in the country. Then, it will have good economic impact to the country in the future. However, when (AI) technology is likely to affect both the productivity and employment components of economic growth in many sectors. Significant public debate has focused on projections of (AI)'s effect on the labor force. However, for instance, some researchers have argued that the rise of (AI) technology and automation will led to significant unemployment as capital is substituted for the low skillful labor. So, they point to the concern that the increasing sophistication of (AI) technology may balance skilled and semi-skilled workers and the reduce the size of the middle class. However, this is not a new argument, due to (AI) technology negatively affecting the labor force and leading to mass unemployment. Because the (AI) technology is the substitution of machinery for human labor. Although, employment in certain industries, has been reduced in the past due to technological advancement. For long term, the labor market has adapted to the introduction of new technology, giving rise to new jobs in new areas. (AI) technology may also be accomplished without a reduction to total employment in the long-term to some Asia countries, such as Hong Kong and Japan. Because Hong Kong and Japan many low skilled labor, e.g. security, cleaner who complaint that employers need them to work long time hours. (abnormal working hours) e.g. one day 12 to 15 working hour per day. Hence, if (AI) machine means invention technology success. Security or cleaning job can be worked from (AI) machine man in some hours every day in order to reduce the long time working hours cleaners or security workers, e.g. one (AI) machine man works 4 hours for cleaning or security job, one day as well as another cleaner or security labor only needs to work 8 hours one day. So total security or cleaning employers can employ 12 hours machine cleaners or security workers and human cleaners or security workers in one day. For long term benefit, Hong Kong or Japan every security or cleaning worker does not need to work 12 hours minimum working hours one day. They won't feel tried and bore and without private with whose families, so who will accept to do these cleaning or security jobs, even they can raise work efficient and performance when who feel happy and health.

So, (AI) technology of machine man invention can raise low skillful labor efficiency and it can help them to avoid abnormal working hours demand in some busy work life countries, such as Hong Kong and Japan. Before, one Japan female labor feel unhappy to work, due to who often needs to work abnormal working hours for her employer and who has less sleeping and without any private time to enjoy her life with her families every day. So this abnormal working hours factor causes her to do commit suicide behavior, then she is die unlucky. So (AI) technology of machine man invention ought avoid abnormal working hours demand for employer in any countries in the future.

The most important occurrence to any employers, some researchers had attempted to do one experiment to find that private research and development , venture capital and public research and development investment all have strong net effect or economic growth with venture capital funding further having the strongest such effect from (AI) technology. The researchers hypothesize the venture capital investment contributes to economic growth through (AI) technology innovation and by the capacity of an economy to use existing (AI) technology knowledge to increase productivity. They predict the impacts of venture capital, business-research and development and public research and development can raise multi factor productivity from (AI) technology introduction.

Can (AI) technology influence the economic development to developing countries? The developing regions of the world contain most of natural resources. If one day, (AI) technology has invent one kind of machine man which can assist any gas or oil workers to seek any new oil/gas natural resource locations easily. I believe that (AI) technology can help these natural resource exploitation countries will gain economic benefit more easily. So, (AI) driven technology can be used to change to create any new opportunities to address poor management or resources and improve human well being, such as Africa Latin America and India can use (AI) technology machine man to seek any oil/gas natural resource countries exploitation activities to attempt to gain much economic benefits.

- Why will (AI) technology grow economic

development ?
Nowadays, increases in capital and labor are no longer driving the levels of economic growth, such as (AI) technology. The ability of increase in capital investment and in labor of traditional drivers of production, have no longer to be enjoyed in most developed economies ,e.g. developed country, US, UK . However, artificial intelligence has the potential to overcome the physical limitation of capital and labor to avoid missing out on this opportunity. So, policy makers and business leaders must prepare for and work toward a future with artificial intelligence. They must do with the idea that (AI) is another simply method to enhance productivity method . Rather they must see (AI) as the tool that can transform thinking about how growth is created.
Economists have always thought of new technologies are as driving growth their ability to enhancing. It can replace labor and capital factor of production. So, it brings this question: What is the factor of production (AI) technology characteristics. They key factor is to see (AI) technology as a capital-labor .
(AI) can replicate labor activities at much greater scale and speed, and to even perform some tasks began the capabilities of human. For example, by using virtual assistants , 1000 legal documents can be reviewed in a matter of days instead of taking three people six moths to complete. Some (AI) technology may be one kind of factor of production in the future. For another example, people will work in workplace digitalization environment. So, in the future, working environment and information management are automated. Such as Konica camera sale company will use workplace digitalization. So , (AI) technology can provide workplace digitalization in order to raise productivity efficiency. (AI) technology will be one kind of production which is replaced by workplace digitalization and it will grow any organization productivity efficiently. Then, (AI) technology will assist overall social economy growth , due to productivity is raised and products can be produced in short time to prepare to sell in consumption market. So, time will be shortened to increase GDP growth fast for the development of (AI) technology countries.

● How can (AI) technology impact to global economic and social and psychological changes?
What will be the development of (AI) technology and predictions

concerning the future evolution? The computers and robots will develop conscious, intelligent and minds into humans, enhancing psychological and behavioral abilities and allowing for direct communication with (AI) minds. (AI) technology will be impacted human life by (AI) technology information communicative and environmental influence. A " world brain" and " world mind", this psychological system will be enhanced and enriched the capacities of both individual and collective cognition by (AI) technology of service industries.

(AI) technology with influence these human needs of service industries changes, such as , biological science, finance, entertainment, business, biological science, transportation, communication military etc. The personal computer evolution, the internet and the world wide web which exploded on the scene, linking business, homes, schools, social organizations which were a completely unpredicted phenomenon to influence human life. Kurzweil (1999) predicts that by 2029 year, most human communication will be with machines. According to Person, by 2100 year, there will be human machine convergence.

How can (AI) technology influence environmental protection to make benefits to farming economic growth? (AI) technology can be applied to predict how to solve environmental pollution challenge to avoid to damage any crop or vegetable or rice or fruit etc. food growth. Because environmental experts can gather global environmental pollution data from an environmental database to build a perform a systematic analysis from (AI) technology. The first step is this broad analysis can include understanding, statistical and data gathering techniques to obtain the relevant data, the correlation among the variables involved, and a list of possible models. The next step is to select a set of methods and models that cover all kinds of knowledge and functionalities needed for the decision making process. Once the models are selected, they must be fully implemented by means of machine learning , data mining, statistical or numerical technique. After that, those models must be integrated to build the whole EDSS. The EDSS must be tested to check its performance, accuracy, usefulness and reliability, both from the user's and (AI) technology/computer scientist's point of view. If these is any wrong feature in any development stage, such as model's integration, models' implementation, selection of models, database, problem analysis etc. the developers must come back in the update th required components. When the evaluation phase is all right, the EDSS is ready to be applied to the environment. The great contribution of artificial intelligence to EDSS the integration of several methods complementing the classical statistical models/simulation , statistical analysis, linear models, etc. and numerical models (control algorithms, optimization techniques etc.) .

This cooperation makes the resulting systems more reliable and powerful in coping with real world environment systems. Date interpretation has been a principal area of research in (AI) technology since the very beginning. The most demanding problem in the environmental assessment context. Knowledge representation permits the definition of the different types of data that the existing methods adapt to the process. There is also a lot of work to clean, repair and transform the huge available quantities of raw data. Apart from this, the availability of meta-information or background knowledge is required to guide the process. Data mining is multi-disciplinary: It covers expert systems, data based technology, statistics, data visualization and unsupervised machine learning. These techniques operate at the level of data and background information, where numerous and often incompatible new commensurate pieces of information from disparate sources have to be brought together (K, Fedra, 1994).

So, it seems that in the future, (AI) technology with the increasing maturity in particular those related to knowledge and engineering, new dimensions can be assisted to users in environmental decision making are available. For example, many environmental systems are characterized both by incomplete models and by limited data. Hence, in the future, (AI) technology will be applied to predict climate change to reduce crop or fruit etc. food agriculture challenge by climate change bad influence.

- Will (AI) technology influence digital economy change to manufacturing industry ?

To understand how the manufacturing business must adapt to prosper in the technology, we need to understand how (AI) technology will change us to shape our daily habits to satisfy our expectation of products to how we shop and even the immediate of the entire process. For example, taxi services are in the crosshairs as on demand transportation services like, available of the touch of a smart phone button expand. In fact, Yellow lab, US country , san Francisco city's largest taxi company is filing for bankruptcy as the industry starts to change faster than almost anyone expected. However, at this point, its more than an app that is changing, some our taxi passengers renting taxi transportation to catch consumption behavior.

(AI) technology will influence digital economy for taxi passenger's individual customer experience, offering a growing renting taxi to catch of service and feedback opportunities when any one taxi passenger who chooses to use mobile phone app online tool to prepaid to rent any taxi more easily.

Also in the long term, (AI) technology can influence vehicles drive themselves of behavior. Already, companies like Google and GM are working on projects to bring fleets of autonomous vehicles to cities at the path of a button.

Moreover, this on-demand service model is beginning to appear across a much broader range of markets. For example , Amazon company is investing in its own fleet of trucks, planes and even drone at the same time as it pushes for same-day delivery of products. As some point, vehicles will be autonomous too. So, it seems that (AI) technique will influence any transportations choose to use digital autonomous driving technology in the future . For Amazon company case, it is not stopping of logistics. It is also aiming to automatically manage the supply of consumer home products with its recently launched Amazon replenishment service, Dash. Dash is a digital service that enables that connected derive to automatically order physical products from Amazon when supplies are running low. So, it seems (AI) technology will be applied to logistic function by digital technology method introduction in the future.

Hence autonomous vehicles will optimize industry supply chains and logistics operations through increased efficiency and flexibility. In fact, fully automated and lean supply chains will keep reduce load sizes and inventory by leveraging smart distribution technologies and smaller autonomous vehicles by machine man assistance. If Amazon continues to grow market share for online sales by reducing effort required by the consumer to place an order, when also contributing the almost immediate delivery of products to the doorstep. So, it will further fuel the trend toward on-demand derive. As Amazon company fuels the on-demand economy, consumers will expect immediacy in more parts of the digital economy. On top of speed, consumers increasing expect more personalization options.

So, (AI) technology will influence digital manufacturing, such as Amazon publishing to monitor every aspect of every process in real -time and communicating to self-optimized deep learning robotics, new methods of high volume and high customization will become possible. Then, as products merge into product platforms and even services, manufacturers have the opportunity to provide components and platforms used by smaller players. So, (AI) technology will influence manufacturing industry to choose automated SMI lines, robots installed, automation engineers.

Another future (AI) technology development can be applied to space science aspect, such as Automation engineering space in manufacturing process to achieve digital manufacturing benefits to any businesses in the future. Such as reducing cost, shortening manufacturing time, raising efficiency, shortening delivery products to client individual time. How can artificial intelligence give the need and advanced fast and evaluation methods benefits for space exploration? When US NASA (space exploration organization) achieves any space exploration missions, it will answer this question:

When is it useful to have a machine use (AI) technology to achieve a decision? After all, after millions of years of space exploration and rough 10,000 years of civilization, humans are usually quite good at making decisions in complex uncertain environments. Through, Johns Hoplains University's Applied Physical Lab. Research in (AI) technology enabled systems, which has identified three general use cases for (AI) technology to explore space mission:

First, for some tasks (AI) technology is more cost effectiveness than human. Second, (AI) technology is better suited than humans at solving some, but not all problems. Third, (AI) technology allows NASA organization's space exploration mission to develop machines that ate capable of responding faster than when a human is in the decision loop (D. Scheidt, 2012, A. Castano et. al. 2008).

So, the use of (AI) technology to enable science by observing the pace of rapidly evolving phenomena was demonstrated. It is more effectively coordinating and (AI) technology utilizing to earn economic benefits to use for space exploration mission.

However, (AI) technology also have current risk for space exploration. Today (AI) technology is immature and requires further development to reach its potential. For instance, the (AI) technology algorithms that detected the dust derive could not have identified whether the Martain weather represented a threat to the cover. Also it can not yet use instrument input to determine what, where and how to autonomously make the next space science measurement. An equally important factor limiting (AI)'s deployment is that lacks the methodology and technology to effectively test (AI) technology. So, the challenge will testing (AI) enabled system is how (AI) performance can be measured. It would be NASA organization's difficulty to find (AI) technology to develop to carry on researching any space exploration missions in the future. However, (AI) technology will be a good economic benefit choice for space exploration mission in the future.

- What is artificial intelligence potential benefits and ethical considerations?

The ability of (AI) technology systems to transform vast amounts of complex information into insight has the potential to help solve manufacturing or service challenges for human needs. However, to reap the societal benefits of (AI) systems, humans will need to trust then and make sure that which follow the same ethical principles, moral values, professional codes and social norms that we humans would follow in the same scenario, research and educational efforts as well as carefully designed regulation in order to achieve the most effort of economic benefits goals. For example, international business machines corporation (IBM) is actively engaged both competitors , in global discussions about how to make (AI) ethical and as beneficial as possible for people as social economic benefits.

(AI) is usually defined as the " capability of a computer program to perform tasks or reasoning processes " that human usually associate to intelligence in a human being. Often, it has to do with the ability to make a good decision, even when there is uncertainty, too much information to handle. As an example, play chess or complex card games of entertainment activities is believed to need some form of intelligence in a human being, as well as choosing the best medical facilities in a difficult medical case, or creating something new, such as mathematical theorem or even some form of act, or even driving automatic machine man (self driving vehicle) replacing human driving in the middle of a crowded city.

(AI) needs depends on what we consider being intelligence in the behavior of a human being act a certain point in time. If human belief about human intelligence changes and we don't believe any longer that a certain task requires intelligence, then a computer program performing that task is no longer part of (AI), it becomes just another boring computer program. So, it means that (AI) technology will replace some old computer programs, if human can invent new generation of (AI) software for any functions or activities to satisfy human needs.

As IBM, it argues intelligence. This means that we aim to build systems that enhance and scale human expertise and skills rather than replacing them.

We therefore focus on practical applications of (AI) capabilities that assist people in performing well-defined tasks of needs by exploiting and wide range of (AI)-based services. We also use the term " cognitive computing" it is mean a comprehensive net of capabilities based on technology. It comprises the fields of machine learning, reasoning and decision technologies, language, speech and vision recognition and processing technologies, high performance and high efficient functions for any industries or individual consumers needs. For example, robotics, which are usually very good at doing what which are supposed to in any environment, much have public shopping center, factory etc. places which need simply services from the robot (machine man), such as cleans the floor of our houses to the robot that can work together with humans in production chains, passing through the warehouse, robots can take care of the tasks of an entire warehouse and the companion robots like Nao, Pepper, Aibo and Giraff, who can entertain use, talk to use and help elderly people to stay connected to their friends, relatives and doctors.

Google company is building automatic machine (self-driving cars) and has acquired more than 10 robotics companies. Facebook had opened whole new research facility only on (AI) research. Apply computer has developed Siri. Microsoft computer company has built a similar personalized assistant. Google has Deep mind, a UK company whose long term aim is to build general (AI) and has already great potential to win game to the world champion and IBM is investing a huge amount of resources in applying its Watson cognitive computing system to the medical domains to finance and to personalized education. In Europe, IBM is establishing new centers in Munich and Milan focused in the application of cognitive computer capabilities to the internet of things and healthcare respectively.

For example, automatic machine man (self-driving cars) are all about (AI), which used to be able to see what happens in the street (signals ,lanes, other cars, pedestrians, traffic lights, which need to able predict what other cars and pedestrians will do, and who need to be able to cope with unforeseen situations. Since, most car accidents are due to human fault, it is estimated that the adoption of self-driving cars will save about half of the lives that are usually last in car accidents.

IBM Watson company has to understand spoken language, make sense of massive amount to text , respond correctly to questions in many categories, as well as assess its own confidence in responding to such questions. In the future, (AI) technology can own question/answering capabilities that

would be very useful, for example, in assisting a doctor when trying to some to the correct diagnosis for a patient and to propose the best therapy .
Intelligent machines can also rely on huge amounts of data to be used to learn how to make better decisions. This data comes from all of us over the years Facebook users have uploaded more than 250 billion pictures and every day who upload about 350 million more. Every second, we submit 40,000 google search queries. So, (AI) technology will be connected through the web from appliances to traffic lights from cars to watches. Other tasks that are very easy for humans are physical and manipulation tasks, such as walking , running, picking up an object to make its shape and location, restricted environment. But (AI) machine man technology still not able to have the general physical and manipulation capabilities even of a 6 year old.
So, it brings this question: Why do (AI) scientists need to concern ethics? Because (AI) technology is complex, information into insight has the potential to reveal long held secrets and help solve some of the world's most difficult problems. (AI) systems can potentially be used to help discover insights to treat disease, predict the whether, and manage the global economy. So, ethic issues is important to and (AI) scientists . If any one new (AI) technology research investigation could success, it will be a secret to and the (AI) scientists can not permit to their loyalty to any competitors to damage the fair (AI) technology products trading market. The country (countries) (AI) technology scientists need to concern ethic issues, who need to keep secrets for their countries economic or/and social benefits. This is moral issues to any countries/country loyalty is whose countries intangible assets. They can not sell (AI) loyalty to any their countries to assist whose economic benefits immorally.

- How can (AI) technology influence to global
health care economy development?

According to (AI) lecturer analysis, when combined key clinical health (AI) application can potentially create $150 billion in annual savings for the US healthcare economy by 2026 year. (AI) technology is re-winning modern conception of healthcare delivery. It enables machines to sense, comprehend, act and learn. So which can perform administrative and clinical healthcare functions (Accenture, 2017).
It will help health care service organizations to reduce health care cost, will improve and raise service quality and access. So, (AI) health market size will be predicted growth. (AI) applications in health care include robot-

assisted surgery, virtual nursing assistant, administrative workflow assistant, fraud detection, error reduction connected machines, clinical trial participant identifier, preliminary diagnosis, automated image diagnosis and cybersecurity.

What kind of benefits (AI) technology can contribute to healthcare service? (AI) technology can deliver what many health care organizations need, such as financial and operational of labor costs, digital expectations from patient consumers how to use (AI) technology to solve interoperability challenges in any healthcare organizations. Also (AI) technology can be applied to wellness an d lifestyle management, diagnostics, delivers financially but also way of organizational and workflow improvement. So, (AI) technology will be continue to become most prevalent and adoption to healthcare organizations , which must need to enhance structure to be position to take full advantages of new (AI) technological capabilities. (AI) technology can change the nature of work and employment is rapidly changing to make the best use of both humans and (AI) talent in healthcare industry in the future. For example, (AI) technology offers a way to fill in gaps and the rising labor shortage in healthcare. According to Accenture analysis, the physicians shortage is increasing. However, (AI) technology will manufacture healthcare machine men to replace physicians in future one day(2017). Hence, (AI) technology will be invented to raise health care service staffs work efficiency and performance in any hospitals or clinics in the future.

In conclusion, (AI) technology will raise efficiency for any service or manufacturing industries in the future, although, it is possible that it will also rise low skillful workers unemployment numbers. But, the most important influence to human technological innovation will be risen and it will influence human life will be changed to be better, e.g. self drive cars, health care physician machine men, machine man cleaners etc. intelligent machine men will be manufactured to serve for our daily life. Furthermore, (AI) technological products will influence countries trading, some low technological development countries manufacturing businessmen can choose to buy any (AI) products to raise whose productivity and efficiency and reducing cost to achieve economic cost saving result. Also, GDP of trading growth income will increase to the (AI) products sale countries. Hence, it will be beneficial to economic development to both developed and developing countries both in the future as well as (AI) scientists time and money spending will be valued to continue to invest (AI) technology development for human life and economy benefits for long term.

In conclusion (AI) technology will raise macro economy growth and it can create many (AI) jobs , but it also raise the low level technological worker unemployment change. In the future, (AI) technology can be applied to digital technology to attempt to invent any new undiscovered (AI) and digital technology. So, it needs any scientists to continue to research how digital and (AI) technology can be mixed to satisfy human's future undiscovered needs.

Online technology and online book technology influences artificial intelligence mind development

Nowadays, online technological invention bring online book technological development. Also, artificial intelligent technological machine men had been invented to link internet to do any jobs, e.g. children can find any data from artificial intelligent machine men when the artificial intelligent machine man had been installed internet and computer function, then children can find any online books to read from the artificial intelligent machine man. Such as Japan artificial intellgent machine men had installed computer and internet function, the Japan family children can find any online books to read from the artificial intelligent machine man at Japan any families' homes conveniently. Hence, it implies that future one day, artificial intelligent machine has possible to be invented to own human's reading and/or writing abilities.

For example,online book publishing is one kind of popular internet technology. For example, Amazon publish is as a business model with many potential advantages, relative to a physical operation. It held out the potential of lower book inventing and distribution costs and reduced overhead. Consumers could find the books, they were looking for more easily and a variety book topic choices could be offered for sale. It can accept and fulfill orders from almost any domestic location with equal ease. And most purchasers made on its site would be exempt from sales tax. One Amazon strategy hand, it would have to make its returns and redress processes transparent and reliable, and offer other ways for clients to learn, as much about the book possible before buying. Future online book market development trend, such as Amazon, Barnes & Noble etc. online book shops.

Hence, online book store technology can be applied to artificial intelligent technology. Such as artificial intelligent machine men can apply computer technology to learn the abilities of reading and/or writing any books either on paper or on computer. Hence, it is possible that artificial intelligent machine men will have similar human's writing and/or reading books ability when they own human's mind ability. However, it bring this questions: Can artificial intelligent machine men own human's mind abilities? If they own human's mind abilities, is it mean that they can write and/or read any books? Can artificial intelligent machine men own human's mind abilities to create to write any books? Can artificial intelligent machine men own human's mind abilities to read and make any judgements or decisions more accurate than human's judgements or decisions? To answer these questions? I shall indicate that online book reading and writing technology can be applied to artificial intelligent machine men reading and writing technology. Because they are similiar computer mind technological development. So, I believe that future artificial intelligence machine men can be invented to own similar human's reading and writing's mind abilities in future one day.

I believe artificial intelligence and online technological reading abilities are very similiar. Nowadays, computer can be invented to attempt to read and write any books by human. Why can not artificial intelligent machine men replace computer to read and write any books? Artificial intelligent machine men can replace human to attempt to write or/and read books, due to artificial intelligent machine men had invented to own human mind to do some jobs and their mind had been invented to be similiar to human behavioral abilities to do these behaviors, e.g. cooking, driving, playing games, singing songs, speaking, listening, frighting etc. different human's abilities. So, it seems that artificial intelligent will be possible to be invented to own human's mind abilities to do any writing or reading behaviors or functions.

Prediction of artificial intelligence
reading and writing abilities

development

What is future trend of artificial intelligence reading and writing abilities development? To answer this question, we need to know what benefits of artificial intelligent machine men can attribute to human's needs when they can own any human's mind to read or/and write any books.

I shall indicate e-books reading and writing example, if artificial intelligent machine men can be invented to own human's mind to write and/or read e-books on computer. Then, it brings this question: Can artificial intelligent machine men assist human to learn to do judgement to solve any challenges?

I believe that when artificial intelligent machine men can be invented to own human mind to write or/and read any books, then they will own human's mind ability to make judgement to solve any challenges more accurately, even their decisions can be more accurate to compare to human's decisions. So, artificial intelligent machine mens' writing and reading ability is the main factor to cause their mind to do any judgement in order to make any decisions more accurately. Consequently, in future one day, artificial intelligent machine mens' writing and reading ability will be invented to similar human's reading and writing abilities as well as their minds can also be invented to similar human's minds as well as their judgement abilities can be invented to similar to human's judgement abilities to make any decisions more accurate.

The influences when AI is invented to own human's mind and judgement abilities

Finally, I shall discuss what are the influences when AI is invented to own human's mind and judgement abilities in our future job market. The achievement of artificial intelligent (AI) machine men achievement requirement of owning human's mind and judgement abilities which requires extensive manual labor, and by augmenting the calling process with machine learning, the process where speed and accuracy are needed to close to human's mind and judgement abilities. Expert human race callers now have better information at artificial intelligent machine men at their fingertips faster.

Hence, if the above those requirements are achieved to satisfy artificial intelligent machine men ind and judgement abilities demand to close or exceed humans' mind and judgement abilities. Then, I believe that future human's some simple jobs must be replaced by (AI) machine men. Even, human's some professonal jobs, e.g. lawyer, accountant, administator, typing etc. professional skillful jobs, which will be either replaced or will be assisted by (AI) machine men. For example, (AI) machine men learn how to type english or other language words to do typing job ; they can learn how to apply accounting knowledge to record any firm's income and expenditure record of accounting job; they can also learn how to assist architects to design any architectural building drawing plans to do architect jobs; they can learn how to analyze any court evidences to judge any criminal or civil cases and assist lawyers to give legal advices to achieve more reasonable judgement for any legal cases; they can also learn how to assist firm's managers or administrators to manage any organization teams efficiently.

Consequently, when (AI) machine men can be invented to achieve to exceed human's mind and judgement abilities level. Then, I believe that they can do instead of human‘ simple jobs, which can do even human's more difficult and more judgement requirement of professional skillful jobs. So, (AI) machine men must need to achieve to do any jobs, they are same, even exceed to human professionals' abilities. Then, it will cause a lot of human's jobs to be disappeared or some human's jobs will be replaced by owning judgement and mind abilities of (AI) machine men to do.

Hence, future many human's jobs will be replaced by technological labors. Employers choose to buy (AI) machine men to replace human labors. The reasons include (AI) machine men have none unhappy, angry emotion to influence their low efficiencies and low productivities. Their judgement and mind abilities can exceed human's abilities or do any jobs to compare better performance to human's abilities. Consequently, different occupation labors need to prepare to learn how to co-operate with (AI) machine men to let future employers feel (AI) machine men will be human's assistant to assist human to do jobs efficiently when human and (AI) machine men work together. It aims to avoid future employers feel (AI) machine men's judgement and mind abilities can exceed any low knowledgeable and skilful occupation labors, even high knowledge and skilful occupation labors. It means that (AI) machine men are only labors‘ assistant if (AI) machine mens' judgement and mind abilities are below under to human labors‘ judgement and mind abilities.

Consequently, to avoid (AI) machine men can replace human to do any simple or complex jobs to cause any future any occupation labors' competitors. I recommend that it is right time labors ought prepare to learn different skills. So, every individual labor does not only concentrate on one kind of skill. Because supposing one kind of the occupation labor's job duties are replaced by (AI) machine men. If the employee had owned more than one kind of occupation skill. Then, I believe that who can avoid the unemployment threat more easier than the employee only owned one kind of occupation skill, when (AI) machine men had invented to own human's mind and judgement abilities in future one day. The most important, I believe that (AI) invention will be applied to be teach how to learn human's skills and mind ability. Such as education industry, teacher won't be replaced by (AI), otherwise, (AI) will be teacher's assistant to help them to do education data gather or teaching jobs. So, teachers won't be replaced by (AI), otherwise, teachers will depend on (AI) data gather or teaching job to give them opinions how to solve student's teaching challenges as well as teachers can concentrate on researching education jobs for schools' benefits if (AI) technology can be invented to on human's mind and judgement and reading and writing abilities in the future.

Online technology and online book technology influences artificial intelligence mind development

Nowadays, online technological invention bring online book technological development. Also, artificial intelligent technological machine men had been invented to link internet to do any jobs, e.g. children can find any data from artificial intelligent machine men when the artificial intelligent machine man had been installed internet and computer function, then children can find any online books to read from the artificial intelligent machine man. Such as Japan artificial intelligent machine men had installed computer and internet function, the Japan family children can find any online books to read from the artificial intelligent machine man at Japan any families' homes conveniently. Hence, it implies that future one day, artificial intelligent machine has possible to be invented to own human's reading and/or writing abilities.

For example,online book publishing is one kind of popular internet technology. For example, Amazon publish is as a business model with many potential advantages, relative to a physical operation. It held out the potential of lower book inventing and distribution costs and reduced overhead. Consumers could find the books, they were looking for more easily and a variety book topic choices could be offered for sale. It can accept and fulfill orders from almost any domestic location with equal ease. And most purchasers made on its site would be exempt from sales tax. One Amazon strategy hand, it would have to make its returns and redress processes transparent and reliable, and offer other ways for clients to learn, as much about the book possible before buying. Future online book market development trend, such as Amazon, Barnes & Noble etc. online book shops.

Hence, online book store technology can be applied to artificial intelligent technology. Such as artificial intelligent machine men can apply computer technology to learn the abilities of reading and/or writing any books either on paper or on computer. Hence, it is possible that artificial intelligent machine men will have similar human's writing and/or reading books ability when they own human's mind ability. However, it bring this questions: Can artificial intelligent machine men own human's mind abilities? If they own human's mind abilities, is it mean that they can write and/or read any books? Can artificial intelligent machine men own human's mind abilities to create to write any books? Can artificial intelligent machine men own human's mind abilities to read and make any judgements or decisions more accurate than human's judgements or decisions? To answer these questions? I shall indicate that online book reading and writing technology can be applied to artificial intelligent machine men reading and writing technology. Because they are similiar computer mind technological development. So, I believe that future artificial intelligence machine men can be invented to own similar human's reading and writing's mind abilities in future one day.

I believe artificial intelligence and online technological reading abilities are very similiar. Nowadays, computer can be invented to attempt to read and write any books by human. Why can not artificial intelligent machine men replace computer to read and write any books? Artificial intelligent machine men can replace human to attempt to write or/and read books, due to artificial intelligent machine men had invented to own human mind to do some jobs and their mind had been invented to be similar to human behavioral abilities to do these behaviors, e.g. cooking, driving, playing games, singing songs, speaking, listening, frighting etc. different human's abilities. So, it seems that artificial intelligent will be possible to be invented to own human's mind abilities to do any writing or reading behaviors or functions.

Prediction of artificial intelligence
reading and writing abilities

development

What is future trend of artificial intelligence reading and writing abilities development? To answer this question, we need to know what benefits of artificial intelligent machine men can attribute to human's needs when they can own any human's mind to read or/and write any books.

I shall indicate e-books reading and writing example, if artificial intelligent machine men can be invented to own human's mind to write and/or read e-books on computer. Then, it brings this question: Can artificial intelligent machine men assist human to learn to do judgement to solve any challenges?

I believe that when artificial intelligent machine men can be invented to own human mind to write or/and read any books, then they will own human's mind ability to make judgement to solve any challenges more accurately, even their decisions can be more accurate to compare to human's decisions. So, artificial intelligent machine mens‘ writing and reading ability is the main factor to cause their mind to do any judgement in order to make any decisions more accurately. Consequently, in future one day, artificial intelligent machine mens' writing and reading ability will be invented to similar human's reading and writing abilities as well as their minds can also be invented to similar human's minds as well as their judgement abilities can be invented to similar to human's judgement abilities to make any decisions more accurate.

The influences when AI is invented to own
human's mind and judgement abilities

Finally, I shall discuss what are the influences when AI is invented to own human's mind and judgement abilities in our future job market. The achievement of artificial intelligent (AI) machine men achievement requirement of owning human's mind and judgement abilities which requires extensive manual labor, and by augmenting the calling process with machine learning, the process where speed and accuracy are needed to close to human's mind and judgement abilities. Expert human race callers now have better information at artificial intelligent machine men at their fingertips faster.

Hence, if the above those requirements are achieved to satisfy artificial intelligent machine men ind and judgement abilities demand to close or exceed humans‘ mind and judgement abilities. Then, I believe that future human's some simple jobs must be replaced by (AI) machine men. Even, human's some professonal jobs, e.g. lawyer, accountant, administator, typing etc. professional skillful jobs, which will be either replaced or will be assisted by (AI) machine men. For example, (AI) machine men learn how to type english or other language words to do typing job ; they can learn how to apply accounting knowledge to record any firm's income and expenditure record of accounting job; they can also learn how to assist architects to design any architectural building drawing plans to do architect jobs; they can learn how to analyze any court evidences to judge any criminal or civil cases and assist lawyers to give legal advices to achieve more reasonable judgement for any legal cases; they can also learn how to assist firm's managers or administrators to manage any organization teams efficiently.

Consequently, when (AI) machine men can be invented to achieve to exceed human's mind and judgement abilities level. Then, I believe that they can do instead of human' simple jobs, which can do even human's more difficult and more judgement requirement of professional skillful jobs. So, (AI) machine men must need to achieve to do any jobs, they are same, even exceed to human professionals' abilities. Then, it will cause a lot of human's jobs to be disappeared or some human's jobs will be replaced by owning judgement and mind abilities of (AI) machine men to do.

Hence, future many human's jobs will be replaced by technological labors. Employers choose to buy (AI) machine men to replace human labors. The reasons include (AI) machine men have none unhappy, angry emotin to influence their low efficiencies and low productivities. Their judgement and mind abilities can exceed human's abilities or do any jobs to compare better performance to human's abilities. Consequently, different occupation labors need to prepare to learn how to co-operate with (AI) machine men to let future employers feel (AI) machine men will be human's assistant to assist human to do jobs efficiently when human and (AI) machine men work together. It aims to avoid future employers feel (AI) machine men's judgement and mind abilities can exceed any low knowledgeable and skilful occupation labors, even high knowledge and skilful occupation labors. It means that (AI) machine men are only labors' assistant if (AI) machine mens' judgement and mind abilities are below under to human labors' judgement and mind abilities.

Consequently, to avoid (AI) machine men can replace human to do any simple or complex jobs to cause any future any occupation labors‘ competitors. I recommend that it is right time labors ought prepare to learn different skills. So, every individual labor does not only concentrate on one kind of skill. Because supposing one kind of the occupation labor's job duties are replaced by (AI) machine men. If the employee had owned more than one kind of occupation skill. Then, I believe that who can avoid the unemployment threat more easier than the employee only owned one kind of occupation skill, when (AI) machine men had invented to own human's mind and judgement abilities in future one day.

How does (AI) robots' brain invention influence our lives

(AI) research modeling the human brain has developed important technologies, and has overcome significant barriers. How will (AI) affect humanity in the near future? How will (AI) change our lives and our societies? Is the evolution of (AI) to humanity, or it represent a threat?

On white collar workers (AI) job replacement aspect, University of Tokyo, Institute of informatics, lecturers who had attempted to do experiments to take (AI) exams over a two year period. The (AI) achieved standard scores of around 50 in each subject, exceeding the norms for humans attempting the tests. The (AI)'s results in subjects emphasizing memorization, such as world history and Japanese history subjects were comparatively high, and the results of the study suggested that an appropriate selection of subjects would give at an 80% chance of passing the entrance exams of 80% of Japan's private universities.

So, if (AI) is applies to human white collar workers‘ job duties aspect, at this level, if white collar workers were replaced by (AI) in the future, around 30% of current staff would be replaced. Whatever, the outcome, large companies will be represented with two choices. One choice will be to protect their employees, but as a result lose their international competitiveness. The latter choice will enable them to reduce the cost of general duties, financial management procedures, accounting etc. general administrative job duties of cost in offices. Hence, it seems that (AI) will be possible to be invented to own human's brain ability to do some mind jobs in future on day.

However, the method called " deep learning" must be developed to cause (AI) to match human's brain ability as well as these were dramatic advances in technologies, such as image recognition and voice recognition, which form the foundation for (AI). Nowadays, this new method called" deep learning" does not reach the matured and stagnated stage. It needs to wait human to continue to invent to let (AI) to match human brain to achieve 100% owning human's mind ability. Nowadays, (AI) industry product include cleaning robots, smart TVs and future (AI) product development market. It will include self-driving vehicles, drones, and nursing robots.

On (AI) weapons applied aspect, if (AI) can be invented to own human's brain judgement and analytical abilities. Then, it is possible that it can be applied to attack enemy to cause war effect. For example, if weapons such as missiles were equipped with (AI) in the future, they would become able to decide on their own targets. Hence, human needs to apply restrictions when necessary.

On (AI) applied to analyzing information collected technological aspect, nowadays, every one will use wearable terminals to connect to the internet to obtain various types of information as well as computers will collect and analyze information on people. Our lives will probably be more reliant on these internet technologies than they are on smartphones today. When, (AI) can match human brain to own mind ability.

Then, (AI) can be applied to do any analyzing information and collection job duties aspect to raise large information restoring and remembering efficiency. For example, (AI) will be generally used and will be extremely useful in analyzing the information collected from wearable devices and stored in the cloud. (AI) will enable wearable devices to be of real assistance in our lives offering their users more intelligent support.

Rather than allowing (AI) to develop on serves, as something separate from humanity. It will be more meaningful to encourage its development via wearable devices, situating it under the control of human intelligence. The intelligence of (AI) will increase rapidly in the future. If this increase in (AI) occurs under human control, enabling humans to increase their own abilities, then surely it will be possible for us to put up a degree of resistance to the opposite scenario, the domination of (AI) over humanity. Hence, if (AI) can be invented to remember and store and make analytical judgement to collect any information from internet. Then, it will bring the effect, such as large international organizations' (AI) internet storage robots can bear in mind factors, such as competitors' privacy or business secret information, such as the loss equality between people and threats to privacy that will be stolen form the owning (AI) storing internet information remembering robots.

Consequently, what is the effect of successful invention of (AI) matching human brain's mind ability? (AI) present computers are adequately able to reproduce the emotional, conceptual and intuitive abilities of humans. Because of this, it is important that we should envision potential future problems that may manifest when we consider how to employ wearable devices. It will be essential to enhance our technologies in order to ensure that we can use (AI) under human control.

However, when a goal has been set. (AI) will implement an appropriate means for its realization. (AI) will be need as a tool by human society. If the capacities of analytical and judgement mind abilities of (AI) brain exceed those of human brain, it is difficult to imagine the type of technological, then singularity is represented by the creation of an (AI) by another (AI). It is important that we rapidly and accurately predict these developments, when image recognition and other individual technologies are functioning at a high level. There will be a considerable matter in different sectors of (AI) industry development.

Today, however, machines have become able to decide for themselves what they will learn, making it difficult to copy human's mind ability. What we must consider when machines exceed humans and (AI) surpasses human capabilities. May technologies exceed human capabilities, cars are faster than humans, planes are able to fly. Consequently, it brings a question that human needs to consider: When does (AI) brain technology be invented to reach the most reasonable stage to be accepted or stopped by humanity?

What is artificial intelligence
human brain invention?

A machine is likely to achieve the ability of a human brain. Does it a scientific story? Some scientists has predicted that a US$1,000 personal computer will match the computing speed and capacity of the human brain by around the year 2020 year. With human reverse engineering, human should have the software insights before 2030 year. it is possible that of machine intelligence and exotic new technology for faster and more powerful computational machines from cellular automata and DNA playing cheese game competition case example, it proves that (AI) had been invented to own human's analytical and judgement ability to exceed the best cheese game human player's brain analytical and judgement ability. Then, it seems that (AI) will have possible to be built machine brains to achieve the exceed level of human brain's analytical and judgement ability in the future one day.

Supposing we scan someone's brain and restate the resulting " mind file" into suitable computing medium. Will the entity that emerges from such an operation be conscious? How have advances in electronic communications changes power relationship? For electronic book publishing case example, a book that looks at the principles companies must adopt to meet the needs and desires of this new kind of client. So, such as paper book can be changed to electronic book for human to read. Why can't human brain be changed to (AI) machine brain to do human's analytical mind and behavioral mind of activities to replace to do any human's daily analytical and behavioral mind activities?

Over the next few decades, machine achieve super intelligence, human will encounter a dramatic phase. Will it be a "WALL" a barrier as conceptually the event of a black hole in space. Such as (AI) brain invention case, an " AI singularity" ruled super-intelligence AIs, or a gentler " surge" into a post human era of agelessness and super-intelligence brain. Will future technology, such as bio-engineered pathogens, self replicating nan robots, and super smart robots run and accelerate out of control, perhaps threatening the human race?

If one day, (AI) brain is invented to achieve agelessness possibility. It means human's brain will be old to lose mind and analytical ability when human's age is increasing. Otherwise, (AI) machine brain age won't lose mind and analytical ability, due to (AI) machine is no age increasing possibility. It is a machine brain. If (AI) machine brain can be built successfully. Scientists need to consider technological ethic matter, such as the challenge of guiding nanotechnology in a constructive direction, advances in nanotechnology and related advanced technologies can not be inevitable, any broad attempt to relinquish nanotechnology would interfere with the benefits. When actually making the dangers worse.

Keeping in mind that intelligence machines are already making their way into our blood stream. There are dozens of projects underway to create blood-stream based " biological micro electronic- system" (bio MES) with a wide range of diagnostic and therapeutic applications BioMEMS devices are being designed to intelligently pathogens and deliver medications in very precise ways. For example, a researcher at the University of Illinois at Chicago has created a ting capsule with pores measuring only seven nanometers. The pores let insulin out in a controlled manner, but prevent antibodies from invading the pancreatic Islet cells inside the capsule. These nano- engineered devices have cured rated with type I diabetes, and there is no reason that the same methodology would fail to work in humans. Similar systems could precisely deliver dopamine to the brain patients, provide blood-clotting factors for patients with hemophilia and deliver cancer drugs directly to tumor sites. A new design provides up to 20 substance-containing reservoirs that can release their cargo at programmed times and locations in the body.

Another brain health technological related invention case, such as Kensall Wise, a professor of electrical engineering at the University of Michigan, who has developed a tiny neural probe that can provide precise monitoring of the electrical activity of patients with neural disease. Future designs are expected to also deliver drugs to precise locations in the brain. Also, kazushi Ishiyama at Tohoku University in Japan has developed micro machines that use microscopic-cancer tumors.

A particularly innovative micro machine developed by Sandia National labs has actual micro teach with a jaw that opens and closes to trap individual cells and then implant them with substances, such as DNA, proteins or drugs. There are already at least four major scientific conferences on bio MES and other approaches to developing micro-and nano-scale machines to go into the body and bloodstream. All these inventions are related to how to apply machines to copy human's brain knowledge in order to achieve to do any human's brain functions.

Finally, for Freitas envisions micron-sized artificial platelets invention case example, who could achieve hemostasis (bleeding control) up to 1,000 times faster than biological platelets. Freitas describes nano-robotic microbivores (white blood cell replacement) that will download software to destroy specific infections hundreds of time faster than antibiotics, and that will be effective against all bacterial, and fungal infections with no limitations of drug resistance.

Consequently, such as above machine health scientific invention cases, there were many scientists had invented any health machines to apply drugs to transfer to human's brain to attempt to reduce human's disease causing risks, such as reducing cancer cell increasing number. Why it is no possible that scientists can attempt to invent (AI) brain which can own human's mind ability to judge or analyze any matters to give opinions in order to exceed human's judgement and analytical ability.

How can artificial intelligent brain

satisfy to human beneficial and
natural needs?

Nowadays, new scientists' most familiar form of this vision in our times is genetic engineering. Specifically, the prospect of designing better human beings by improving their biological systems of a small, serious and accomplished group of tailors in the field of artificial intelligence and robotics. Their goal is a simply new age of post-biological life, a world of intelligence without bodies, immortal identity without the limitations of disease, death and unfulfilled desire. If human can understand why this fate is presented as both necessary and desirable, human might understand modern science can help us to enter the good life and good society stage when (AI) brain is invented by scientists successfully in our future life.

How can (AI) beneficial brain satisfy to human natural need? For relatively recent example, similarly as a long term trend beginning with the first mechanical calculators, the evaluation of computing capacity increases in speed over time and decrease in cost. From biological evolution has been invented to influence human brain, an electronic chemical machine with a great, but finite number of computer neuron connections, the product of which we call mind or consciousness. As an electro-chemical machine, the brain obeys the laws of physics, all of its functions can be understood and duplicated. And since computers already operate at far faster speeds then the brain, they soon will rival or surpass the brain in their capacity to store and process information. When happens, the computer will at the vary least, be capable of responding to stimuli in ways that are indistinguishable for human responses. At that point, we would be justified in calling the machine intelligent, we would have the same evidence to call it conscious that human now have when giving such a label to any consciousness other than our own.

At the same time, the study of human brain will allow us to duplicate its functions in machine circuitry. Advances in brain imaging will allow us to " map out" brain functions, allowing individual minds to be duplicated in some combination of hardware and software. The result, will be a world that is remade and reconstructed at the atomic level through nanotechnology, a world whose organization will be shaped by an intelligence that surpasses all human comprehension.

Whether or not today's humans are willing or able to " download" their brains into machines, there will come a time when all human beings will be intelligent machines in the future. Computer hardware will continue to get faster, cheaper and more powerful computer software will increase in sophistication. Brain research will continue to explore the " mechanics" of consciousness. Nanotechnology will continue to develop.

There are powerful incentives, commercial, military, medical and intellectual that will drive many of the advances that the extinctions desire if for very different reasons. Much of the work in artificial intelligence and robotics is open to the same defense that is made on behalf of biotechnology: If we don't do it, they will and why suffer or be unhappy when some new agent or invention is available that will solve the problem.

Finally, we already accept significant artificial argumentation and replacement of natural body parts when those parts are missing or defective. Over time indistinguishable from or " superior" to their biological counterparts as they employ increasing computer processing power. There are powerful incentives, commercial, military, medical and intellectual that will drive many of the advances that the extinctions desire, if for very different reasons. Much of the work in artificial intelligence and robotics is open to the same defense that is made on behalf of biotechnological if we don't do it, they will and why suffer or be unhappy, when some new agent or invention is available. That will cure the problem.

Finally, we already accept significant artificial augmentation and replacement of natural body parts when those parts are missing or deductive. Over time, such replacements are only likely to get more useful and perhaps eventually indistinguishable from or superior to their biological counterparts, as they employ increasing computer processing power. Nor is there an obvious distinction between using manufactured chemicals to fight disease and using " smart" nanotechnology. The extinction project is begun by offering new routes to fulfilling old promises about doing good for human beings. But, it doesn't necessary end.

In connection with machine intelligence, it does not seem very promising to try to limit the power or ability of computers. The danger (or promise) that computers might develop characteristics that lead some people to call them conscious and that this age of intelligent machines would mean our extinction seems remote when compared with their practical benefits. We already rely so heavily on computers that the incentives to make them easier to use and more powerful are very great. Computers already do a great many things better than we can, and there seems to be no natural place to enforce a stopping point to further abilities. Certainly mechanistic and reductionist assumptions about society, ethics and psychology the notion that we are atoms or animals, driven by chance or instinct, run deep in the present world.

Artificial intelligent brain future

innovation and attribution (AI) brain invention successful factors

(AI) brain will bring what attribution to influence human's positive impact. How (AI) brain will be invented to apply to any businesses‘ needs. By how much the (AI) brains might exceed us remain unknown, but it could potentially be by a very significant degree. Future (AI) brain invention will have noted similar growth in everything from hard-drive storage density to the price and speed of DNA sequencing. On key feature of this technological growth that has not been adequately measured in the degree to which technology is becoming more intelligent.

(AI) brain test experiment

When there is an intuitive sense that (AI) programs/brains today are more capable than those of age, and that those were considerably " smarter" than the serial instructions that passed through the first supercomputers. Scientists will carry on testing (AI) to do any experiments to improve (AI) brain development. They will assess the progress of artificial (general) intelligence, but the need for intelligence tests and tests for other cognitive abilities will be tested in the forthcoming decades for bots, robots, avators, " animats" etc. and any collective system of these and biological systems (humans and non-human animals).

When (AI) brain technology is invented successfully, the idea of a super intelligent computer means invention successfully also. Whether super intelligent computer or (AI) brain can be invented successfully. Similarly, many think that the future beyond the technological singularity is unknowable or even unimaginable. Since its conception, the idea has been examined and explored by technologists. (AI) brain invention will be mean human-equivalent (AI) vs human-level(AI). Many machine intelligence tests is the exclusive focus on identifying systems that achieve human equivalence. Considering our experience with studying non-human animal intelligence.

The need to distinguish human equivalent (AI) from human level (AI) seems critical. Perfect human intelligence , such as (AI) brain invention is likely to be extremely difficult to achieve. Potentially every aspect of the biological processes involved would need to be translated with very high fidelity.

Human level (AI), such as (AI) brain invention is another matter. Achieving capabilities that are equivalent to those of the human mind could be very feasible if it is not limited to perfectly processes involves. For instance, some pattern recognition algorithms are already superior to human abilities. This machine ability is not achieved by duplicating the processes our brains use, through some of the methods have been inspired by them. If researchers had been limited to replicating the brain's mind processes, We would still be waiting for the development of a (AI) brain machine equivalent.

Tests that would seen to have a reasonable chance of successfully testing non-human intelligence are those that use mathematics to define the value of a given challenges for (AI) brain invention. Such as Capability-test has some potential to generate meaningful data about (AI) machine intelligence, e.g. others in complexity theory test, it presents a series of abduction and prediction problems, similar to those in standard IQ tests to (AI) brain. Hence, IQ test and C-test will be potential tests to test (AI) brain ability.

(AI) brain test goals include that to identify a range of possible types of mind such as: super-fast human mind, mind with operational access to its source code, any mind capable of general intelligence and self awareness, general intelligence without self-awareness, self-awareness without general intelligence, super-logic , machine without emotion, mind capable of imaging greater mind or creating greater mind to compare human's brain abilities. Thus, any IQ or Capability test experiments aim to evaluate whether (AI) brain mind ability which can exceed to human brain mind ability. Thus, if future one day, scientists could prove (AI) brain mind ability can exceed to human brain mind ability. Then, they believe (AI) brain invention has ensured to achieve success.

(AI) brain invention successful factors

Hence, scientists want to invent (AI) brain successfully. They need to solve these challenges. Such as How robots and computers have progressively supplemented humans, initially only in relatively simple computational and manipulation tasks, but more recently in higher cognitive tasks that used to be the pre negative of the human brain, including language, mathematics, probabilistic reasoning and decision making.

An important challenge is how to enhance the productive interactions between humans and artificial intelligence? The important challenge include these major successful factors to invent (AI) brain technology, such as:

What is the state of the art in (AI) software and machine learning?

Can all aspects of brain function be manufactured by artificial system?

What is the proper form of mathematics that may capture the operation of minds and brains?

How to make (AI) brain feels consciousness?

What would it be taken for a machine to pose a sense of art in (AI) brain software and (AI) brain machine learning by artificial system?

Will machines soon surpass us in all domains of human competence?

What is the proper form of mathematic that may capture the operation of minds and brains?

What is consciousness to (AI) brain invention?

Could a machine be endowed with an artificial consciousness?

What would it take for a machine to posses a sense of self?

Will intelligence machines soon pose a danger to humanity of (AI) brain is invented to reach the mature stage successfully?

Is it possible to design and construct an intelligent robot with an artificial brain sense of ethics?

How can we enhance the humanitarian uses of artificial intelligence brain and owning mind ability of robotics, in particular in the field of education, health and emergencies?

Consequently, above all these challenges, I recommend scientists need to solve to achieve (AI) brain invention in order to reach (AI) brain invention mature stage easily.

Artificial intelligence brain invention opportunities and challenges

If scientists focus wrong direction to invent (AI) brain, it will bring wrong marketing development to attribute any benefits to human. So, they need to reduce a mismatch of timescales between the pace of commercial innovation and (AI) brain invention process, reduce an underappreciation of the fundamental unpredictability of (AI) brain autonomous systems and reduce a lack of a university agreed upon conceptual framework for any (AI) brain invention and reduce a disconnect between the (AI) brain design of any kind of (AI) autonomous robots. Thus, scientists need examine these gapes, provide a roadmap of opportunities and challenges and identify areas of any (AI) beneficial functions to be attributed to human to use for our daily life needs.

Future (AI) brain market opportunities, it is rapidly growing innovations in digital -electronic and information technology had development of new intelligence, surveillance, and reconnaissance platform and battle management capabilities, precision-strike weapons, stealth aircraft, smart weapons and sensors and tactical exploitation of space (e.g. GPS).

Any one of these aspects will be (AI) brain future marketing development opportunities. Future (AI) brain invention of so called " narrow AI", (i.e. non-sentient artificial intelligence, whose problem-solving capability is confined to one narrow task. For example, (AI) brain needs to find the best method to win any one of chess player in any both human and (AI) robot chess playing game.

In smart weapon strategy industry, (AI) brain is needed to design how to analyze or mind to protect whose country to avoid enemy attack in any war by the best weapon protection strategy. In education industry, (AI) brain is needed to design how to analyze or mind how to assist teachers to educate whose students by the best education method. In aircraft industry, how to design (AI) brain to analyze or mind to assist pilot to make the most correct flying direction judgement to fly in the most safe way. In space exploitation industry, (AI) brain is needed to design how to find undiscovered natural resources to supply to human to use in anywhere space.

Thus, future (AI) brain invention needs have these features/characteristics to be designed. They include: (AI) learned on its own, where to find the information it needs to accomplish a specific task, (AI) can predict the immediate future from studying any matter, (AI) automatically needs to be inferred the rules that govern the behavior of individual robots within a robotic swarm simply by watching, (AI) needs to be learned how to navigation the acquired memories and experiences, much like a human brain, (AI) speech recognition needs to be reach human parity in conversational speech, (AI) communication system needs to be invented its own encryption scheme, without being taught specific cryptographic algorithms (and without revealing to researchers how its method works, (AI) translation algorithm needs to be invented to remember fluent language to more effectively translate between any two languages (without being taught to do so by humans), (AI) brain system interacted with its environment (via virtual environment) to learn and solve problems in the same ways that a human child can do, (AI) based medical diagnosis system needs to be achieved 99% percent accuracy in any medical reviewing

researches (at a rate minimum 30 times faster than humans), (AI) poker playing program brain development needs to be defeated some of the world's best human poker players during a minimum three-week-long tour, (AI) brain development needs to be effectively " read minds" of human test subjects looking at pictures of faces, via functional magnetic reasonable images of brain activity.
Consequently, (AI) future brain development needs to follow above directions to be invented to attribute to human's satisfactory needs.

(AI) brain legal remembering attribution

Future, (AI) robots can assist lawyers to deal any legal cases more efficient. If human understands that smart (AI) technology is not to replace human lawyers, but to make a better lawyer that forces who to use, emotional intelligence, and capital on lawyers' mind, then human lawyer have made the first step in future, proofing whose legal service business from (AI) legal robots' assistance. (AI) promises to be a real advantage for today and tomorrow' lawyers having to deal with the rate of legislative evolution and technological change.
In future, for the better with regard to technology in any law firms. According to the ALM 205 law tech. survey 95% of firm leaders and technologist respondents agreed with recent decisions by management regarding the firm's technology in legal service profession.
How can (AI) robots be applied to legal service industry by legal service firms? The (AI) reality in the legal world, it includes in relation to the four key elements of legal service provision, such as commodity, research, reasoning and judgement, exist and can support or replace certain aspects of every lawyer individual jobs both fee earning processes and business processes can be supported and/or replaced by expert systems, cognitive computing, robotics automated systems, (AI) and the machine learning, clients demand and expect more speedy, accurate, expert, creative, intuitive and accessible legal advice, it can assist young lawyers to innovate / tech. focused firm, reducing pressure both from within law firms (or in house teams) and from clients to respond to the demand for client-designed service from (AI) robots assistance, technology related projects that are both user and client -centric need to be implemented successfully.
Due to the deployment of (AI) robots in the legal ecosystem where lawyers, firms, general counsel and clients are beginning to believe (AI) capability technologies, (AI) robots can assist lawyers to increasingly become more

productive, efficient, accurate, better quality, less labor intensive and time intensive and the role of the lawyer is gradually changing. If we break down a lawyers' tasks in a legal project from beginning that can handle the majority of these four tasks far more quickly and accurately than human lawyer. (AI) robots can handle legal task in the four aspects as below:

First in legal aspect, it can be used for deep research and processing, such as extracting specific pieces of information from land registry documents, (AI) technology is placed top of a document set including client guidelines and similar forms. It searches through documents and extracts key data points to provide a report of data for improved coordination with clients.

Second on managed services technology aspect, (AI) platform which could have a huge advantage for general counsel and law departments in corporations and for clients of all company sizes.

Third on reading aspect, (AI) brain program that reads and analyzes , e.g. clauses in loan agreements. Its program helps its lawyers through transactions and points. Then toward the correct precedents of each stage of a process.

Fourth, on academics aspect, (AI) robots can assess the merits of personal injury cases. It can automatically review high volumes of contract documents to identify provisions that could potentially be impacted by contract law regulation.

Thus, all of these systems can handle large quantities of structured and unstructured data, and assist with the process management, research, and reasoning elements related to legal issues. Thus, in future, (AI) brain development can be invented to apply to knowledge research job, such as legal industry.

Artificial legal intelligence presents a thought-provoking approach to both computational models of legal reasoning and the use of evolutionary thinking about the law. The visions of computerized artificial legal intelligence , a vision of developments in both technology and legal history. A number of creative research projects have applied artificial intelligence techniques to the domain of legal reasoning.

Consequently, (AI) brain for legal industry marketing development ought concentrate on those three fields of artificial intelligence at most relevant to work in the legal areas in order to achieve the excellent attribution. Such as case-based reasoning, expert systems and neural networks. Artificial intelligence program, such as the legal reasoning programs. Thus, (AI) brain invention needs to own these human legal concept knowledge in order to achieve (AI) legal brain program development successfully.

Whether human mind can create to (AI) brain mind

How can (AI) scientists build a machine that think? In fact, there was general agreement that minds can be existence on non-biological substrates and that algorithms are of central importance to the existence of minds. However, there are much debate about the raw hardware power present in organic brains, such as (AI) brain.

I think (AI) scientists need to invent powerful hand ware, e.g. commercial digital signal processing might be, giving an appcarance even to digital operations, but nothing would ever make up the intellectual runaway that is the essence of the singularity.

I also think raw hardware power is not be able to organize the parts to behave in a super-human way as well as I also think powerful software complexity is the main factor to solve (AI) brain mind invention challenge. Hence, future super-human (AI) brain invention will ought consider how to invent superhuman software more than hardware, because software can store any memory, i.e. human mind. When, (AI) brain invention which can achieve to own human mind ability. Then, (AI) scientists need to consider ethic matter: Does the future of (AI) pose an existential threat to humanity? How do we present learning algorithms from morally objectionable biases? Should autonomous (AI) be used to kill in warfare? How should (AI) systems be in our social relations? Is it permissible to fall in love with an (AI) system? What sort of ethical rules should (AI) like a self-driving car use? Can (AI) systems suffer moral harms? All those ethic matters. I think (AI) scientists need to consider after (AI) brain owns human's mind ability because it is possible that (AI) robots will harm human if they are educated to do any wrong or illegal or immoral mind ability. Thus, (AI) scientists need to consider (AI) robot's moral mind and judgement behavior.

Brain-inspired intelligent robotics

How to solve fundamental problems in the areas of brain sciences and brain-inspired intelligence technology? One way scientists seek to accomplished the mission is to develop brain-inspired hardware including intelligent devices, chips, robotic systems and brain inspired computing systems. (AI) scientists ultimate goal, but since the robot's memory and learning after the human brain, there is still much to learn about neurobiology before that goal is attached.

In (AI) brain university research aspect, two schools of thought have emerged in robotics: bio-logically robots that include a body, sensor and actuators, and brain-inspired computing robot.

Robots have found increasing applications in industry, service and medicine, due in large part to advances achieved in robotics research over the past decades, such as the ability to accomplish complex manipulations that are essential for automated product assembly. However, robots still have these weaknesses which need to be solved if (AI) scientists expect (AI) brain invention can be success. Robots still lack truly flexible movement, have limited intellectual perception and control, and not yet able to carry out natural interactions with human. These deficits are especially critical in service robots. A critical concern of government, academia, and industry is how to advance research and development for the key technologies that can bring about the next generation of robots. Developing robots with more flexible manipulation, improved learning ability and increased intellectual perception will achieve the main goals for (AI) scientists' solutions.

Consequently future (AI) brain -inspired intelligent robotic invention needs have these competitive or attractive abilities or strengths to compare computer storage ability. Such as (AI) brain needs have perception to exceed computation ability, adaptation exceeds computing speed, flexibility exceeds, computer memory access speed, cognition exceeds computer memory lifetime, learning exceeds computer memory capacity and innovation exceeds computer memory storage abilities. Hence, (AI) brain innovation must need to exceed general computer storage, lifetime, capacity, learning abilities if (AI) scientists expect (AI) robots will be popular to be applied by any service, manufacturing, education industries.

(AI) influences the automation working changing aspect, as companies increasingly use robots on production lines or algorithms to optimize their logistics manage inventory, any carry out other core business functions. Technological advances are creating a new automation age in which ever-smarter and more flexible machines will be deployed on an ever larger scale in the marketplace. However, researching artificial intelligence with how influences human working nature. We need to answer these questions:

How will automation transform the workplace?

What will the implications for employment?

What is likely to be its impact both on productivity in the global economy and on employment?

Advances in robotics, artificial intelligence, and machine learning are growing in a new age of automation as machines match or outperform human performance in a range of work activities, including ones requiring cognitive capabilities.

What factors are determined the changing in workplace adoption by artificial intelligence innovation?

What advantages are automation?

Automation of activities can be enabled businesses to improve performance by reducing errors and improving quality and speed, and achieving outcomes that go beyond human capabilities.

Some scientists indicated based on their scenario modeling. They estimated automation could raise producing growth globally by 0.8 to 1.4 percent annually. Almost, the activities people are paid almost $16 trillion in wages to do in global economy have the potential to be automated by adopting currently demonstrated technology. According to their analysis of more than 2,000 work activities across 800 occupations. When less than 5% of all occupations have of least 30% of activities that could be automated. They also indicated that technical economic and social factors will determine automation. Continued technical progress, for example, in areas such as natural language processing is a key factor beyond technical feasibility , the cost of technology, competition with labor including skills, and supply and demand dynamics, performance benefits including and beyond labor cost savings and social and regulatory acceptance will affect (alter) the scope of automation.

Other some scientists also indicate U.S. country for example, the anticipate shift in the activities in labor force of a similar order of magnitude as the long term sight away from agriculture and decreases in manufacturing. Share of employment in the United States both which were achieved. So, those factors can influence why artificial intelligence technology needs. So, it is possible that future agriculture and manufacturing both industries will apply (AI) technology manufacturer-kind of job nature to raise productivity instead of farmers, fruit picking workers, farming transportation labours as well as factory manufacturing workers and supervisors etc. human-kind of job nature.

Not just intelligence, but also debating, if machines are capable of having a conscious minds. Artificial intelligence has those characteristics as below:

On functionalism aspect, artificial intelligence inputs mental states, sensory inputs, (beliefs, desires being in pain feeling) and behavioral outputs. Since mental states are identified by a functional role, which are thoughts to be manifested in various systems. Even, perhaps computers which are physical devices with electronic substrate that inform computations on inputs to give outputs similar to brains which are artificial intelligence composed of part any intrinsic relationship to each other. Thus, artificial intelligence activities is not the whole itself, but into parts or on external influence on the parts.

On dualism aspect, artificial intelligence is a set of views about the relationship between mind are matter. On materialism aspect, it builds the only thing that exists is matter, including consciousness.

On biological naturalism aspect, it is similar a human brain than feels pains makes mental situation. So, artificial intelligence is similar biologist which might to be excited to human labor work. Hence, it seems artificial intelligence can change (alter) or replace human labor work of nature in order to raise efficiency and productivity in possible any working environment when it own human mind and effort absolutely.

On technological innovation reason view point, the history development of artificial intelligence studying the intelligence is one of most ancient scientific discipline. The history development of artificial intelligence what aims to achieve human use to sense, learn remember and think, logic probability, decision making and calculation develop from mathematics, instead of replacement human labor functions.

Artificial intelligence history development aim is the scientific analysis of skills in connection and practice with the appearance of computers from 1950 year beginning. The artificial intelligence (AI) can deal with the ultimate challenges. How can (either biological or electronic) mind sense, understand and manipulate a world that is much simple and more complex than itself? And what if would human like to construct something with such capabilities?

The general-purpose software of the early period of (AI) were only able to solve simple tasks effectively and failed when which should be used in a wider range or an more difficult tasks. One of the sources of difficulty was that early software had very few or mix knowledge about the problems which handled, and activities successes by simply syntactic manipulation. Moreover, the other difficulty was that many problems that were tried to solve by the (AI) were untreatable.

The early (AI) software whether trying step sequences based on the basic facts about the problem that should be solved, experimented with different combinations till which found a solution. From the end the 1960 year, developing the so-called expert systems were emphasized. These systems had (sue-based) knowledge base about the field which handled. Till to the beginning of the 1970 year, (Prolog) the logical programming language was born, which was built in the computation realization of a version of the resolution calculus. (Prolog) is a remarkably prevalent tool in developing expert systems (on medical, judiciary and other scopes), but natural language parsers were implemented in this language. Then, in 1981 s, the Japanese announced the fifth generation computer system project, a 10 years plan to build an intelligent computer system that use the (Prolog) language as a machine code. Nowadays, (AI) can be applied any industries, such as car manufacturing industry can use (AI) technological machine-men manufacture car, instead of replacing human labors in factory. Even, in the future, using (AI) machine-men drivers can drive any private cars or public transportation tools, instead of replacing human drivers, e.g. bus, train, tram, ferry etc. Also in the future, machine-men can replace housewives to serve families to do housekeeping clean job , e.g. cleaning toilets, bathrooms, kitchens, even cooking functions at home. So (AI) machine-man can reduce housewives works at home. Moreover, (AI) machine man can take care old people , when who are living at homes or elder care centers.

So, it seems artificial intelligence (AI) will be possible developed to manufacture a new generation machine-man to assist (serve) families to do any simply cleaning or cooking jobs at homes. Moreover, the overall demand of (AI) general social needs will also rise, such as security, driving transportation tools, restaurant cleaning, elder centers care service etc. (AI) will have chance often to practise to do its tasks every day. It is possible that it can improve worker individual simple job duty to raise productivity and efficiency to be fast.

First, On machine-man satisfactory demand aspect view point, it makes computers that think, it is the automation of activities. We associate with human thinking: like decision making, learning. It is the act of creating machine that perform function that require intelligence when performed by people. It is the study of mental faculties through the use of computational models. It is the study of computations that make it possible to perceive, reason and act. It is a branch of computer science that is concerned with the automation of intelligent behavior. It is anything in computing service that

human don't yet know how to do property.
Second, on thought aspect artificial intelligence means systems thank think like humans, systems that think rationally.
Third, on behavioral aspect, artificial intelligence systems that act like human and that systems act rationally. However, the basic objective of (AI) is to represent human's thought processes in computation . These machines are supposed to exhibit behavior that. It is performed by a human being, would be considered intelligent. However, some authors feel (AI) has disadvantages, such as it is not creative, it is excited in the use of sensory devices, it can't make use of a very wide context of experiences and it does not use common sense.
For speech recognition and understanding function needs example, (AI) can be applied in speech recognition and understanding function, which (AI) speech or voice recognition is a data input method. For example, the computer recognizes and understands one (or a few) word commands. Speech understanding on the other hand is the computer's ability to understanding a spoken language. That is , the computer understands the meaning of sentences, an paragraphs through (AI).
So, (AI) can be attempted to learn human language how to speak. It is similar to translate human language skill, instead of actual human speaking skill. Also, (AI) can assist handicap learning or language student how to listen different languages by machine-man sounds from computers more accurately.
So, it seems that it (AI) can replace human language teachers speaking function and can change teaching language nature of job in language speaking and listening education industry. IT will improve its language speaking performance to teach students to raise teaching efficience and teaching performance to satisfy student learning needs in short time.

How AI excites future new technological leisure activites need increases? Advances in artificial intelligence (AI) technology and related fields have opened up new markets and new opportunities progress in critical areas, such as health, education, energy, economic development, social welfare and the environment pollution.
(AI) automation will continue to create wealth and expand the global economy development in the future. However, when many will benefits that growth won't be costless and will be accompanied by changes in the skills, that workers need to increase productivity in the economy and structural changes in the economy. So, in the skills that workers need to succeed in the

economy and structural changes.
I shall indicate why aggressive policy action will be needed to help Americans who are disadvantaged by these changes , due to (AI) technology is caused. For automation industry change example, artificial intelligence (AI) capabilities will enable automation of some tasks that have long required human labor. These artificial intelligence technology introduction can increase new opportunities for individuals. The economy and society, but (AI) has also the potential to disrupt be current livelihoods of many Americans. However, (AI) leads to unemployment and increase in inequality over the long run depends not only on the (AI) technology itself, but also on the institutions and policies that are changed.
Thus, it is possible that (AI) technology will raise some countries unemployment number if the employer apply (AI) technology workers to replace human labor in their factories, but it can also raise productivities for these employers, when (AI) can spend less time to compare labor to do any human's same tasks in order to raise productivity.

Technological progress is main driver of growth of GDP per capita, allowing output to increase faster than labor and capital . However, technology can increase productivity, but also decrease the number of labor hours needed to create a unit of output. So (AI) causes unequal to labor wage decreases, even reduces the number of labor to manufacture, e.g. artificial intelligence technology of automation car manufacturing industry; clothing manufacturing industry; plane manufacturing etc. high technology of artificial intelligence manufacturing method. But (AI) should be potential environment benefit, although it raises unemployment ratio. Moreover, it can rise production , due to many skilled craft were replaced by the combination of machines and lower-skilled labor. The result of (AI) technology introduction , it causes output per hour risen when inequality declined, driving up average living standards, but the labor of some high-skill workers was no longer as valuable in the market. Otherwise, if (AI) technology is continue developed to be success. Some routine intensive occupations will be loss, which focused on predictable, e.g. easily programmable tasks, such as switchboard operators, filing clerks, travel agents, and assembly line workers would be particularly replaced by new (AI) technology. However, at the same time, (AI) technology development will bring these benefits: improvement in education (training (AI) technology scientists) , due to (AI) manufacturing technology needs are

raising to businesses and institutional changes, such as the reduction in unionization and raising in the minimum wage to the (AI) manufacturing technology skilled labor in factories.
Because (AI) technology is not a single technology, but rather a collection of technologies that are applied to specific tasks, the effects of (AI) will be felt unevenly though the economy. It will bring some tasks will be most easily automated than others , and some jobs will be affected more than others, both negatively and positively. Finally, new jobs are likely to be directly created in areas , such as the development and supervision of (AI) as well as indirectly created in a range areas though out the economy as higher incomes lead to expanded demand.
However, if (AI) technology could dominate global labor markets. If labor productivity increases, do not influence to wage increases, then the large economic gains brought about by (AI) technology could be increased wealth inequality, due to employers can reduce production cost, but workers (labors) wages will not be increased, even will be decreased. Hence, it seems the (AI) technology will bring disadvantages to labor market to cause unemployment or reduce wages in possible, although it can reduce employer individual salary (wage) expenditure and it can raise productivity.

Artificial intelligence (AI) technology is a branch of computer science that aims to create intelligent machines that work and react like humans. So, (AI) is a technology that appears to impact (influence) human preference by learning, understanding complex contents, enhancing humans in executing both routine and non-routine tasks. In the future, (AI) technology that can be virtual personal assistant, as well as it may exist, such as robots with human-like processing capabilities.
How can (AI) technology impact global economy growth over the next 10 years? During this time period, (AI) technology is predicted to have wide-ranging applications including: Machine learning that automates analytical model building by using algorithms that allow machines to operate without human assistance.
In global education aspect, potential applications include predicting cause-and-effect relationships from biological data, identifying new drugs, self-driving cars, and protecting against fraud, improved natural language processing that allows computers to continue to better analysis, understand and generate language to interface with humans using natural human

languages. For example, transcribing notes dictated by physicians, automatically drafting articles and translating text and speech. So (AI) technology can be applied to education aspect to improve humans‘ knowledge level.

In visual art aspect, (AI) machine vision that allows computers to identify objects, scenes and activities in images. Current applications of (AI) machine vision include providing objective descriptions for the blind seeing(visual) needs.

We except the economic effects of (AI) technology to include both direct GDP growth from sectors that develop or manufacture. (AI) technology and indirect GDP growth through increased productivity in existing sectors that employ some form of (AI). If (AI) technology is an increasingly critical component of more products, it will become an integral part of many people's lives. Thus, (AI)'s ability to influence economic activity, rather than the economic or development status of the region. (AI) has the potential to impact income classes and to bring significant gains to both developed and developing countries. For example, (AI) has the potential to optimize good production around the world by analyzing agricultural regions and identifying what is necessary to improve crop yields.

In estimating the future economic effects by (AI) technology innovation, it is important to note that it is challenging to accurately predict which applications of (AI) will ultimately be commercially successful. In micro level economic influence, we need to apply methodologies to estimate the economic effects of investment in firms developing (AI) technology since investment levels in a technology are a telling sign of the future potential of that (AI) technology.

How (AI)'s development may affect the global economy over the next ten years. In fact, (AI) technology has the potential to affect business across the global in a wide range of industries in ways only a number of technologies have done in the parts. For example, (AI) technology's expected to be a useful tool for enhancing human capabilities and in some instances replacing functions, such as driving a car, adoption of broadband internet, mobile telephone, industrial robotic automation have served to enhance human capabilities.

However, significant public debate has focused on projections of (AI) technology's effect on the labor force. However, large companies prefer to invest in (AI) technological industry. For example, face book's (AI) research lab., google machine intelligence lab. and micro soft machine learning and artificial intelligence research division are all making advances in (AI) technology and investing in the industry's top talent. Additionally, between 2010 year and 2015 year, nearly $5 billion in venture capital funding invested in firms across the global developing and employing (AI) technology (Facebook (AI) Research).

Modern information technologies and the labor economy growth of machines is powered by artificial intelligence have already strongly influenced the world of work in the 21 ST century. Computers, algorithms and software simplify every tasks and it is impossible to image how most of our life could be managed without them. How can be the information economy characterized by exponential growth replaces the most production industry based on economy of scales? What will the future world of work look like and how long will it take to get? Will the future world of work be a world where humans spend less time earning their livelihood? Alternatively, are mass unemployment, mass poverty and social distortions also possible scenario for the future, where robots, artificial intelligence systems play an increasingly central role? These questions concern how artificial intelligence further development . Can influence labor economy growth on workplace ? When the labor market has widespread impact on intelligence property, information technology, product liability, competition and labor and employment laws.

How (AI) technology impacts on labor workplace.

The future influence any organizations how labor economies use of (AI) can be analyzed, such as deep machine learning is based on a set of model high level data. Unlike human workers, the machines are connected the whole time in workplace. If one machine makes a mistake, all autonomous systems will keep this in mind and will avoid the same mistake the next time.

Over the long run intelligent machines will win against every human expert. Production robots have been replacing employees because of the (AI) technology. They work more precisely than humans and cost loss. Creative solutions like 3D printers and the self learning ability of these production robots will replace human workers, the automatic data recording and data processing, traditional back office activities are no longer in demand. Autonomous software will collect necessary information and will send it to the employee who needs it. Additionally, dematerialization leads to the phenomenon that traditional physical products are becoming software. For example, CD or DVDs are being replaced by streaming services. The replacement of traditional event ticket, e-travel ticket service products or hard cash will be the next step, due to the possibility of payment by smartphone. So, (AI) technology will impact human's daily life consumption behaviors in the future. For another example, transportation tools, such as boats and ferries and private vehicles will use sensors and navigating without human input. Taxi and truck drivers will become obsolete, the stock store applies to stock managers and postal carriers of the delivery is distributed by (AI) machine delivery methods.

Nowadays , (AI) is a technology almost as old as the computer industry itself, it is similar with the advent of personal assistants function to businesses and personal promotion channel, such as (Amazon's Alexa, Apple's Siri, Google's Assistant) image recognition (face book), personalized recommendations (Netflix , Amazon). Those innovations have been driven by a increase in processing power, lower cost hardware, and the exploding creation and availability of data. It seems, (AI) technology can impact global customer service management method.

How to forecast economic impact modeling to (AI) will affect global economy? Can human forecast business revcnue growth and job creation (or destruction) based on (AI) applied to customer relationship management (CRM) activities? In addition to the economic impact on (AI) or (CRM) which can include an estimate of the economic impact attributable to sales forces customer base. What can economic benefits be brought to (CRM) from (AI) technology?

Artificial intelligence(AI) comprises a set of technologies that use natural language processing, machine learning, knowledge graphs, and other tools to answer questions, discover insights and provide recommendations. Computer systems can use (AI) hypothesize and formulate possible answers based on available evidence can be trained through the ingestion of vast amounts of content, and automatically adapt and learn from (AI) self mistakes and failures.

So, any business organizations (customer service departments) can provide efficient and effective customer relationship management of excellent customer service quality if which applied (AI) technology system. The different type of (AI) systems include: (AI) system platforms, machine learning (AI) based data preparation and enrichment tools, machine vision/ image recognition, voice speech recognition, text analysis and natural language processing, bots , e.g. face book website and virtual digital assistance solutions, social media pattern analysis , sentiment analysis, advanced numerical analysis (e.g. IOT streaming , machine logs), supporting technologies, knowledge base dialog management, Q&A processing etc. different (AI) technology system customer relationship management (CRM) tools.

(AI) (CRM) of activity can include these categories, such as: corporate marketing, marketing operation, field marketing, customer support, digital commerce, customer analytics, customer influenced product or service design, product or service pricing, finance information, presentation, customer billing, inventory , logistics and fulfilment support, partner management etc. different CRM tools.

(AI) technology of CRM has been carrying on plan different stages to achieve CRM personal assistant tool for businesses. The stages are such as, in the beginning stage of (AI) projects in place, implement now, pilot phase next year in the final stage of (AI) customer relationship management tools are foreseeable future. So, this CRM technology has been improved to plan in different stages every year to prepare to achieve full capacity of CRM service quality for businesses to use in the future.

Hence, how to develop an estimate prediction of the economic impact (AI) technologies could have CRM activities, which depends on gathering macroeconomic information on business revenue and the basic marketing of business revenue and the basic markup of business expenses by major functions (customer support, marketing and sales , production etc.)

An economic impact model that can gather data together and forecast the results how (AI) artificial intelligence technology brings (CRM) customer relationship management benefits to businesses, e.g. surveys investigation includes IT spending by sample countries, GDP and population estimates and forecasts, revenue per employee and ratios of IT spend to GDP. Surveys (questionnaire questions) of forecast results are influenced by (AI) impact can include: results are projected from surveys and rely on estimates are made by respondents on the expected financial improvements in categories of (AI) –assisted customer relationship management activities. The forecast assumes that these estimates are correct; financial estimates are based on estimates of “first year” improvement from full (AI) implementation; forecasts are from planning to implement any artificial intelligence of customer relationship management (CRM) projects, the improvement forecast is of categories of activity , e.g. corporate marketing , digital commerce, and customer analytics. They are not estimates of ROI for the (AI) software. They rely on conservative estimates to which each of these entities might affect company revenue, expenses or productivity. They also rely on estimates of the penetration of software in customer relationship management activities . Net new jobs created are based on the ratio of new revenue to jobs required to support that revenue . They can assume that 50% of the net new revenue will support increases in labor and the rest will go for capital and other operating expenses that may replace jobs lost to automation.

In the future, some of the ways in micro economic benefits to any organizations. (AI) technology is expected to impact CRM activities include: Spending up sales cycles, improving lead generation and qualification solving customer support problems faster (raising service quality), helping companies improve brand campaigns and recognition, lowering costs of support calls when increasing resolution rates, lowering the cost of recruiting employees and partners, increasing revenue from optimized product marketing, optimizing price, distribution logistics and preventing loss through fraud detection. So, micro economic benefits view point, it seems that (AI) CRM technology can raise any companies economic benefits for care term.

Artificial intelligence enables machines or the in-build software to behave like human beings which allows these decisions and act. The advent of (AI) is leading , talking, making decisions and act. The advent of (AI) is leading to new technologies advances and transforming the economic and employment opportunities for humans in a positive way. (AI) related technologies can facilitate our live. For example, industrial robotics, robotic medical assistants, smart games, financial forecasting software, big data analysis, algorithms in health and bioinformatics, pilotless cargo places, drone ambulances and general purpose and workplace robots and others. (Disruptors technologies: Advances that will transform life, business and the global economy).

Artificial intelligence also known as computational intelligence is defined as " the human –like intelligence exhibited by machines or software. It is theorized that intelligence of humans can be described and intelligence machines or software can simulate it. These machines software can be reasonable , learn, perceive and process information, like human mind and thus facilitate human life. They can think and act for us. So, artificial intelligence is an interdisciplinary field of study including computer science, neuroscience, psychology, linguistics and philosophy.

However, (AI) research and developments have economically impacted

many industries, such as robotics, telecommunications, computer applications , health, finance, heavy manufacturing, transportation, aviation, e-service and e-commerce, military , music and movie, toys and games entertainment etc. industries.
In fact, many ideas, systems and technologies have been developing in the world of (AI) technology. However, which are net called or considered (AI) products, rather which are mentioned with their specific names, such as smart graphics, machine learning, e-commerce etc. (i.e. this is called (AI) effect).

Nowadays, (AI) related industrial applications will replace most human power in fields, including call centers, customer services and air cargo transportation. (AI) technologies also help weather forecasting based on repeated rainfall pattern (data) recognition, through robotics (i.e. floor cleaning, moving lawns etc.) transporting people and products with unmanned vehicles, sending space unmanned smart shuttles, developing robotic arms, predicting market values in stock exchanges by internet, making homes safer, helping elderly and disabled using robotic servants etc.

Among the (AI) related technologies , there are a few that significance for the impact on society and especially on digital economy . (AI) is particularly influential in machine learning. Such as robotics, transportation, finance, health and bioinformatics, e-commerce , e-games, big online data gathering and internet-of-things. For example, machine e-learning is based in bioinformatics and robots that can learn new skills for better caregiving in healthcare. What is machine e-learning? Machines can e-learn from e-data gathering, coming up generalizations and making decisions to act in certain ways from internet.
There are important applications , such as e-machine perception, electronic online natural language learning processing, online search engines, online bioinformatics, online brain –computer interface, online game playing, online robot locomotion, online advertising, online computations finances, online health monitoring, online DNA classification and decision making, online in chemistry –cheminformatics . So, online machine learning can positively impact productivity and it can enhance information and analytical system from (AI) online channel.
What is robotics? Robotics is one of the most strongly influenced fields in (AI). For example, heavy manufacturing industries, robots and used and

man power is replaced for effectiveness, precision, and accuracy, especially in respective or dangerous tasks, including welding, assembling , picking and placing .

So, robots can acquire new skills or adapt the changing dynamic environment. Also, artificial intelligence can be applied in developing transportation. For example, automated vehicles, driver assistance systems , safety systems, collision avoidance systems and public transportation. Moreover, (AI) technology has proven to produce some of the best tools to predict stock market fluctuations from internet data gathering method. It's predictions are based on ever-evolving predictions algorithms and systems learn new models and make connections between historical data and new data to measure stock market trading more accurate from internet data gathering channel.

In health field, especially in health data processing , analysis, decision making support and medical diagnosis. So, online data can show which patients will need what treatment and what alternative drugs could be used more accurate from (AI) online data gathering method. Bioinformatics is an interdisciplinary field combining statistics, (AI) online technology can help in discovering data patterns and modeling through the application of machine learning, artificial neural networks and genetic algorithms. For example, further (AI) technology development of human genome project of online data sequences.

Online shopping can be facilitated by virtual assistants developed through (AI) technology and these assistants can offer the best advice. (AI) online purchase coming after every product image recommendations and personalization bring important revenue to shopping online sites, like Amazon . Smart computer graphics and games, artificial intelligence is useful in smarter computer, graphics, scene modeling , scene rendering processes in order to create, for example, effective human –robot interactions , online machine learning, online strategic games techniques etc. online computer related (AI) software.

So, online big data analysis and big data does have a critical need in the world of online intelligence machines and software in our future. In other words, (AI) offers online technology to enable online big data analysis to provide industrial organizations with valuable information for effective decision making in short time. For example, what IBM's Watson achieved: this machine used 200 million of structured and unstructured content with a special technology of hypothesis generation, massive evidence gathering, analysis and scoring from internet channel.

Finally, (AI) online technology another related internet invention (internet of things) (IOT) is the network of machines or objects connected through internet. These connected objects can sense their internal and external environment, communicate with each other, can send critical data and finally can make decisions to act or correct their environment from (AI) online technology. For example, factories can monitor and automatically change production processes, hospitals can monitor and regulate the health conditions of their patients , schools can collect data from facilities and cars can send data to car makers from (AI) online technology.

Partner predicts that (IOT) market will create about trillion amount value by 2020 year. Although machines collect big data from their environment, whether which gain an insight or learn from these online data largely depends on the (AI) online machine learning principals and (AI) online technology. In 2013, Mckinsey estimated that disruptive technologies closely related with potential economic impact in 2025 year between $7.1 to $13.1 trillion amount (automation of knowledge work, advanced robotics, autonomous or near-autonomous vehicles).

Can (AI) technology influence developing countries new technology of leisure need increases? Could China workers be affected and jobs made up of routine work activities and predictable? Will programmable tasks be particularly impact to China employment market ? When impact on labor market is likely to be gradual at the aggregate level, it can be sudden and dramatic at the level of specific work activities, rending some job obsolete fairly. Overall (AI) technology will raise digital skills when reducing demand for medium incomer inequality for China workers. It seems (AI) technology's effect on productivity could be crucial to China's future economic growth as the population ages are increasing.

In China, some biggest technological companies driving significant investments in research and development. Moreover, China is one of the leading global (AI) technology development county. However, China will need to focus on building its innovation capacity. For example, United States and United Kingdom are currently producing more influential (AI) technological research. However, if China planed to achieve (AI) technology success, it's traditional industries will need to develop technical know-how –to and overcoming implementation costs prepare to develop (AI) . When (AI) technology is introduced into China society, China government needs to raise concerning ethical, legal, technological security etc. business questions. Also, surrounding issues include privacy, discrimination, legal liability and regulation. It aims to encourage overseas investors to choose to invest (AI) technological industry to raise GDP growth and manufacturing industries income growth for long term in China. If China encouraged overseas (AI) technology investment in its country. It is possible to influence China employment market to be changed. Because (AI) technology will impact to influence China people daily life. Due to (AI) technology is introduced to China society, many rich people will prefer to spend to buy any high (AI) technological products for entertainment or learning or machine man driving etc. daily necessity activities. Then it will raise GDP growth and will raise (AI) manufacturers or related-(AI) technological manufacturers profit. It is beneficial to China because it can become one high knowledgeable and (AI) technological economical society. But it will bring bad influences to raise unemployment chance for the low skillful labor. In labor economy aspect influence , how (AI) technology can influence China low skillful labor unemployment ratio raising. The raising low skill labor unemployment reason is because China low skillful human labors are argued or are replaced by (AI) technology creating new challenges to introduce to influence China society of simply human manufacturing job nature to be changed to be high (AI) technology manufacturing job nature in any China factories. Moreover, when (AI) technology introduction to China, it will cause other related social challenges in China. The varied (AI) related challenges, including the difficulty of creating safe and reliable hardware for sensing and affecting (transportation and education), the challenges of gaining public trust, a low resource comities and public safety and security, the challenges of overcoming fears or marginalizing humans in China employment and workplace and the risk of diminishing interpersonal trust because the low skillful labors won't believe any China employers will give chance to employ them , due to (AI) technology will replace their skills and man manufacturing of productivity is much less to compare to (AI) technology manufacturing method.

Are future nature of jobs changed to computerization from (AI) technology? Where are the probability of computing occupations from (AI) technology influence? What is expected impacts of future computing on labor market from (AI) technology influence? John Maynard Keynes's frequently cited prediction of widespread technological unemployment " du to our discovery of means of economic the use of labor outrunning the pace of which we can find new used of labor" (Keynes, 1933, p.3).

In the future, (AI) technology will impact some nature of occupations to change computing. This chance will also influence some countries' economic change. For example, some factory human labors hand routine manufacturing tasks will be changed to computerization of routine manufacturing tasks by (AI) technological machine men hand manufacturing method. it will cause a structured shift in the labor market, with workers reallocating their labor supply from middle-income manufacturing to low-income service occupations.

Arguably, this is because the manual tasks of service occupations are less computerization, as who require a higher degree of flexibility and physical adaptability. So, (AI) technology will influence the human hand labor skillful occupation nature of task cheaper , such as vehicle manufacturing , ship manufacturing, computer manufacturing, steel manufacturing, television, radio etc. home electronic products of heavy machine industry change. Due to (AI) technology machine man will be proper to be used to manufacturing these electronic products when the (AI) technology innovation can develop to the mature stage. Then, any countries manufacturers will choose to use (AI) technology machine man, instead of human hand production.

Supposing the future prices of computing are fallen, seriously, problem solving skills are becoming relatively productive, explaining the substantial employment growth in manufacturing occupations, involving cognitive tasks where skilled labor has a comparative advantage, as well as the increase education needs for (AI) technology computing of machine man subject study.

Prediction of education needs for (AI) technology student numbers will increase, due to manufacturing industry needs many (AI) technology students in future employment market. Another (AI) technology influence if the future (AI) technological innovation, e.g. machine man manufacturing or machine man service industries will both increase demand, then with more sophistic software technologies will be disrupted labor markets by marketing workers redundant.

For publishing industry, what is striking about the case in paper book publishing industry will be unpopular? Due to the electronic book publishing industry will be popular, e.g. Amazon publish . (AI) technology can influence paper book manufacturing method which is replaced by machine man electronic book manufacturing method as well as it will cause the computerization is no longer confined to routine manufacturing tasks. Due to (AI) machine man manufacturing technology will be proper to be used to manufacture any products in short time efficiently and effectively , e.g. electronic book products. In the future, if it is fact to occur this case, such as (AI) technological machine man manufacturing method will be adopted (applied) to manufacture electronic books or any products in possible. (AI) technology will cause many manufacturing workers are unemployed. It is beneficial to employers, who can reduce to spend much wages expenditure to employ manufacturing workers, but it will cause many manufacturing workers loss jobs and reduce income to support whose families lives. It will cause social challenges, e.g. increasing stealing crimes if the manufacturing workers had not other skills to find other jobs to do easily. So, manufacturers need to concern over technological unemployment which will be hardly future phenomenon if who decided to dismiss all manufacturing workers, due to (AI) technology machine men replace to them.

If (AI) technology can be innovated to produce any kinds of machine man to serve any service or manufacturing industries successfully. Then, it will bring these questions: Can future that workers be influenced to be automation employment and productivity by (AI) technology influence? Does it impact to influence the (AI) technology countries‘ productivity and growth and natural resources development and labor markets and evolution of global financial markets and economic impact of technology and innovation and urbanization etc. issues? How will automation transform the workplace? What will be the implication for employment? What is likely to be its impact both on productivity in the global economy and on employment?

In fact, automatic of activities can enable businesses to improve performance by reducing errors chance and improving quality and speed, and same cases achieving outcomes that go beyond human capabilities. Some economists indicate (AI) technology would give a needed boost to economic growth and prosperity have of the working age population in many countries. Based on the scenario modeling, they estimate automation could raise productivity growth globally by 0.8 to 1.4 % annually. They also indicated that almost half the activities people are almost $1.6 trillion in wages to do in the global economy have the potential to be automated adapting current demonstrates technology, according to their analysis of more than 2,000 work activities across 800 occupations. When less than 5% of all occupations can be automated entirely using demonstrated technology, about 60% of all occupations have at least 30% of worker made activities, that would be automated. More occupation will change to be automated. They also indicated for business performance benefits of automation are relatively clear, but the issues are more complicated by policy making to attract foreign investors. Beyond technical feasibility, the cost of technology, competition labor will include skills and supply and demand dynamics, performance benefits and beyond labor cost savings and social and regulatory acceptance will affect the automation. Their predictions suggest that half of today work activities could be automated by 2055 year, but this could happen 10 to 20 years earlier or latter depending on the various factors in addition to their wider economic condition.

Some scientists suggest (AI) technology is finally starting to deliver real-life business benefits. Computer power is growing significantly , algorithms are becoming more sophisticated and perhaps most important of all, the world is generating vast quantities of the fuel that powers (AI) technology data billions of gigabytes of it every day. Also, online firms are digital natives, such as Google online search service company is investing on (AI) technology. For new though most of the news if coming from the suppliers of (AI) technologies. And many new users are only in the experimental phase. Few products are on the market or are likely to arrive these soon to drive immediate and widespread adoption. As a result, analysts believe (AI) technology's potential will give true economic benefit in the future. (AI) industry will introduce to suppliers and users to raise economic potential of (AI) technology.

In the future, (AI) technology systems can solve business problems. Some scientists categorized those into five technology systems that are key areas of (AI) technology development: robotics and autonomous vehicles, computer vision language virtual agents and machine learning , which is based on algorithms that learn from data without replying on rules-based programming in order to draw conclusions or direct an action.

Such as computer vision and language includes natural language processing, analytics, speech recognition technology, some are about learning from information, such as about machine learning and others are related to acting on information, such as robotics, autonomous vehicles and virtual agents, which are computer programs that can converse with humans. Machine learning and a subfield called deep learning are artificial intelligence applications.

Artificial intelligence (AI) is a term first defined in 1956 year. It is a branch of computer science that aims to create intelligent machines that work and react like humans. In contrast today, 60 years later, (AI) is characterized by a number of applications, including computers playing games against humans and understanding human languages, virtual personal assistants, and robotics which involve computers seeing , hearing and reacting to sensory stimuli. In the future, technologists predict for (AI) technology ranging from (AI) being used as a tool to aid relatively simple processes for robots with human like mental capabilities, who expect (AI) technology can emulate human performance by learning, coming to mind its own conclusions, understanding complex content, engaging in dialog with people, enhancing human cognitive performance or replacing humans in executing both routine and non-routine tasks. In existing industry, (AI) technology is used , such as targeted advertising and virtual used personal assistant as well as the (AI) technology that my exist in the future, such as robots with human vehicle processing capabilities.

The range of (AI) technology's progress in the future will determine the economic impact future of (AI) technology on the global economy with more limited advances and applications (i.e. weak (AI) only) corresponding to more limited economic impacts and more substantial progress, i.e. strong (AI) technology is corresponding to more significant economic impact.

(AI) technology learning that automates analytical model, including predicting cause-and-effect relationship from biological data, identifying new drugs, self-driving cars and protecting against fraud etc. functions. Also (AI) learning can improve natural language processing that allows computers to continue to better analyze, understand and generate language to interface with human using the natural human language, virtual personal assistant, helps users by providing scheduling appointment, reminds organizing personal finance and finding providers of various services, machine vision allows (AI) machine man to identify object, scenes and activities in detect pedestrians and bicyclists.

We expect the economic effects of (AI) technology to include both direct GDP growth from sectors that develop or manufacture (AI) technology and indirect GDP growth through increased productivity in existing sectors that employ some from of (AI) technology. If (AI) producing sectors could grow, then it could lead to increase revenues and employment of (AI) technological professionals within these existing firms as well as the potential creation of entirely new economic activities to any countries' societies productivity improvement in existing sectors could be realized through faster and move efficient processes and decision making as well as increased (AI) technological knowledge and access to information available in societies easily.

In the future, if (AI) technology is an increasingly critical component of more products, it will become an integral part of necessary products of many people's lives. The extent of (AI)'s economy effort is also likely to vary from region to region, thought variation may be more dependent on the predominate economic activity of a region and the (AI) ability can influence economic activity, rather then the economic or developmental status of the regions. (AI) technology can move accessibility and can use source development to do international business between one country and another country.

So (AI) technology has the potential to give benefits to different income chooses and to bring significant gains to both developed and developing countries. For agricultural technology, (AI) has the potential to optimize food production around the world by analyzing agricultural regions and identifying what is necessary to improve crop yield. In total, (AI) technology gives greater economic impact to any countries agricultural regions if which implemented (AI) technology to grow crop , fruit etc. food production in the farms.

Investment in (AI) technology is such as capital investment to any countries‘ public or private enterprises. So, it will have large economic impact to the future . If the (AI) technology is reasonable invested to the different needs aspect by the public or private enterprises in the country. Then, it will have good economic impact to the country in the future. However, when (AI) technology is likely to affect both the productivity and employment components of economic growth in many sectors. Significant public debate has focused on projections of (AI)'s effect on the labor force. However, for instance, some researchers have argued that the rise of (AI) technology and automation will led to significant unemployment as capital is substituted for the low skillful labor. So, they point to the concern that the increasing sophistication of (AI) technology may balance skilled and semi-skilled workers and the reduce the size of the middle class. However, this is not a new argument, due to (AI) technology negatively affecting the labor force and leading to mass unemployment. Because the (AI) technology is the substitution of machinery for human labor. Although, employment in certain industries, has been reduced in the past due to technological advancement. For long term, the labor market has adapted to the introduction of new technology, giving rise to new jobs in new areas. (AI) technology may also be accomplished without a reduction to total employment in the long-term to some Asia countries, such as Hong Kong and Japan. Because Hong Kong and Japan many low skilled labor, e.g. security, cleaner who complaint that employers need them to work long time hours. (abnormal working hours) e.g. one day 12 to 15 working hour per day. Hence, if (AI) machine means invention technology success. Security or cleaning job can be worked from (AI) machine man in some hours every day in order to reduce the long time working hours cleaners or security workers, e.g. one (AI) machine man works 4 hours for cleaning or security job, one day as well as another cleaner or security labor only needs to work 8 hours one day. So total security or cleaning employers can employ 12 hours machine cleaners or security workers and human cleaners or security workers in one day. For long term benefit, Hong Kong or Japan every security or cleaning worker does not need to work 12 hours minimum working hours one day. They won't feel tried and bore and without private with whose families, so who will accept to do these cleaning or security jobs, even they can raise work efficient and performance when who feel happy and health.

So, (AI) technology of machine man invention can raise low skillful labor efficiency and it can help them to avoid abnormal working hours demand in some busy work life countries, such as Hong Kong and Japan. Before, one Japan female labor feel unhappy to work, due to who often needs to work abnormal working hours for her employer and who has less sleeping and without any private time to enjoy her life with her families every day. So this abnormal working hours factor causes her to do commit suicide behavior, then she is die unlucky. So (AI) technology of machine man invention ought avoid abnormal working hours demand for employer in any countries in the future.

The most important occurrence to any employers, some researchers had attempted to do one experiment to find that private research and development , venture capital and public research and development investment all have strong net effect or economic growth with venture capital funding further having the strongest such effect from (AI) technology. The researchers hypothesize the venture capital investment contributes to economic growth through (AI) technology innovation and by the capacity of an economy to use existing (AI) technology knowledge to increase productivity. They predict the impacts of venture capital, business-research and development and public research and development can raise multi factor productivity from (AI) technology introduction.

Can (AI) technology influence the economic development to developing countries? The developing regions of the world contain most of natural resources. If one day, (AI) technology has invent one kind of machine man which can assist any gas or oil workers to seek any new oil/gas natural resource locations easily. I believe that (AI) technology can help these natural resource exploitation countries will gain economic benefit more easily. So, (AI) driven technology can be used to change to create any new opportunities to address poor management or resources and improve human well being, such as Africa Latin America and India can use (AI) technology machine man to seek any oil/gas natural resource countries exploitation activities to attempt to gain much economic benefits.

Nowadays, increases in capital and labor are no longer driving the levels of economic growth, such as (AI) technology. The ability of increase in capital investment and in labor of traditional drivers of production, have no longer to be enjoyed in most developed economies ,e.g. developed country, US, UK . However, artificial intelligence has the potential to overcome the physical limitation of capital and labor to avoid missing out on this opportunity. So, policy makers and business leaders must prepare for and work toward a future with artificial intelligence. They must do with the idea that (AI) is another simply method to enhance productivity method . Rather they must see (AI) as the tool that can transform thinking about how growth is created.

Economists have always thought of new technologies are as driving growth their ability to enhancing. It can replace labor and capital factor of production. So, it brings this question: What is the factor of production (AI) technology characteristics. They key factor is to see (AI) technology as a capital-labor .

(AI) can replicate labor activities at much greater scale and speed, and to even perform some tasks began the capabilities of human. For example, by using virtual assistants , 1000 legal documents can be reviewed in a matter of days instead of taking three people six moths to complete. Some (AI) technology may be one kind of factor of production in the future. For another example, people will work in workplace digitalization environment.

So, in the future, working environment and information management are automated. Such as Konica camera sale company will use workplace digitalization. So , (AI) technology can provide workplace digitalization in order to raise productivity efficiency. (AI) technology will be one kind of production which is replaced by workplace digitalization and it will grow any organization productivity efficiently. Then, (AI) technology will assist overall social economy growth , due to productivity is raised and products can be produced in short time to prepare to sell in consumption market. So, time will be shortened to increase GDP growth fast for the development of (AI) technology countries.

What will be the development of (AI) technology and predictions concerning the future evolution? The computers and robots will develop conscious, intelligent and minds into humans, enhancing psychological and behavioral abilities and allowing for direct communication with (AI) minds. (AI) technology will be impacted human life by (AI) technology information communicative and environmental influence. A " world brain" and " world mind", this psychological system will be enhanced and enriched the capacities of both individual and collective cognition by (AI) technology of service industries.

(AI) technology with influence these human needs of service industries changes, such as , biological science, finance, entertainment, business, biological science, transportation, communication military etc. The personal computer evolution, the internet and the world wide web which exploded on the scene, linking business, homes, schools, social organizations which were a completely unpredicted phenomenon to influence human life. Kurzweil (1999) predicts that by 2029 year, most human communication will be with machines. According to Person, by 2100 year, there will be human machine convergence.

How can (AI) technology influence environmental protection to make benefits to farming economic growth? (AI) technology can be applied to predict how to solve environmental pollution challenge to avoid to damage any crop or vegetable or rice or fruit etc. food growth. Because environmental experts can gather global environmental pollution data from an environmental database to build a perform a systematic analysis from (AI) technology. The first step is this broad analysis can include understanding, statistical and data gathering techniques to obtain the relevant data, the correlation among the variables involved, and a list of possible models. The next step is to select a set of methods and models that cover all kinds of knowledge and functionalities needed for the decision making process. Once the models are selected, they must be fully implemented by means of machine learning , data mining, statistical or numerical technique. After that, those models must be integrated to build the whole EDSS. The EDSS must be tested to check its performance, accuracy, usefulness and reliability, both from the user's and (AI) technology/computer scientist's point of view. If these is any wrong feature in any development stage, such as model's integration, models' implementation, selection of models, database, problem analysis etc. the developers must come back in the update th required components. When the evaluation phase is all right, the EDSS is ready to be applied to the environment. The great contribution of artificial intelligence to EDSS the integration of several methods complementing the classical statistical models/simulation , statistical analysis, linear models, etc. and numerical models (control algorithms, optimization techniques etc.) .

This cooperation makes the resulting systems more reliable and powerful in coping with real world environment systems. Date interpretation has been a principal area of research in (AI) technology since the very beginning. The most demanding problem in the environmental assessment context. Knowledge representation permits the definition of the different types of data that the existing methods adapt to the process. There is also a lot of work to clean, repair and transform the huge available quantities of raw data. Apart from this, the availability of meta-information or background knowledge is required to guide the process. Data mining is multi-disciplinary: It covers expert systems, data based technology, statistics, data visualization and unsupervised machine learning. These techniques operate at the level of data and background information, where numerous and often incompatible new commensurate pieces of information from disparate sources have to be brought together (K, Fedra, 1994).

So, it seems that in the future, (AI) technology with the increasing maturity in particular those related to knowledge and engineering, new dimensions can be assisted to users in environmental decision making are available. For example, many environmental systems are characterized both by incomplete models and by limited data. Hence, in the future, (AI) technology will be applied to predict climate change to reduce crop or fruit etc. food agriculture challenge by climate change bad influence.

To understand how the manufacturing business must adapt to prosper in the technology, we need to understand how (AI) technology will change us to shape our daily habits to satisfy our expectation of products to how we shop and even the immediate of the entire process. For example, taxi services are in the crosshairs as on demand transportation services like, available of the touch of a smart phone button expand. In fact, Yellow lab, US country , san Francisco city's largest taxi company is filing for bankruptcy as the industry starts to change faster than almost anyone expected. However, at this point, its more than an app that is changing, some our taxi passengers renting taxi transportation to catch consumption behavior.

(AI) technology will influence digital economy for taxi passenger's individual customer experience, offering a growing renting taxi to catch of service and feedback opportunities when any one taxi passenger who chooses to use mobile phone app online tool to prepaid to rent any taxi more easily.

Also in the long term, (AI) technology can influence vehicles drive themselves of behavior. Already, companies like Google and GM are working on projects to bring fleets of autonomous vehicles to cities at the path of a button.

Moreover, this on-demand service model is beginning to appear across a much broader range of markets. For example , Amazon company is investing in its own fleet of trucks, planes and even drone at the same time as it pushes for same-day delivery of products. As some point, vehicles will be autonomous too. So, it seems that (AI) technique will influence any transportations choose to use digital autonomous driving technology in the future . For Amazon company case, it is not stopping of logistics. It is also aiming to automatically manage the supply of consumer home products with its recently launched Amazon replenishment service, Dash. Dash is a digital service that enables that connected derive to automatically order physical products from Amazon when supplies are running low. So, it seems (AI) technology will be applied to logistic function by digital technology method introduction in the future.

Hence autonomous vehicles will optimize industry supply chains and logistics operations through increased efficiency and flexibility. In fact, fully automated and lean supply chains will keep reduce load sizes and inventory by leveraging smart distribution technologies and smaller

autonomous vehicles by machine man assistance. If Amazon continues to grow market share for online sales by reducing effort required by the consumer to place an order, when also contributing the almost immediate delivery of products to the doorstep. So, it will further fuel the trend toward on-demand derive. As Amazon company fuels the on-demand economy, consumers will expect immediacy in more parts of the digital economy. On top of speed, consumers increasing expect more personalization options.
So, (AI) technology will influence digital manufacturing, such as Amazon publishing to monitor every aspect of every process in real -time and communicating to self-optimized deep learning robotics, new methods of high volume and high customization will become possible. Then, as products merge into product platforms and even services, manufacturers have the opportunity to provide components and platforms used by smaller players. So, (AI) technology will influence manufacturing industry to choose automated SMI lines, robots installed, automation engineers.

Another future (AI) technology development can be applied to space science aspect, such as Automation engineering space in manufacturing process to achieve digital manufacturing benefits to any businesses in the future. Such as reducing cost, shortening manufacturing time, raising efficiency, shortening delivery products to client individual time. How can artificial intelligence give the need and advanced fast and evaluation methods benefits for space exploration? When US NASA (space exploration organization) achieves any space exploration missions, it will answer this question:
When is it useful to have a machine use (AI) technology to achieve a decision? After all, after millions of years of space exploration and rough 10,000 years of civilization, humans are usually quite good at making decisions in complex uncertain environments. Through, Johns Hoplains University's Applied Physical Lab. Research in (AI) technology enabled systems, which has identified three general use cases for (AI) technology to explore space mission:
First, for some tasks (AI) technology is more cost effectiveness than human. Second, (AI) technology is better suited than humans at solving some, but not all problems. Third, (AI) technology allows NASA organization's space exploration mission to develop machines that ate capable of responding faster than when a human is in the decision loop (D. Scheidt, 2012, A. Castano et. al. 2008).

So, the use of (AI) technology to enable science by observing the pace of rapidly evolving phenomena was demonstrated. It is more effectively coordinating and (AI) technology utilizing to earn economic benefits to use for space exploration mission.
However, (AI) technology also have current risk for space exploration. Today (AI) technology is immature and requires further development to reach its potential. For instance, the (AI) technology algorithms that detected the dust derive could not have identified whether the Martain weather represented a threat to the cover. Also it can not yet use instrument input to determine what, where and how to autonomously make the next space science measurement. An equally important factor limiting (AI)'s deployment is that lacks the methodology and technology to effectively test (AI) technology. So, the challenge will testing (AI) enabled system is how (AI) performance can be measured. It would be NASA organization's difficulty to find (AI) technology to develop to carry on researching any space exploration missions in the future. However, (AI) technology will be a good economic benefit choice for space exploration mission in the future.

The ability of (AI) technology systems to transform vast amounts of complex information into insight has the potential to help solve manufacturing or service challenges for human needs. However, to reap the societal benefits of (AI) systems, humans will need to trust then and make sure that which follow the same ethical principles, moral values, professional codes and social norms that we humans would follow in the same scenario, research and educational efforts as well as carefully designed regulation in order to achieve the most effort of economic benefits goals. For example, international business machines corporation (IBM) is actively engaged both competitors , in global discussions about how to make (AI) ethical and as beneficial as possible for people as social economic benefits.
(AI) is usually defined as the " capability of a computer program to perform tasks or reasoning processes " that human usually associate to intelligence in a human being. Often, it has to do with the ability to make a good decision, even when there is uncertainty, too much information to handle. As an example, play chess or complex card games of entertainment activities is believed to need some form of intelligence in a human being, as well as choosing the best medical facilities in a difficult medical case, or creating something new, such as mathematical theorem or even some form of act, or even driving automatic machine man (self driving vehicle) replacing

human driving in the middle of a crowded city.

(AI) needs depends on what we consider being intelligence in the behavior of a human being act a certain point in time. If human belief about human intelligence changes and we don't believe any longer that a certain task requires intelligence, then a computer program performing that task is no longer part of (AI), it becomes just another boring computer program. So, it means that (AI) technology will replace some old computer programs, if human can invent new generation of (AI) software for any functions or activities to satisfy human needs.

As IBM, it argues intelligence. This means that we aim to build systems that enhance and scale human expertise and skills rather than replacing them. We therefore focus on practical applications of (AI) capabilities that assist people in performing well-defined tasks of needs by exploiting and wide range of (AI)-based services. We also use the term " cognitive computing" it is mean a comprehensive net of capabilities based on technology. It comprises the fields of machine learning, reasoning and decision technologies, language, speech and vision recognition and processing technologies, high performance and high efficient functions for any industries or individual consumers needs. For example, robotics, which are usually very good at doing what which are supposed to in any environment, much have public shopping center, factory etc. places which need simply services from the robot (machine man), such as cleans the floor of our houses to the robot that can work together with humans in production chains, passing through the warehouse, robots can take care of the tasks of an entire warehouse and the companion robots like Nao, Pepper, Aibo and Giraff, who can entertain use, talk to use and help elderly people to stay connected to their friends, relatives and doctors.

Google company is building automatic machine (self-driving cars) and has acquired more than 10 robotics companies. Facebook had opened whole new research facility only on (AI) research. Apply computer has developed Siri. Microsoft computer company has built a similar personalized assistant. Google has Deep mind, a UK company whose long term aim is to build general (AI) and has already great potential to win game to the world champion and IBM is investing a huge amount of resources in applying its Watson cognitive computing system to the medical domains to finance and to personalized education. In Europe, IBM is establishing new centers in Munich and Milan focused in the application of cognitive computer capabilities to the internet of things and healthcare respectively.

For example, automatic machine man (self-driving cars) are all about (AI), which used to be able to see what happens in the street (signals ,lanes, other cars, pedestrians, traffic lights, which need to able predict what other cars and pedestrians will do, and who need to be able to cope with unforeseen situations. Since, most car accidents are due to human fault, it is estimated that the adoption of self-driving cars will save about half of the lives that are usually last in car accidents.

IBM Watson company has to understand spoken language, make sense of massive amount to text , respond correctly to questions in many categories, as well as assess its own confidence in responding to such questions. In the future, (AI) technology can own question/answering capabilities that would be very useful, for example, in assisting a doctor when trying to some to the correct diagnosis for a patient and to propose the best therapy .

Intelligent machines can also rely on huge amounts of data to be used to learn how to make better decisions. This data comes from all of us over the years Facebook users have uploaded more than 250 billion pictures and every day who upload about 350 million more. Every second, we submit 40,000 google search queries. So, (AI) technology will be connected through the web from appliances to traffic lights from cars to watches. Other tasks that are very easy for humans are physical and manipulation tasks, such as walking , running, picking up an object to make its shape and location, restricted environment. But (AI) machine man technology still not able to have the general physical and manipulation capabilities even of a 6 year old.

So, it brings this question: Why do (AI) scientists need to concern ethics? Because (AI) technology is complex, information into insight has the potential to reveal long held secrets and help solve some of the world's most difficult problems. (AI) systems can potentially be used to help discover insights to treat disease, predict the whether, and manage the global economy. So, ethic issues is important to and (AI) scientists . If any one new (AI) technology research investigation could success, it will be a secret to and the (AI) scientists can not permit to their loyalty to any competitors to damage the fair (AI) technology products trading market. The country (countries) (AI) technology scientists need to concern ethic issues, who need to keep secrets for their countries economic or/and social benefits. This is moral issues to any countries/country loyalty is whose countries intangible assets. They can not sell (AI) loyalty to any their countries to assist whose economic benefits immorally.

According to (AI) lecturer analysis, when combined key clinical health (AI) application can potentially create $150 billion in annual savings for the US healthcare economy by 2026 year. (AI) technology is re-winning modern conception of healthcare delivery. It enables machines to sense, comprehend, act and learn. So which can perform administrative and clinical healthcare functions (Accenture, 2017).

It will help health care service organizations to reduce health care cost, will improve and raise service quality and access. So, (AI) health market size will be predicted growth. (AI) applications in health care include robot-assisted surgery, virtual nursing assistant, administrative workflow assistant, fraud detection, error reduction connected machines, clinical trial participant identifier, preliminary diagnosis, automated image diagnosis and cybersecurity.

What kind of benefits (AI) technology can contribute to healthcare service? (AI) technology can deliver what many health care organizations need, such as financial and operational of labor costs, digital expectations from patient consumers how to use (AI) technology to solve interoperability challenges in any healthcare organizations. Also (AI) technology can be applied to wellness an d lifestyle management, diagnostics, delivers financially but also way of organizational and workflow improvement. So, (AI) technology will be continue to become most prevalent and adoption to healthcare organizations , which must need to enhance structure to be position to take full advantages of new (AI) technological capabilities. (AI) technology can change the nature of work and employment is rapidly changing to make the best use of both humans and (AI) talent in healthcare industry in the future. For example, (AI) technology offers a way to fill in gaps and the rising labor shortage in healthcare. According to Accenture analysis, the physicians shortage is increasing. However, (AI) technology will manufacture healthcare machine men to replace physicians in future one day(2017). Hence, (AI) technology will be invented to raise health care service staffs work efficiency and performance in any hospitals or clinics in the future.

In conclusion, (AI) technology will raise efficiency for any service or manufacturing industries in the future, although, it is possible that it will also rise low skillful workers unemployment numbers. But, the most important influence to human technological innovation will be risen and it will influence human life will be changed to be better, e.g. self drive cars, health care physician machine men, machine man cleaners etc. intelligent machine men will be manufactured to serve for our daily life. Furthermore, (AI) technological products will influence countries trading, some low technological development countries manufacturing businessmen can choose to buy any (AI) products to raise whose productivity and efficiency and reducing cost to achieve economic cost saving result. Also, GDP of trading growth income will increase to the (AI) products sale countries. Hence, it will be beneficial to economic development to both developed and developing countries both in the future as well as (AI) scientists time and money spending will be valued to continue to invest (AI) technology development for human life and economy benefits for long term.

In consequent, when (AI) can spend more time to attempt to do human's any tasks every day, then it have possible to raise productivity and efficiency better than human.

Reference

A. Castano et. al. " Automatic detection of dust devils and clouds at Mars" Machine vision and applications, Oct. 2008, vol. 19, no 5-6, pp. 467-482.

Accenture, " Why artificial intelligence is the future of growth"(2017) <http://www.accenture.com/us-en/insight-a rtificial-intelligence-future-growth>.

D. Schedidt , Unmanned Air Vehicle Command And Control, Handbook Of Unmanned Air Vehicles, Springer-Verlag, 2014. Facebook (AI) Research Available at https://research.facebook.com/ai, research at google, machine intelligence available at http://research.google.com/pubs/machineintellige nce.html; micro soft research-machine learning and artificial intelligence available at http://research.microsoft.com/en-us/research- areas/machine-learning-ai.aspx.

K, Fedra , "GIS and environmental modelling" in environmental modelling with GIS, edited by M.F. Goodchild.B.O. Parks and L.T. Steyaert, Oxford University press, pp. 35-50, 1994.

Keynes, J.M. (1933). Economic possibilities for our grandchildren (1930). Essays in persuasion, pp.358-73.

Mckinsey & Company (2013, May). Disruptive technologies: Advices that will transform life, business and the global economy , USA.

Ray Kurzweil , The age of spiritual machines (1999) is cited numerously through this chapter: Kurzweilai.net http://www.kurzweilai.net

Rich, Elaine & Knight, Kevin, Artificial Intelligence Second Edition, 1991, New York; Mc-Graw-Hill.

What is (AI) consumer behavioral prediction tool? How any why will (AI) tool assist manufactures to attempt to predict consumer behavior before and after consumption occurrence? First, I shall indicate how to apply (AI) tool to predict vehicle product consumer behavior case example.

Nowadays, many vehicle manufacturers hope their vehicles can attract to vehicle buyers to choose to buy their vehicles. However, there are many different brands of vehicles to provide to them to choose, so the vehicle market competition is very serious.

How to judge their different kinds of vehicle price which is reasonable acceptance to attract vehicle buyers to choose to buy the brand of vehicle manufacturers' any kinds of vehicles, e.g. fast speed sport style vehicles, comfortable and slow speed common cars, for four passengers common small size or more than four passengers common large car size? How to evaluate the vehicle prices issue is important factor to influence vehicle buyers' choices. Either if the brand of vehicle price is too high to compare brands, it will influence many vehicle buyers choose to buy other brands' vehicles or if the brand of vehicle price is too low, it will influence vehicle buyers feel this brand's vehicle's quality is worse to compare to other vehicle brands' similar vehicle products.

Thus, if the brand of vehicle manufacturers can predict how to design vehicles which can attract many vehicle buyers to choose to buy whose any vehicle products. What are future vehicle buyers' favorable vehicle styles? Then, the vehicle manufacturer can concentrate on manufacturing the kind style of vehicle products to sell already. It will reduce its vehicle manufacturing investment risk.

How to apply (AI) tools to predict vehicle buyers' behavioral consumption model? Whether artificial intelligent tools can predict automotive buyers' behavioral consumption model and predict future trend. In fact, automotive brands and dealerships are facing an increasingly competition when attempting to manually gathering the vast quantities of data required to create customer focused programs that increase retention, ultimately new sales and service automotive business. Building a based on that client's intrinsic needs and interests to any kinds of automotive vehicles at any given time. This is especially true in the automotive industry where the time span between purchases is measured in years. Because vehicle buyers would not like often to change their old vehicle to another new one. So, their decisions to buying another new vehicle, the time is usually after one year, even longer time. Hence, it seems any vehicles won't be frequent consumption products to the owned at least one vehicle family consumers (vehicle buyers).

Hence, how to predict vehicle consumers' taste or preferable which styles of vehicle choices issues is very important. If the vehicle manufacturers can not manufacture any attractive vehicles to sell easily in this year. Then, it will lose time, money in this year because it won't know when the owned least one vehicle users or non-owned any vehicle users who will decide to buy one new vehicle or change another new vehicle ensure. The different brand vehicle dealers will possible wait more than one year to attract them to buy their vehicles if their styles are not attractive to compare other brands of vehicle competitors.

However, artificial intelligence and machine learning can help any vehicle manufacturers to find solution to solve patterns in highly to solve patterns in highly complex data-sets that are beyond the capability of a human brain, and then building and automatically acting on the customer insights it generates.

Given the automotive customer need for individualized communications, this technology is positioned to become a critical component of any successful vehicle retailer's domestic or/and overseas vehicle markets. How can vehicle manufacturers and retailers use (AI) to enhance their vehicle marketing campaigns? How will (AI) affect their vehicle sale marketing strategy? What criteria would they use when selecting on (AI) solution?

Vehicle consumers today are able to quickly access different brands of vehicle information, research vehicle products and reviews, negotiate prices and compare one vehicle brand or retailer to another resulting of the brands of vehicle customers. At the same time, the rise of " big -data mining", wearable devices that track user's every move and preference and greater contextualization in advertising and social media has resulted in consumer expectations of individualized. Thus, it seems that (AI) tools can be used to gather " big-data" and then they can make human's mind to analyze how to design kinds of vehicles to satisfy vehicle buyers' needs.

As automotive vehicle marketers can apply (AI) tools to achieve messaging strategies to meet the needs of this new generation of informed vehicle consumers, using data from a variety of sources to move from a variety of sources to move from mass- messaging to more personalized messages aimed at particular vehicle buyer segments, e.g. fast speed sport vehicle buyer segment, slow speed comfortable small size or large size of buyer segment. However, when 90% of vehicle marketers believe having a single vehicle buyer view is important, only 6% have achieved it.

However, one of the main issues vehicle marketers facing is the lack of capacity to efficiently sift through and analyze the massive vehicle buyer amounts of data required to create vehicle buyer individualized vehicle customer experiences easily. This is especially difficult for automotive dealers, the long periods between purchase cycles, and the highly considered nature of the vehicle purchase means that each vehicle dealer needs to not only track a large number of potential vehicle customers for an extremely long period of time, but each of those vehicle customers will generate a huge amount of different kinds of vehicle behavioral consumption data as they research their next vehicle purchase. However, by choosing the right (AI) technological tools and programs , vehicle dealers can solve this big data gathering challenge into a major advantage.

For Forrester vehicle brand example, vehicle consumers have more power over the Forrester vehicle brand's reputation than ever before. Mayne, L. (2014) indicated that Forrester calls this new (AI) tools is the " age of the vehicle customer", a 20 year business cycle in which the most successful vehicle enterprises will reinvent themselves to systematically understand and serve increasingly powerful vehicle consumers. To win in this new age, Forrester declares companies must become vehicle customer obsessed and the only sustainable competitive advantage is knowledge and engagement with customers, such as (AI) gathering data knowledge.

Thus, the biggest challenge vehicle businesses currently face is not the collection of a large quantity of vehicle consumer data, but what to do with that data once they have it. Even at a large vehicle data research firm, the data sets are often too big for a single analyze, or even a team of analysts to sort through and draw conclusion from. However, enter artificial intelligence and machine learning , an efficient technology solution that can continuously find patterns in highly complex data sets that are way beyond the capacity of a human brain and then automatic drive action based on the customer insights is generated.

What is (AI) machine learning tool? Machine learning is a type of (AI) that learns from data and is not explicitly program. Think Amazon, face book. Machine learning serves up relevant content based on an individual vehicle purchase behavior and experiences. More simply, machine learning is a computer program that can learn relationships between data, subject those learnings to errors functions, and then learn from its errors. The program in effect, trains itself.

Lee, T. (2016) explained that "Thus, (AI) tools can learn deep a more advanced branch of machine learning inspired by how our brain's nervous function, has also been found to be especial effective in identifying patterns from data."

When this way sound is complicated from a vehicle dealer perspective, the implementation of a marketing program driven by artificial intelligence can take care of these tasks in an automatic vehicle fashion with little to no manual intervention required from the staff at time vehicle stores.

In practice at a vehicle dealership, the program will continue track vehicle customer behavior online, merging that data with any offline source (like CRM or DMS data) and then analyze this aggregated vehicle buyer data set to predict what vehicle customer may be shopping for and what information they might like to

relevance from different kinds style of vehicle design photos.

1.1 Why can (AI) be applied to predict consumer behaviors?

Artificial intelligence refers to complex in vehicle market, machine learning that posses the same characteristics of human intelligence and that have all our sense, all our reason and think just like human do. Besides, machine learning is the practice of using algorithms to collect and examine data, learn from it, and then make a determination or prediction about something in the world.

The machine is " trained" using large amounts of data and algorithms that give it the ability to learn how to automatically perform a task with increasing accuracy. Otherwise, deep learning is primarily based on artificial neural networks inspired by our understanding of the biology of human's brains.

Deep learning breaks down tasks in ways that enables machines to assist us with increasingly complex tasks, driverless cars, better preventive healthcare and more accurate product recommendation (including vehicle recommendations). So, such as why (AI) technology can be applied to predict how vehicle consumer behavior changes to bring to judge whether vehicle consumer will like what kinds of vehicle styles next year. Then, vehicle manufacturers can gather overall vehicle consumer data to analyze and conclude the more accurate vehicle design direction for next year any new design vehicle manufacturing products.

Thus, (AI) machine learning can help vehicle manufacturers to solve how to design any new vehicle products challenge. A vehicle is both one of the most important and carefully considered purchases the majority of people will ever make in their lifetime. It is also a purchase that tends to be fundamentally tied to a person's identify and view of themselves. As the same time, vehicle consumers changing lifestyles result in changing vehicle needs, e.g. the young sport car enthusiast matures into the family driver.

Automotive dealers need to remember that vehicle customers and prospects are individual human beings with risk, complex and ever-changing lives factors, these factors will influence every vehicle consumer why who feels has vehicle purchase need, and how who choose to buy the first vehicle if who decided to buy the first vehicle.

The (AI) technological customer behavioral prediction tool seems to be the best vehicle salespeople in the world are those that know every one of their vehicle customers. Their likes and dislikes which style of vehicle design, preferences and changing tastes to vehicle choices. The capacity of the human brain, however, limits us from achieving this type of vehicle sales and frequent turnover at vehicle dealerships often results in the further loss of vehicle salespeople along with their vehicle customer relationships and knowledge. In this competitive vehicle environment, machine learning enables platforms to assist the vehicle sales team by tracking the vehicle consumer behaviors of each vehicle customer, learning and memorizing their preferences and predicting their future vehicle purchase needs.

Finally, I recommend that for a vehicle dealerships marketing platform to make their customer engagement efficient and fully-functional, I should be able to: applying (AI) tools to track every vehicle customer behavior across the web, connecting to a society of data sources, CRM, DMS, third-party, web vehicle brands, social email, click etc., aggregating and accurately cross-reference data from a variety of sources, leveraging this data to drive insights on a mass scale, as well as on an individualized basis, driving actions and automatically direct customer engagement via multiple channels based on where each customer is in their individual lifecycle.

How can (AI) provide businesses with better-informed decisions

I shall explain how (AI) technology can provide businesses with better-informed decisions to drive top-line growth, deliver meaningful experience for customers and smooth their path along the consumer journey. The widely understood definition of (AI) involves the ability of machines or computers to learn human thinking, reasoning and decision-making abilities.

A Narrative science study in 2015 year identified that (AI) was being used primarily in voice recognition, machine learning virtual assistants and decision support. This study also highlighted the many branches of (AI) and that techniques and their definition are used interchangeably. It is possible that (AI) can be used to gather big data , then to analyze to help businesses to predict consumer behaviors. For example, one of the most common techniques is machine learning, where algorithms are used to perform tasks

- How (AI) influences organizational change

Consequently creative and social intelligence will be in even greater demand as (AI) makes in management and the workforce. This development will represent a long term trend in labor markets , one characterized by intensifying demand and reward for social skills with a growing desire for creative capabilities, managers will seek to fashion of ideas and hypotheses from inside and outside of the enterprise to shape solutions to their most pressing business problems. Thus, (AI) will influence overall organizational team members who have chance to participate any decision to make more accurate business judgment.

Many managers mistakenly view judgment work as only an individual discipline, failing to appreciate that it can also involve decide interpersonal and organizational practices. In more complex settings, judgment is typically a collective outcome of individuals' and teams' diverse perspectives, insights and experiences. And often , the resulting choices are better informed than decisions that an individual would have arrived at on his or her own.

Thus, when any organizations apply (AI) technology to assist managers to gather data and ideas to make any judgment. In these cases, organizations can create the conditions for effective collective judgment by establishing structures , such as " shadow advisory boards" that prompt managers and employees to source and synthesize multiple perspectives. Thus, a traditional organization (firm) might freshen its thinking is t put together a shadow advisory board, comprised of young, digital people who can apply (AI) machine assistance to make judgment work more accurate whether related to people development, problem-solving or strategizing and innovating for considerable degrees of creative and social intelligence.

Thus, on the one hand, (AI) technology machine augmentation and automation can give these advantages to human (organization managers) , e.g. developing people and community, solving problems and collaborating, coordinating and controlling work, shaping strategy and leading innovation. Besides, on the other hand, the next generation managers need have these individual attitude to treat intelligent machines to be as colleagues.

When, judgment is a human skill, intelligent machines can accelerate human learning that supports it, assisting in data -driven simulations, scenarios and search and discovery activities. Focuses on judgment work, some decisions require insight beyond what data can tell them. This is the sweet sport for human judgment, the application of experience and expertise to critical business decisions and practices. Thus, managers will also need to find ways to learn how to use digital (AI) technologies to tap into the knowledge and judgment of partners, customer external stakeholders and role models in other industries after the (AI) machine had been implemented to the organization.

Future works change:Automation, employment and productivity

2.1 How (AI) influences employment

Human future " micro to macro" industry trends will be affected business strategy and public policy by (AI) technology. In the future (AI) technology will influence those six themes: productivity and growth, natural resources, labor markets, the evolution of global financial markets, the economic impact of technology and innovation and urbanization. However, (AI) technology will bring economic benefits of tackling gender inequality, a new global competition, Chinese innovation and digital globalization.

Nowadays, advances in robotics artificial intelligence, and machine learning are in a new age of automation, as machines match or outperform human performance in a development to any countries. For example, automation of activities can enable businesses to improve performance by reducing errors and improving quality and speed, and in some cases achieving outcomes that go beyond human capabilities. For example, some research indicated automation could raise productivity growth globally by 0.8 to 1.4 % annually; more than 2,000 work activities across 800 occupations. When less than 5% of all occupations can be automated using demonstrated technologies about 60% of all occupations have at least 30% of constituent activities that could be automated. Many occupations will change that will be automated away: Activities most susceptible to automation involve physical activities, in highly structured and predictable environments, as well as the collection and processing of data. They are most prevalent in manufacturing , accommodation and food service and retail trade and include some middle-skill jobs. For example, such as natural language processing is a key factor. Beyond technical feasibility, the cost of technology competition with labor including skills and supply and demand dynamics, performance benefits including and beyond labor cost savings, and social and regulatory acceptance will be affected by (AI) automation technology. Thus, (AI) automation will impact to influence global employment in those aspects as below:

Firstly, assuming that people are displaced by automation will find other employment. The anticipated shift in the activities in the labor force is of a similar order as the long-term shift away from agriculture and decreases in manufacturing share of employment. Both of manufacturing and agriculture industries which would be accompanied by the creation of new types of work not foreseen at the time.

Secondly, for business, the performance benefits of automation are relatively clear. Thus, the businessmen have opportunities for their micro economies to benefits from the productivity growth potential and macro economics to benefit to encourage continued progress and innovation , investment and market incentives. At the same time, employers must innovate policies to help workers and institutions adapt to the impact on employment.

This will likely include rethinking education and training, income support and safety nets , as well as support for those dislocated, when employees need to leave themselves homes to move to other cities to learn new (AI) automation works. Thus, individuals in the workplace will need to engage move comprehensively with machines as part of their everyday activities, and acquire new skills that will be in demand in the new automation age. Consequently , the scale of shifts in the labor force over many decades that automation technologies can be a similar order to the long -term technology -enables shifts in the developed countries' workforces away from agriculture in the 21 th century. Those shifts did not result in long-term mass unemployment because they were accompanied by the creation of new types of work not foreseen at the time. However, human will still be needed in the workforce when the total productivity gains are caused by (AI) technology.

2.2 What occupations will be influenced by (AI) technology.

In the future, scientists predict that these occupations will be influenced by (AI) technology mostly. They include : retail salespeople, food and beverage service workers, language or translation teachers, health practitioners. Since these work activities have a more relevant occupations are made up of a range of activities with different potential for (AI) automation . For example, a retail salesperson will spend more time interacting with customers, stocking shelves , or ringing up sales. Each of these activities is distinct and requires different capabilities to perform successfully.

Thus, these job activities have similar simple control characteristics. Simple activities include greet customers, answer questions about products and services, clean and maintain work areas, demonstrate product feature process sales and transactions. All these activities can have similar simple activities in order to (AI) machines can be learn how to do these activities from (AI) technology . For example, the capability perception includes sensory perception, cognitive capabilities, such as retrieving automation, recognizing known patterns(supervised learning), logical reasoning problem solving.

Thus, (AI) machine is such human, which has feeling and emotion, such as social and emotional sensing, judgement reasoning methods, natural language understanding and physical capabilities, such as mobility , navigation, gross motor skill, fine motor skills. It seems that the future, (AI) human invents machines which will have these human characteristics to do human similar behavioral job duties more easily and efficiently. It implies these above human occupations will be replaced by (AI) human invention machines in the future. Due to (AI) creation, it is possible to cause unemployment number of these above workers will increase because (AI) machines can do their similar job behavioral activities.

Consequently, employers won't need to employ many of these skillful labor. Otherwise, they can buy less number (AI) machines to attempt to do whose job activities more easily and efficiently. So, it seems (AI) machines will have more high work performance to replace these occupation workers' work performance. Finally, these occupation worker unemployment number will only increase when the (AI) machines had been invented to achieve to do their work behavioral activities absolutely success in the future.

2.3 Whether (A) technology machine labor

will replace human worker more or assist
human worker more

There is no single agreed definition of a robot how outcome of a task that is completed without human intervention. When some definitions require the task to be completed by a physical machine moves and respond to its environment, other definitions use the term robot in connection with tasks completed by software , without physical embodiment.
However, to answer the question : Whether (AI) technology machine labor will replace human worker more or assist human worker more. I shall indicate some examples to let readers to judge whether (AI) technology can create new jobs or reduce old jobs.
Firstly, I shall explain what (AI) function is. (AI) is a service robot that performs useful tasks for humans or equipment excluding industrial automation application . Thus, the classification of a robot into industrial robot or service robot is done according to its intended application. It is also a personal service robot or a service robot for personal used for a non commercial task, usually by lay persons . Examples are domestic servant robot, and pet exercising robot. It is also a professional service robot or a service robot for professional used for a commercial task, usually operated by a properly trained operator. Examples, are cleaning robot for public places, delivery robot in offices or hospitals, fire-fighting robot, rehabilitation robot and surgery robot in hospitals. Thus, these functions will be future (AI) application to our daily life necessaries or business necessaries.
However, some authors agree (AI) will bring negative outcomes of automation, due to raise competiveness, reduce human job nature. Otherwise, other authors argue (AI) will bring positive outcomes of automation, due to raise productivities, job creation, assist humans work.
On the positive outcome hand, robots can increase productivity . This is particularly important for small-to medium sized businesses both are in developed and developing countries economies. It also enables large companies to increase their competitiveness through faster product development and delivery. Increased use of robot is also enabling companies in high cost countries to re shore, or bring back to their domestic base parts of the supply chain that will have previously outsourced to sources of cheaper labor. Currently , the greater threat to employment is not a automation, but an inability to remain competitive. Automation has

led overall to an increase in labor demand and positive impact on wages. The reason is that the middle-income/middle-skilled jobs have reduced as a proportion of overall contribution to employment and earnings leading to fears of increasing income inequality, the skills range within the middle income bracket is large. Thus, robots are driving an increase in demand for workers at the higher -skilled and with a positive impact on wages. This issue is how to enable middle-income earners in the lower-income range to unskilled or retain. Finally, the (AI) positive impact supporter who argue the future will be robots and humans can work together.

However, on the negative outcome hand, robots can substitute labor activities, but don't replace jobs. They believe that less than 10% of jobs are fully automatable. Increasingly , robots are used to complement and augment labor activities, the net impact on jobs and the quality of work is positive. Automation can provide the opportunity for humans to focus on higher-skilled, higher-quality and higher-paid tasks. Robots can improve productivity when they are applied to tasks that which perform more efficiently and to a higher and more consistent level of quality than humans. For example, increased productivity is enabling some firms, such as Whirlpool, Caterpillar and Ford Motors company in the US restructure their supply chains, bringing back parts of the manufacturing process to the country of origin. Thus, productivity gains due to robotics and automation are important not just at the company level, but also for build industry and nation competitiveness.

I suppose that productivity can be raised. What are the impacts of robots on employment? Firstly, the main focus of development has been on personal entertainment, which does not drive worker productivity (manufacturing production). When the internet (information and communication technology (ICT)) innovation. This is borne and by findings that manufacturing productivity, which has been driven by innovations in automation rather than consumer technologies, has government strongly than productivity in the services sectors of the economy in most nature economies. It seems (AI) automation will create many jobs in internet communication entertainment game industry. For example, many young people like to use internet to play any electronic games from computer or mobile at home or outside home conveniently. Thus, (AI) automation will increase demand to be invented to any new entertainment game from internet channel. It will need to employ many (AI) entertainment game inventors to create many automation entertainment games. Thus, (AI) automation in internet entertainment game industry will need human (AI) entertainment game inventors to invent the knowledge-based capital of (AI) automation entertainment games. The (AI) entertainment game inventors will need own research and development skills, form specific skills, organizational know-how skills, databased knowledge, design and various forms of intellectual property to do these (AI) automation entertainment game invention occupations in the future.

International Federation Of Robotics(2016) indicated that China will be as a major robotics manufacturer and user of robots, benefiting from jobs created by robot manufacturing and productivity gains from robot use. Chins had sold of robots to any one single market every year since 2017 year. The Chinese government has included a focus on robotics in its 10 year strategy. In order to achieve its target of a robot density of 150 units per 10, 000 workers by 2020 year. Thus, Chinese companies will have to install around 650,000 new industrial robots between 2016 to 2020 year, 2.5 times more than installed globally in 2015 year.

Hence, China (AI) manufacturing industry will need to employ many workers . It implies (AI) manufacturing industry will create many new occupations in China. Also, ministry of economy, trade and industry (2015) also showed that Japan currently has the largest stock of industrial robots in operations, primarily in the automation industry. Driven by a rapidly aging population and low productivity rates, the Japanese government has sights on a 20-fold increase in the use of robots in the non-manufacturing sector and a three-fold growth rate of labor productivity in the service sector both by 2020 year. Thus, it also implies Japan will need many robots to be provide to service industry. Due to robots will provide to serve any businessmen's clients. Thus, it is possible that the service workers won't be dismissed as well as it is depended on the serving job nature to decide whether Japan's service workers can still serve to their employer when the service (AI) robots are applied to whose employers.

Consequently, it seems that (AI) can create employment, Ministry of economy, trade and industry (2015) showed that such as China will develop the major (AI) automation manufacturing industry. The (AI) employers will need to employ many workers to manufacture any these different kinds of (AI) robots to satisfy China or overseas individual or business buyers needs. But, (AI) can also cause unemployment to the low skillful service workers. Such as if Japan some service businesses choose to buy any (AI) service robots to replace their service staffs to serve their clients. It is possible that the service staffs will be dismissed, due to (AI) robots can do such as their same service job duties to achieve better service performance. Thus, today, it is increasingly common for people to use robots in various situations at home and in retail stores, hotels and hospitals these service industries. Robots are classified into server types based on their functionality (service and utility robots or those designed to communicate with humans) and appearance (humanoid robots or mechanical robots). The type of robot, to which each country allocated particular importance in the advance of robotics, reflects the sense of values and preferences of its population. Thus, if the country has high population needs to use robots, then they will influence either more new jobs creation or more old job loss in the country's (AI) manufacturing or (AI) service industries both. For example, Japan respondents often associate the term " robot " with humanoid robots that can communicate with human and they have a high level of familiarity with robot. The US has the highest level of robot utilization at home and in retail stores with its people being the most enthusiastic about the future use of robots. Germany shows a strong tendency to consider robots for industrial purposes and its people feel strong effort to the presence of robots in their households.

In conclusion, to judge whether how (AI) will influence the country's employment to be better or worse. It will depend on the country home buyers (users) or business buyers (users) how to use (AI) for their daily needs. If the country , such as US retail stores need to use (AI) , it will have possible to reduce some or many retail service workers. Even, if the country , such as Japan has many home users need to use (AI) , it will not influence the employment market. Otherwise, it will raise (AI) salespeople numbers. Even, if the country, such as Germany and China will have many (AI) manufacturers, then it will create many (AI) manufacturing occupations for these (AI) manufactory workers.

Consequently, (AI) robots manufacturing and service needs will have positive or negative impact to any country's employment. It will depend on the (AI) service provision and service workers' job nature as well as the manufacturing workers of (AI) knowledge level to decide their employment chance in their country's employment market.

● Can (AI) impact human leisure need changes?

Human need concern this question: Will artificial intelligence (AI) reduce some human jobs in order to instead of replacing machines to do? Due to artificial intelligence is the ability of machines to do thing, that people would require intelligence. For example, artificial intelligence machine man driving(self-driver), it (AI) machine man driving research is an attempt to discover and describe aspects of human intelligence that can be simulated by driving machine functions. Alternatively, (AI) mathematical research may be another viewed as an attempt to develop a mathematical theory function to describe the abilities and actions of things (natural or man-made) exhibiting intelligent behavior and server as a design of intelligent calculation machine function.

Why do humans need artificial intelligence machines to instead of traditional human service job? For example, can artificial intelligence machine man (self-driving) driver drive to replace human driver? I shall compare the differences between humans and computers : The characteristics of humans are good at recognizing various things, either seen before or not, recognizing the relationship patterns between things. Human thinking is common sense reasoning, combining all types of sensory input, acting appropriately in novel situations, learning new things and changing behavior patterns, making decisions , even when given incomplete information, working with noisy, incomplete information gathering behaviors . However, characteristics of computers are good at: The tasks humans do naturally are extremely difficult for a computer program as intelligent, which must be able to do the same kind of tack as humans do naturally.

Hence, (AI) is an combination of many different success and technologies: Linguistics - computational and socio, philosophy-logic, philosophy of mind and of language, electronical engineering -image and speech processing, pattern recognition, robotics, machine learning, neural networks, optimization scheduling, management information system and decision making. So, it is possible that (AI) can impact human job nature to instead of human working behavior in the future.

How can (AI) influence labor market?

- How can human society job nature

to be changed to artificial intelligent society?

From the first intelligent perspective reason view point, artificial intelligence is making machines " intelligent" acting as humans expect people to act. Artificial intelligence has ability to distinguish computer responses from human responses, it owns knowledge to solve expert problem. From another research perspective reason view point, artificial intelligence is the study of how to make computers do things which, at the moment, people do better (Rich & Knight, 1991, p.3).

(AI) researchers are native in a variety of domains, e.g. formal tasks (mathematics, games), tasks (perception, robotics, natural language, common sense reasoning), expert tasks (financial analysis, medical diagnostics, engineering, scientific analysis and other areas).

From the second business perspective reason view point, (AI) is a set of many powerful tools, and methodologies for using those tools to solve business problems. From a programming perspective reason view point, (AI) includes the study of symbolic programming problem solving and search .

From the third human technological perspective reason view point, today's computer can do many well-defined tasks, for example, arithmetic operations, are much faster and more accurate than human beings. However, the computers' interaction with their environment is not very sophisticated yet. How can human test whether a computer has reached the general intelligence level of a human being? Can a computer convince a human interrogator that it is a human? But before thinking of such advanced kinds of machines, human will start developing our own extremely simple " intelligent" machines.

So, it is possible that human society job nature will to be changed to artificial intelligent society when (AI) technology is developed to the mature stage in the future.

- Why does human need artificial intelligence machines?

One of major division in (AI) is between humans who think (AI) is the only serious way of finding out how we (human) work and human who want companies to do very smart things, independently of how we (human) work. This is the important distinction between cognitive scientists vs engineers. One of another major division in (AI) is between symbolic (AI), which represents information through symbols and their relationships. Specific Algorithms are used to process these symbols to solve problems or deduce new knowledge and connectionist. So (AI) , which represents information in network. Biological processes underlying learning, task performance and problem solving are imitated from human mind behaviors. Thus, it is possible that artificial intelligence machines can do the better judgicious behavior to compare human.

- How does artificial intelligence influence future working changing in automation employment and productivity aspects?

In the automation changing influence aspect, as companies increasingly use robots on production lines or algorithms to optimize their logistics manage inventory, any carry out other core business functions. Technological advances are creating a new automation age in which ever-smarter and more flexible machines will be deployed on an ever larger scale in the marketplace. However, researching artificial intelligence with how influences human working nature. We need to answer these questions: How will automation transform the workplace? What will the implications for employment? And what is likely to be its impact both on productivity in the global economy and on employment?

Advances in robotics, artificial intelligence, and machine learning are growing in a new age of automation as machines match or outperform human performance in a range of work activities, including ones requiring cognitive capabilities. What factors are determined the changing in workplace adoption by artificial intelligence innovation? What advantages are automation? Automation of activities can be enabled businesses to improve performance by reducing errors and improving quality and speed, and achieving outcomes that go beyond human capabilities.

Some scientists indicated based on their scenario modeling. They estimated automation could raise producing growth globally by 0.8 to 1.4 percent annually. Almost, the activities people are paid almost $16 trillion in wages to do in global economy have the potential to be automated by adopting currently demonstrated technology. According to their analysis of more than 2,000 work activities across 800 occupations. When less than 5% of all occupations have of least 30% of activities that could be automated. They also indicated that technical economic and social factors will determine automation. Continued technical progress, for example, in areas such as natural language processing is a key factor beyond technical feasibility , the cost of technology, competition with labor including skills, and supply and demand dynamics, performance benefits including and beyond labor cost savings and social and regulatory acceptance will affect (alter) the scope of automation.

Other some scientists also indicate U.S. country for example, the anticipate shift in the activities in labor force of a similar order of magnitude as the long term sight away from agriculture and decreases in manufacturing. Share of employment in the United States both which were achieved. So, those factors can influence why artificial intelligence technology needs. So, it is possible that future agriculture and manufacturing both industries will apply (AI) technology manufacturer-kind of job nature to raise productivity instead of farmers, fruit picking workers, farming transportation labours as well as factory manufacturing workers and supervisors etc. human-kind of job nature.

● Is artificial intelligence possible to replace labor ?

Not just intelligence, but also debating, if machines are capable of having a conscious minds. Artificial intelligence has those characteristics as below:
On functionalism aspect, artificial intelligence inputs mental states, sensory inputs, (beliefs, desires being in pain feeling) and behavioral outputs. Since mental states are identified by a functional role, which are thoughts to be manifested in various systems. Even, perhaps computers which are physical devices with electronic substrate that inform computations on inputs to give outputs similar to brains which are artificial intelligence composed of part any intrinsic relationship to each other. Thus, artificial intelligence activities is not the whole itself, but into parts or on external influence on the parts.

On dualism aspect, artificial intelligence is a set of views about the relationship between mind are matter. On materialism aspect, it builds the only thing that exists is matter, including consciousness.

On biological naturalism aspect, it is similar a human brain than feels pains makes mental situation. So, artificial intelligence is similar biologist which might to be excited to human labor work. Hence, it seems artificial intelligence can change (alter) or replace human labor work of nature in possible in the future.

● Can (AI) technology replace human labour nature of work?

On technological innovation reason view point, the history development of artificial intelligence studying the intelligence is one of most ancient scientific discipline. The history development of artificial intelligence what aims to achieve human use to sense, learn remember and think, logic probability, decision making and calculation develop from mathematics, instead of replacement human labor functions.

Artificial intelligence history development aim is the scientific analysis of skills in connection and practice with the appearance of computers from 1950 year beginning. The artificial intelligence (AI) can deal with the ultimate challenges. How can (either biological or electronic) mind sense, understand and manipulate a world that is much simple and more complex than itself? And what if would human like to construct something with such capabilities?

The general-purpose software of the early period of (AI) were only able to solve simple tasks effectively and failed when which should be used in a wider range or an more difficult tasks. One of the sources of difficulty was that early software had very few or mix knowledge about the problems which handled, and activities successes by simply syntactic manipulation. Moreover, the other difficulty was that many problems that were tried to solve by the (AI) were untreatable.

The early (AI) software whether trying step sequences based on the basic facts about the problem that should be solved, experimented with different combinations till which found a solution. From the end the 1960 year, developing the so-called expert systems were emphasized. These systems had (sue-based) knowledge base about the field which handled. Till to the beginning of the 1970 year, (Prolog) the logical programming language was born, which was built in the computation realization of a version of the resolution calculus. (Prolog) is a remarkably prevalent tool in developing expert systems (on medical, judiciary and other scopes), but natural language parsers were implemented in this language. Then, in 1981 s, the Japanese announced the fifth generation computer system project, a 10 years plan to build an intelligent computer system that use the (Prolog) language as a machine code. Nowadays, (AI) can be applied any industries, such as car manufacturing industry can use (AI) technological machine-men manufacture car, instead of replacing human labors in factory. Even, in the future, using (AI) machine-men drivers can drive any private cars or public transportation tools, instead of replacing human drivers, e.g. bus, train, tram, ferry etc. Also in the future, machine-men can replace housewives to serve families to do housekeeping clean job , e.g. cleaning toilets, bathrooms, kitchens, even cooking functions at home. So (AI) machine-man can reduce housewives works at home. Moreover, (AI) machine man can take care old people , when who are living at homes or elder care centers.

So, it seems artificial intelligence (AI) will be possible developed to manufacture a new generation machine-man to assist (serve) families to do any simply cleaning or cooking jobs at homes. Moreover, the overall demand of (AI) general social needs will also rise, such as security, driving transportation tools, restaurant cleaning, elder centers care service etc. So, it seems that individual or families or social needs of (AI) will be increase in the future. Thus, it will influence macro economy growth (GDP) if there are large house family consumer group and hotel or bus or taxis or ferry etc. different business consumer group demand any artificial intelligence machine numbers increasing. Then, the artificial intelligence products and material manufacturers must need to buy many artificaial intelligence materials to produce any kinds of artificial intelligence machines to prepare to satisfy consumer individual needs. Consequently, macro economy will grow to the owned artificial intelligence development countries, e.g. US, China, UK.

First, On machine-man satisfactory demand aspect view point, it makes computers that think, it is the automation of activities. We associate with human thinking: like decision making, learning. It is the act of creating machine that perform function that require intelligence when performed by people. It is the study of mental faculties through the use of computational models. It is the study of computations that make it possible to perceive, reason and act. It is a branch of computer science that is concerned with the automation of intelligent behavior. It is anything in computing service that human don't yet know how to do property.

Second, on thought aspect artificial intelligence means systems thank think like humans, systems that think rationally.

Third, on behavioral aspect, artificial intelligence systems that act like human and that systems act rationally. However, the basic objective of (AI) is to represent human's thought processes in computation . These machines are supposed to exhibit behavior that. It is performed by a human being, would be considered intelligent. However, some authors feel (AI) has disadvantages, such as it is not creative, it is excited in the use of sensory devices, it can't make use of a very wide context of experiences and it does not use common sense.

For speech recognition and understanding function needs example, (AI) can be applied in speech recognition and understanding function, which (AI) speech or voice recognition is a data input method. For example, the computer recognizes and understands one (or a few) word commands. Speech understanding on the other hand is the computer's ability to understanding a spoken language. That is , the computer understands the meaning of sentences, an paragraphs through (AI).

So, (AI) can be attempted to learn human language how to speak. It is similar to translate human language skill, instead of actual human speaking skill. Also, (AI) can assist handicap learning or language student how to listen different languages by machine-man sounds from computers more accurately. So, it seems that it (AI) can replace human language teachers speaking function and can change teaching language nature of job in language speaking and listening education industry.

Nowadays, new technology development is popular. However, artificial intelligence is one kind of new technology choice among different technologies innovation. So it brings this question: Is artificial intelligence technology value to invest? To answer this question. I shall indicate some other new technology developments to compare (AI) technology development to judge which has urgent needs to achieve human expectation nowadays.

For example, why is green peace interested in new technologies? New technologies features prominently in our ongoing campaigns against genetic modified crops and number power. However, which are also an integral part of our solutions to environmental challenges, including renewable energy technologies, such as solar, wind and wave (water) power energy as well as waste treatment technologies, such as mechanical, biological treatment.

It seems humans need concern how to apply (AI) technology to solve environment pollution challenges in our future. So, environment protective, agriculture, natural energy technology will be popular demand to attempt to apply (AI) technology to solve their challenges or apply (AI) to assist to develop their industry.

Advances in artificial intelligence (AI) technology and related fields have opened up new markets and new opportunities progress in critical areas, such as health, education, energy, economic development, social welfare and the environment pollution.

(AI) automation will continue to create wealth and expand the global economy development in the future. However, when many will benefits that growth won't be costless and will be accompanied by changes in the skills, that workers need to increase productivity in the economy and structural changes in the economy. So, in the skills that workers need to succeed in the economy and structural changes.

I shall indicate why aggressive policy action will be needed to help Americans who are disadvantaged by these changes , due to (AI) technology is caused. For automation industry change example, artificial intelligence (AI) capabilities will enable automation of some tasks that have long required human labor. These artificial intelligence technology introduction can increase new opportunities for individuals. The economy and society, but (AI) has also the potential to disrupt be current livelihoods of many Americans. However, (AI) leads to unemployment and increase in inequality over the long run depends not only on the (AI) technology itself, but also on the institutions and policies that are changed.

Thus, it is possible that (AI) technology will raise some countries unemployment number if the employer apply (AI) technology workers to work instead of human labor in their factories, but it can also raise productivities for these employers.

- Can (AI) influence global economy growth?

Technological progress is main driver of growth of GDP per capita, allowing output to increase faster than labor and capital . However, technology can increase productivity, but also decrease the number of labor hours needed to create a unit of output. So (AI) causes unequal to labor wage decreases, even reduces the number of labor to manufacture, e.g. artificial intelligence technology of automation car manufacturing industry; clothing manufacturing industry; plane manufacturing etc. high technology of artificial intelligence manufacturing method. But (AI) should be potential environment benefit, although it raises unemployment ratio. Moreover, it can rise production , due to many skilled craft were replaced by the combination of machines and lower-skilled labor. The result of (AI) technology introduction , it causes output per hour risen when inequality declined, driving up average living standards, but the labor of some high-skill workers was no longer as valuable in the market. Otherwise, if (AI) technology is continue developed to be success. Some routine intensive occupations will be loss, which focused on predictable, e.g. easily programmable tasks, such as switchboard operators, filing clerks, travel agents, and assembly line workers would be particularly replaced by new (AI) technology. However, at the same time, (AI) technology development will bring these benefits: improvement in education (training (AI) technology scientists) , due to (AI) manufacturing technology needs are raising to businesses and institutional changes, such as the reduction in unionization and raising in the minimum wage to the (AI) manufacturing technology skilled labor in factories.

Because (AI) technology is not a single technology, but rather a collection of technologies that are applied to specific tasks, the effects of (AI) will be felt unevenly though the economy. It will bring some tasks will be most easily automated than others , and some jobs will be affected more than others, both negatively and positively. Finally, new jobs are likely to be directly created in areas , such as the development and supervision of (AI) as well as indirectly created in a range areas though out the economy as higher incomes lead to expanded demand.

However, if (AI) technology could dominate global labor markets. If labor productivity increases, do not influence into wage increases, then the large economic gains brought about by (AI) technology could be increased wealth inequality, due to employers can reduce production cost, but workers (labors) wages will not be increased, even will be decreased. Hence, it seems the (AI) technology will bring disadvantages to labor market to cause unemployment or reduce wages in possible, although it can reduce employer individual salary (wage) expenditure and it can raise productivity.

- How can artificial intelligence impact global economy growth?

Artificial intelligence (AI) technology is a branch of computer science that aims to create intelligent machines that work and react like humans. So, (AI) is a technology that appears to impact (influence) human preference by learning, understanding complex contents, enhancing humans in executing both routine and non-routine tasks. In the future, (AI) technology that can be virtual personal assistant, as well as it may exist, such as robots with human-like processing capabilities.

How can (AI) technology impact global economy growth over the next 10 years? During this time period, (AI) technology is predicted to have wide-ranging applications including: Machine learning that automates analytical model building by using algorithms that allow machines to operate without human assistance.

In global education aspect, potential applications include predicting cause-and-effect relationships from biological data, identifying new drugs, self-driving cars, and protecting against fraud, improved natural language processing that allows computers to continue to better analysis, understand and generate language to interface with humans using natural human languages. For example, transcribing notes dictated by physicians, automatically drafting articles and translating text and speech. So (AI) technology can be applied to education aspect to improve humans' knowledge level.

In visual art aspect, (AI) machine vision that allows computers to identify objects, scenes and activities in images. Current applications of (AI) machine vision include providing objective descriptions for the blind seeing(visual) needs.

We except the economic effects of (AI) technology to include both direct GDP growth from sectors that develop or manufacture. (AI) technology and indirect GDP growth through increased productivity in existing sectors that employ some form of (AI). If (AI) technology is an increasingly critical component of more products, it will become an integral part of many people's lives. Thus, (AI)'s ability to influence economic activity, rather than the economic or development status of the region. (AI) has the potential to impact income classes and to bring significant gains to both developed and developing countries. For example, (AI) has the potential to optimize good production around the world by analyzing agricultural regions and identifying what is necessary to improve crop yields.

In estimating the future economic effects by (AI) technology innovation, it is important to note that it is challenging to accurately predict which applications of (AI) will ultimately be commercially successful. In micro level economic influence, we need to apply methodologies to estimate the economic effects of investment in firms developing (AI) technology since investment levels in a technology are a telling sign of the future potential of that (AI) technology.

How (AI)'s development may affect the global economy over the next ten years. In fact, (AI) technology has the potential to affect business across the global in a wide range of industries in ways only a number of technologies have done in the parts. For example, (AI) technology's expected to be a useful tool for enhancing human capabilities and in some instances replacing functions, such as driving a car, adoption of broadband internet, mobile telephone, industrial robotic automation have served to enhance human capabilities.

However, significant public debate has focused on projections of (AI) technology's effect on the labor force. However, large companies prefer to invest in (AI) technological industry. For example, face book's (AI) research lab., google machine intelligence lab. and micro soft machine learning and artificial intelligence research division are all making advances in (AI) technology and investing in the industry's top talent. Additionally, between 2010 year and 2015 year, nearly $5 billion in venture capital funding invested in firms across the global developing and employing (AI) technology (Facebook (AI) Research).

- How can artificial intelligence impact on workplace?

Modern information technologies and the labor economy growth of machines is powered by artificial intelligence have already strongly influenced the world of work in the 21 ST century. Computers, algorithms and software simplify every tasks and it is impossible to image how most of our life could be managed without them. How can be the information economy characterized by exponential growth replaces the most production industry based on economy of scales? What will the future world of work look like and how long will it take to get? Will the future world of work be a world where humans spend less time earning their livelihood? Alternatively, are mass unemployment, mass poverty and social distortions also possible scenario for the future, where robots, artificial intelligence systems play an increasingly central role? These questions concern how artificial intelligence further development . Can influence labor economy growth on workplace ? When the labor market has widespread impact on intelligence property, information technology, product liability, competition and labor and employment laws.

How (AI) technology impacts on labor workplace.

The future influence any organizations how labor economies use of (AI) can be analyzed, such as deep machine learning is based on a set of model high level data. Unlike human workers, the machines are connected the whole time in workplace. If one machine makes a mistake, all autonomous systems will keep this in mind and will avoid the same mistake the next time.

Over the long run intelligent machines will win against every human expert. Production robots have been replacing employees because of the (AI) technology. They work more precisely than humans and cost loss. Creative solutions like 3D printers and the self learning ability of these production robots will replace human workers, the automatic data recording and data processing, traditional back office activities are no longer in demand. Autonomous software will collect necessary information and will send it to the employee who needs it. Additionally, dematerialization leads to the phenomenon that traditional physical products are becoming software. For example, CD or DVDs are being replaced by streaming services. The replacement of traditional event ticket, e-travel ticket service products or hard cash will be the next step, due to the possibility of payment by smartphone. So, (AI) technology will impact human's daily life consumption behaviors in the future. For another example, transportation tools, such as boats and ferries and private vehicles will use sensors and navigating without human input. Taxi and truck drivers will become obsolete, the stock store applies to stock managers and postal carriers of the delivery is distributed by (AI) machine delivery method.

Nowadays , (AI) is a technology almost as old as the computer industry itself, it is similar with the advent of personal assistants function to businesses and personal promotion channel, such as (Amazon's Alexa, Apple's Siri, Google's Assistant) image recognition (face book), personalized recommendations (Netflix , Amazon). Those innovations have been driven by a increase in processing power, lower cost hardware, and the exploding creation and availability of data. It seems, (AI) technology can impact global customer service management method.

How to forecast economic impact modeling to (AI) will affect global economy? Can human forecast business revenue growth and job creation (or destruction) based on (AI) applied to customer relationship management (CRM) activities? In addition to the economic impact on (AI) or (CRM) which can include an estimate of the economic impact attributable to sales forces customer base. What can economic benefits be brought to (CRM) from (AI) technology?

Artificial intelligence(AI) comprises a set of technologies that use natural language processing, machine learning, knowledge graphs, and other tools to answer questions, discover insights and provide recommendations. Computer systems can use (AI) hypothesize and formulate possible answers based on available evidence can be trained through the ingestion of vast amounts of content, and automatically adapt and learn from (AI) self mistakes and failures.

So, any business organizations (customer service departments) can provide efficient and effective customer relationship management of excellent customer service quality if which applied (AI) technology system. The different type of (AI) systems include: (AI) system platforms, machine learning (AI) based data preparation and enrichment tools, machine vision/ image recognition, voice speech recognition, text analysis and natural language processing, bots , e.g. face book website and virtual digital assistance solutions, social media pattern analysis , sentiment analysis, advanced numerical analysis (e.g. IOT streaming , machine logs), supporting technologies, knowledge base dialog management, Q&A processing etc. different (AI) technology system customer relationship management (CRM) tools.

(AI) (CRM) of activity can include these categories, such as: corporate marketing, marketing operation, field marketing, customer support, digital commerce, customer analytics, customer influenced product or service design, product or service pricing, finance information, presentation, customer billing, inventory , logistics and fulfilment support, partner management etc. different CRM tools.

(AI) technology of CRM has been carrying on plan different stages to achieve CRM personal assistant tool for businesses. The stages are such as, in the beginning stage of (AI) projects in place, implement now, pilot phase next year in the final stage of (AI) customer relationship management tools are foreseeable future. So, this CRM technology has been improved to plan in different stages every year to prepare to achieve full capacity of CRM service quality for businesses to use in the future.

Hence, how to develop an estimate prediction of the economic impact (AI) technologies could have CRM activities, which depends on gathering macroeconomic information on business revenue and the basic marketing of business revenue and the basic markup of business expenses by major functions (customer support, marketing and sales , production etc.)

An economic impact model that can gather data together and forecast the results how (AI) artificial intelligence technology brings (CRM) customer relationship management benefits to businesses, e.g. surveys investigation includes IT spending by sample countries, GDP and population estimates and forecasts, revenue per employee and ratios of IT spend to GDP. Surveys (questionnaire questions) of forecast results are influenced by (AI) impact can include: results are projected from surveys and rely on estimates are made by respondents on the expected financial improvements in categories of (AI) –assisted customer relationship management activities. The forecast assumes that these estimates are correct; financial estimates are based on estimates of “first year” improvement from full (AI) implementation; forecasts are from planning to implement any artificial intelligence of customer relationship management (CRM) projects, the improvement forecast is of categories of activity , e.g. corporate marketing , digital commerce, and customer analytics. They are not estimates of ROI for the (AI) software. They rely on conservative estimates to which each of these entities might affect company revenue, expenses or productivity. They also rely on estimates of the penetration of software in customer relationship management activities . Net new jobs created are based on the ratio of new revenue to jobs required to support that revenue . They can assume that 50% of the net new revenue will support increases in labor and the rest will go for capital and other operating expenses that may replace jobs lost to automation.

In the future, some of the ways in micro economic benefits to any organizations. (AI) technology is expected to impact CRM activities include: Spending up sales cycles, improving lead generation and qualification solving customer support problems faster (raising service quality), helping companies improve brand campaigns and recognition, lowering costs of support calls when increasing resolution rates, lowering the cost of recruiting employees and partners, increasing revenue from optimized product marketing, optimizing price, distribution logistics and preventing loss through fraud detection. So, micro economic benefits view point, it seems that (AI) CRM technology can raise any companies economic benefits for care term.

Artificial intelligence enables machines or the in-build software to behave like human beings which allows these decisions and act. The advent of (AI) is leading , talking, making decisions and act. The advent of (AI) is leading to new technologies advances and transforming the economic and employment opportunities for humans in a positive way. (AI) related technologies can facilitate our live. For example, industrial robotics, robotic medical assistants, smart games, financial forecasting software, big data analysis, algorithms in health and bioinformatics, pilotless cargo places, drone ambulances and general purpose and workplace robots and others. (Disruptors technologies: Advances that will transform life, business and the global economy).

Artificial intelligence also known as computational intelligence is defined as " the human –like intelligence exhibited by machines or software. It is theorized that intelligence of humans can be described and intelligence machines or software can simulate it. These machines software can be reasonable , learn, perceive and process information, like human mind and thus facilitate human life. They can think and act for us. So, artificial intelligence is an interdisciplinary field of study including computer science, neuroscience, psychology, linguistics and philosophy.

However, (AI) research and developments have economically impacted many industries, such as robotics, telecommunications, computer applications , health, finance, heavy manufacturing, transportation, aviation, e-service and e-commerce, military , music and movie, toys and games entertainment etc. industries.

In fact, many ideas, systems and technologies have been developing in the world of (AI) technology. However, which are net called or considered (AI) products, rather which are mentioned with their specific names, such as smart graphics, machine learning, e-commerce etc. (i.e. this is called (AI)

effect).
Nowadays, (AI) related industrial applications will replace most human power in fields, including call centers, customer services and air cargo transportation. (AI) technologies also help weather forecasting based on repeated rainfall pattern (data) recognition, through robotics (i.e. floor cleaning, moving lawns etc.) transporting people and products with unmanned vehicles, sending space unmanned smart shuttles, developing robotic arms, predicting market values in stock exchanges by internet, making homes safer, helping elderly and disabled using robotic servants etc.

Among the (AI) related technologies , there are a few that significance for the impact on society and especially on digital economy . (AI) is particularly influential in machine learning. Such as robotics, transportation, finance, health and bioinformatics, e-commerce , e-games, big online data gathering and internet-of-things. For example, machine e-learning is based in bioinformatics and robots that can learn new skills for better caregiving in healthcare. What is machine e-learning? Machines can e-learn from e-data gathering, coming up generalizations and making decisions to act in certain ways from internet.
There are important applications , such as e-machine perception, electronic online natural language learning processing, online search engines, online bioinformatics, online brain –computer interface, online game playing, online robot locomotion, online advertising, online computations finances, online health monitoring, online DNA classification and decision making, online in chemistry –cheminformatics . So, online machine learning can positively impact productivity and it can enhance information and analytical system from (AI) online channel.
What is robotics? Robotics is one of the most strongly influenced fields in (AI). For example, heavy manufacturing industries, robots and used and man power is replaced for effectiveness, precision, and accuracy, especially in respective or dangerous tasks, including welding, assembling , picking and placing .
So, robots can acquire new skills or adapt the changing dynamic environment. Also, artificial intelligence can be applied in developing transportation. For example, automated vehicles, driver assistance systems , safety systems, collision avoidance systems and public transportation. Moreover, (AI) technology has proven to produce some of the best tools to predict stock market fluctuations from internet data gathering method. It's

predictions are based on ever-evolving predictions algorithms and systems learn new models and make connections between historical data and new data to measure stock market trading more accurate from internet data gathering channel.

In health field, especially in health data processing , analysis, decision making support and medical diagnosis. So, online data can show which patients will need what treatment and what alternative drugs could be used more accurate from (AI) online data gathering method. Bioinformatics is an interdisciplinary field combining statistics, (AI) online technology can help in discovering data patterns and modeling through the application of machine learning, artificial neural networks and genetic algorithms. For example, further (AI) technology development of human genome project of online data sequences.

Online shopping can be facilitated by virtual assistants developed through (AI) technology and these assistants can offer the best advice. (AI) online purchase coming after every product image recommendations and personalization bring important revenue to shopping online sites, like Amazon . Smart computer graphics and games, artificial intelligence is useful in smarter computer, graphics, scene modeling , scene rendering processes in order to create, for example, effective human –robot interactions , online machine learning, online strategic games techniques etc. online computer related (AI) software.

So, online big data analysis and big data does have a critical need in the world of online intelligence machines and software in our future. In other words, (AI) offers online technology to enable online big data analysis to provide industrial organizations with valuable information for effective decision making in short time. For example, what IBM's Watson achieved: this machine used 200 million of structured and unstructured content with a special technology of hypothesis generation, massive evidence gathering, analysis and scoring from internet channel.

Finally, (AI) online technology another related internet invention (internet of things) (IOT) is the network of machines or objects connected through internet. These connected objects can sense their internal and external environment, communicate with each other, can send critical data and finally can make decisions to act or correct their environment from (AI) online technology. For example, factories can monitor and automatically change production processes, hospitals can monitor and regulate the health conditions of their patients , schools can collect data from facilities and cars can send data to car makers from (AI) online technology.

Partner predicts that (IOT) market will create about trillion amount value by 2020 year. Although machines collect big data from their environment, whether which gain an insight or learn from these online data largely depends on the (AI) online machine learning principals and (AI) online technology. In 2013, Mckinsey estimated that disruptive technologies closely related with potential economic impact in 2025 year between $7.1 to $13.1 trillion amount (automation of knowledge work, advanced robotics, autonomous or near-autonomous vehicles).

Can (AI) technology influence China economy? Could China workers be affected and jobs made up of routine work activities and predictable? Will programmable tasks be particularly impact to China employment market ? When impact on labor market is likely to be gradual at the aggregate level, it can be sudden and dramatic at the level of specific work activities, rending some job obsolete fairly. Overall (AI) technology will raise digital skills when reducing demand for medium incomer inequality for China workers. It seems (AI) technology's effect on productivity could be crucial to China's future economic growth as the population ages are increasing.

In China, some biggest technological companies driving significant investments in research and development. Moreover, China is one of the leading global (AI) technology development county. However, China will need to focus on building its innovation capacity. For example, United States and United Kingdom are currently producing more influential (AI) technological research. However, if China planed to achieve (AI) technology success, it's traditional industries will need to develop technical know-how –to and overcoming implementation costs prepare to develop (AI) . When (AI) technology is introduced into China society, China government needs to raise concerning ethical, legal, technological security etc. business questions. Also, surrounding issues include privacy, discrimination, legal liability and regulation. It aims to encourage overseas investors to choose to invest (AI) technological industry to raise GDP growth and manufacturing industries income growth for long term in China. If China encouraged overseas (AI) technology investment in its country. It is possible to influence China employment market to be changed. Because (AI) technology will impact to influence China people daily life. Due to (AI) technology is introduced to China society, many rich people will prefer to spend to buy any high (AI) technological products for entertainment or learning or machine man driving etc. daily necessity activities. Then it will raise GDP growth and will raise (AI) manufacturers or related-(AI) technological manufacturers profit. It is beneficial to China because it can become one high knowledgeable and (AI) technological economical society. But it will bring bad influences to raise unemployment chance for the low skillful labor. In labor economy aspect influence , how (AI) technology can influence China low skillful labor unemployment ratio raising. The raising low skill labor unemployment reason is because China low skillful human labors are argued or are replaced by (AI) technology creating new challenges to introduce to influence China society of simply human manufacturing job nature to be changed to be high (AI) technology manufacturing job nature in any China factories. Moreover, when (AI) technology introduction to China, it will cause other related social challenges in China. The varied (AI) related challenges, including the difficulty of creating safe and reliable hardware for sensing and affecting (transportation and education), the challenges of gaining public trust, a low resource comities and public safety and security, the challenges of overcoming fears or marginalizing humans in China employment and workplace and the risk of diminishing interpersonal trust because the low skillful labors won't believe any China employers will give chance to employ them , due to (AI) technology will replace their skills and man manufacturing of productivity is much less to compare to (AI) technology manufacturing method.

Are future nature of jobs changed to computerization from (AI) technology? Where are the probability of computing occupations from (AI) technology influence? What is expected impacts of future computing on labor market from (AI) technology influence? John Maynard Keynes's frequently cited prediction of widespread technological unemployment " du to our discovery of means of economic the use of labor outrunning the pace of which we can find new used of labor" (Keynes, 1933, p.3).

In the future, (AI) technology will impact some nature of occupations to change computing. This chance will also influence some countries' economic change. For example, some factory human labors hand routine manufacturing tasks will be changed to computerization of routine manufacturing tasks by (AI) technological machine men hand manufacturing method. it will cause a structured shift in the labor market, with workers reallocating their labor supply from middle-income manufacturing to low-income service occupations.

Arguably, this is because the manual tasks of service occupations are less computerization, as who require a higher degree of flexibility and physical adaptability. So, (AI) technology will influence the human hand labor skillful occupation nature of task cheaper , such as vehicle manufacturing , ship manufacturing, computer manufacturing, steel manufacturing, television, radio etc. home electronic products of heavy machine industry change. Due to (AI) technology machine man will be proper to be used to manufacturing these electronic products when the (AI) technology innovation can develop to the mature stage. Then, any countries manufacturers will choose to use (AI) technology machine man, instead of human hand production.

Supposing the future prices of computing are fallen, seriously, problem solving skills are becoming relatively productive, explaining the substantial employment growth in manufacturing occupations, involving cognitive tasks where skilled labor has a comparative advantage, as well as the increase education needs for (AI) technology computing of machine man subject study.

Prediction of education needs for (AI) technology student numbers will increase, due to manufacturing industry needs many (AI) technology students in future employment market. Another (AI) technology influence if the future (AI) technological innovation, e.g. machine man manufacturing or machine man service industries will both increase demand, then with more sophistic software technologies will be disrupted labor markets by marketing workers redundant.

For publishing industry, what is striking about the case in paper book publishing industry will be unpopular? Due to the electronic book publishing industry will be popular, e.g. Amazon publish . (AI) technology can influence paper book manufacturing method which is replaced by machine man electronic book manufacturing method as well as it will cause the computerization is no longer confined to routine manufacturing tasks. Due to (AI) machine man manufacturing technology will be proper to be used to manufacture any products in short time efficiently and effectively , e.g. electronic book products. In the future, if it is fact to occur this case, such as (AI) technological machine man manufacturing method will be adopted (applied) to manufacture electronic books or any products in possible. (AI) technology will cause many manufacturing workers are unemployed. It is beneficial to employers, who can reduce to spend much wages expenditure to employ manufacturing workers, but it will cause many manufacturing workers loss jobs and reduce income to support whose families lives. It will cause social challenges, e.g. increasing stealing crimes if the manufacturing workers had not other skills to find other jobs to do easily. So, manufacturers need to concern over technological unemployment which will be hardly future phenomenon if who decided to dismiss all manufacturing workers, due to (AI) technology machine men replace to them.

If (AI) technology can be innovated to produce any kinds of machine man to serve any service or manufacturing industries successfully. Then, it will bring these questions: Can future that workers be influenced to be automation employment and productivity by (AI) technology influence? Does it impact to influence the (AI) technology countries' productivity and growth and natural resources development and labor markets and evolution of global financial markets and economic impact of technology and innovation and urbanization etc. issues? How will automation transform the workplace? What will be the implication for employment? What is likely to be its impact both on productivity in the global economy and on employment?

In fact, automatic of activities can enable businesses to improve performance by reducing errors chance and improving quality and speed, and same cases achieving outcomes that go beyond human capabilities. Some economists indicate (AI) technology would give a needed boost to economic growth and prosperity have of the working age population in many countries. Based on the scenario modeling, they estimate automation could raise productivity growth globally by 0.8 to 1.4 % annually. They also indicated that almost half the activities people are almost $1.6 trillion in wages to do in the global economy have the potential to be automated adapting current demonstrates technology, according to their analysis of more than 2,000 work activities across 800 occupations. When less than 5% of all occupations can be automated entirely using demonstrated technology, about 60% of all occupations have at least 30% of worker made activities, that would be automated. More occupation will change to be automated. They also indicated for business performance benefits of automation are relatively clear, but the issues are more complicated by policy making to attract foreign investors. Beyond technical feasibility, the cost of technology, competition labor will include skills and supply and demand dynamics, performance benefits and beyond labor cost savings and social and regulatory acceptance will affect the automation. Their predictions suggest that half of today work activities could be automated by

2055 year, but this could happen 10 to 20 years earlier or latter depending on the various factors in addition to their wider economic condition.
Some scientists suggest (AI) technology is finally starting to deliver real-life business benefits. Computer power is growing significantly , algorithms are becoming more sophisticated and perhaps most important of all, the world is generating vast quantities of the fuel that powers (AI) technology data billions of gigabytes of it every day. Also, online firms are digital natives, such as Google online search service company is investing on (AI) technology. For new though most of the news if coming from the suppliers of (AI) technologies. And many new users are only in the experimental phase. Few products are on the market or are likely to arrive these soon to drive immediate and widespread adoption. As a result, analysts believe (AI) technology's potential will give true economic benefit in the future. (AI) industry will introduce to suppliers and users to raise economic potential of (AI) technology.
In the future, (AI) technology systems can solve business problems. Some scientists categorized those into five technology systems that are key areas of (AI) technology development: robotics and autonomous vehicles, computer vision language virtual agents and machine learning , which is based on algorithms that learn from data without replying on rules-based programming in order to draw conclusions or direct an action.
Such as computer vision and language includes natural language processing, analytics, speech recognition technology, some are about learning from information, such as about machine learning and others are related to acting on information, such as robotics, autonomous vehicles and virtual agents, which are computer programs that can converse with humans. Machine learning and a subfield called deep learning are artificial intelligence applications.

Can AI excite online leisure industry development?
Artificial intelligence (AI) is a term first defined in 1956 year. It is a branch of computer science that aims to create intelligent machines that work and react like humans. In contrast today, 60 years later, (AI) is characterized by a number of applications, including computers playing games against humans and understanding human languages, virtual personal assistants, and robotics which involve computers seeing , hearing and reacting to sensory stimuli. In the future, technologists predict for (AI) technology ranging from (AI) being used as a tool to aid relatively simple processes

for robots with human like mental capabilities, who expect (AI) technology can emulate human performance by learning, coming to mind its own conclusions, understanding complex content, engaging in dialog with people, enhancing human cognitive performance or replacing humans in executing both routine and non-routine tasks. In existing industry, (AI) technology is used , such as targeted advertising and virtual used personal assistant as well as the (AI) technology that my exist in the future, such as robots with human vehicle processing capabilities.

The range of (AI) technology's progress in the future will determine the economic impact future of (AI) technology on the global economy with more limited advances and applications (i.e. weak (AI) only) corresponding to more limited economic impacts and more substantial progress, i.e. strong (AI) technology is corresponding to more significant economic impact.

(AI) technology learning that automates analytical model, including predicting cause-and-effect relationship from biological data, identifying new drugs, self-driving cars and protecting against fraud etc. functions. Also (AI) learning can improve natural language processing that allows computers to continue to better analyze, understand and generate language to interface with human using the natural human language, virtual personal assistant, helps users by providing scheduling appointment, reminds organizing personal finance and finding providers of various services, machine vision allows (AI) machine man to identify object, scenes and activities in detect pedestrians and bicyclists.

We expect the economic effects of (AI) technology to include both direct GDP growth from sectors that develop or manufacture (AI) technology and indirect GDP growth through increased productivity in existing sectors that employ some from of (AI) technology. If (AI) producing sectors could grow, then it could lead to increase revenues and employment of (AI) technological professionals within these existing firms as well as the potential creation of entirely new economic activities to any countries' societies productivity improvement in existing sectors could be realized through faster and move efficient processes and decision making as well as increased (AI) technological knowledge and access to information available in societies easily.

In the future, if (AI) technology is an increasingly critical component of more products, it will become an integral part of necessary products of many people's lives. The extent of (AI)'s economy effort is also likely to vary from region to region, thought variation may be more dependent on the predominate economic activity of a region and the (AI) ability can influence economic activity, rather then the economic or developmental status of the regions. (AI) technology can move accessibility and can use source development to do international business between one country and another country.

So (AI) technology has the potential to give benefits to different income chooses and to bring significant gains to both developed and developing countries. For agricultural technology, (AI) has the potential to optimize food production around the world by analyzing agricultural regions and identifying what is necessary to improve crop yield. In total, (AI) technology gives greater economic impact to any countries agricultural regions if which implemented (AI) technology to grow crop , fruit etc. food production in the farms.

Investment in (AI) technology is such as capital investment to any countries' public or private enterprises. So, it will have large economic impact to the future . If the (AI) technology is reasonable invested to the different needs aspect by the public or private enterprises in the country. Then, it will have good economic impact to the country in the future. However, when (AI) technology is likely to affect both the productivity and employment components of economic growth in many sectors. Significant public debate has focused on projections of (AI)'s effect on the labor force. However, for instance, some researchers have argued that the rise of (AI) technology and automation will led to significant unemployment as capital is substituted for the low skillful labor. So, they point to the concern that the increasing sophistication of (AI) technology may balance skilled and semi-skilled workers and the reduce the size of the middle class. However, this is not a new argument, due to (AI) technology negatively affecting the labor force and leading to mass unemployment. Because the (AI) technology is the substitution of machinery for human labor. Although, employment in certain industries, has been reduced in the past due to technological advancement. For long term, the labor market has adapted to the introduction of new technology, giving rise to new jobs in new areas. (AI) technology may also be accomplished without a reduction to total employment in the long-term to some Asia countries, such as Hong Kong and Japan. Because Hong Kong and Japan many low skilled labor, e.g. security, cleaner who complaint that employers need them to work long time hours. (abnormal working hours) e.g. one day 12 to 15 working hour per day. Hence, if (AI) machine means invention technology success. Security or cleaning job can be worked from (AI) machine man in some hours every day in order to reduce the long time working hours cleaners or security workers, e.g. one (AI) machine man works 4 hours for cleaning or security job, one day as well as another cleaner or security labor only needs to work 8 hours one day. So total security or cleaning employers can employ 12 hours machine cleaners or security workers and human cleaners or security workers in one day. For long term benefit, Hong Kong or Japan every security or cleaning worker does not need to work 12 hours minimum working hours one day. They won't feel tried and bore and without private with whose families, so who will accept to do these cleaning or security jobs, even they can raise work efficient and performance when who feel happy and health.

So, (AI) technology of machine man invention can raise low skillful labor efficiency and it can help them to avoid abnormal working hours demand in some busy work life countries, such as Hong Kong and Japan. Before, one Japan female labor feel unhappy to work, due to who often needs to work abnormal working hours for her employer and who has less sleeping and without any private time to enjoy her life with her families every day. So this abnormal working hours factor causes her to do commit suicide behavior, then she is die unlucky. So (AI) technology of machine man invention ought avoid abnormal working hours demand for employer in any countries in the future.

The most important occurrence to any employers, some researchers had attempted to do one experiment to find that private research and development , venture capital and public research and development investment all have strong net effect or economic growth with venture capital funding further having the strongest such effect from (AI) technology. The researchers hypothesize the venture capital investment contributes to economic growth through (AI) technology innovation and by the capacity of an economy to use existing (AI) technology knowledge to increase productivity. They predict the impacts of venture capital, business-research and development and public research and development can raise multi factor productivity from (AI) technology introduction.

Can (AI) technology influence the economic development to developing countries? The developing regions of the world contain most of natural resources. If one day, (AI) technology has invent one kind of machine man which can assist any gas or oil workers to seek any new oil/gas natural resource locations easily. I believe that (AI) technology can help these natural resource exploitation countries will gain economic benefit more easily. So, (AI) driven technology can be used to change to create any new opportunities to address poor management or resources and improve human well being, such as Africa Latin America and India can use (AI) technology machine man to seek any oil/gas natural resource countries exploitation activities to attempt to gain much economic benefits.

- Why will (AI) technology grow economic development ?

Nowadays, increases in capital and labor are no longer driving the levels of economic growth, such as (AI) technology. The ability of increase in capital investment and in labor of traditional drivers of production, have no longer to be enjoyed in most developed economies ,e.g. developed country, US, UK . However, artificial intelligence has the potential to overcome the physical limitation of capital and labor to avoid missing out on this opportunity. So, policy makers and business leaders must prepare for and work toward a future with artificial intelligence. They must do with the idea that (AI) is another simply method to enhance productivity method . Rather they must see (AI) as the tool that can transform thinking about how growth is created.

Economists have always thought of new technologies are as driving growth their ability to enhancing. It can replace labor and capital factor of production. So, it brings this question: What is the factor of production (AI) technology characteristics. They key factor is to see (AI) technology as a capital-labor .

(AI) can replicate labor activities at much greater scale and speed, and to even perform some tasks began the capabilities of human. For example, by using virtual assistants , 1000 legal documents can be reviewed in a matter of days instead of taking three people six moths to complete. Some (AI) technology may be one kind of factor of production in the future. For another example, people will work in workplace digitalization environment. So, in the future, working environment and information management are automated. Such as Konica camera sale company will use workplace digitalization. So , (AI) technology can provide workplace digitalization in order to raise productivity efficiency. (AI) technology will be one kind of production which is replaced by workplace digitalization and it will grow any organization productivity efficiently. Then, (AI) technology will assist overall social economy growth , due to productivity is raised and products can be produced in short time to prepare to sell in consumption market. So, time will be shortened to increase GDP growth fast for the development of (AI) technology countries.

● How can (AI) technology impact to global economic and social and psychological changes?

What will be the development of (AI) technology and predictions concerning the future evolution? The computers and robots will develop conscious, intelligent and minds into humans, enhancing psychological and behavioral abilities and allowing for direct communication with (AI) minds. (AI) technology will be impacted human life by (AI) technology information communicative and environmental influence. A " world brain" and " world mind", this psychological system will be enhanced and enriched the capacities of both individual and collective cognition by (AI) technology of service industries.

(AI) technology with influence these human needs of service industries changes, such as , biological science, finance, entertainment, business, biological science, transportation, communication military etc. The personal computer evolution, the internet and the world wide web which exploded on the scene, linking business, homes, schools, social organizations which were a completely unpredicted phenomenon to influence human life. Kurzweil (1999) predicts that by 2029 year, most human communication will be with machines. According to Person, by 2100 year, there will be human machine convergence.

How can (AI) technology influence environmental protection to make benefits to farming economic growth? (AI) technology can be applied to predict how to solve environmental pollution challenge to avoid to damage any crop or vegetable or rice or fruit etc. food growth. Because environmental experts can gather global environmental pollution data from an environmental database to build a perform a systematic analysis from (AI) technology. The first step is this broad analysis can include understanding, statistical and data gathering techniques to obtain the relevant data, the correlation among the variables involved, and a list of possible models. The next step is to select a set of methods and models that cover all kinds of knowledge and functionalities needed for the decision making process. Once the models are selected, they must be fully implemented by means of machine learning , data mining, statistical or numerical technique. After that, those models must be integrated to build the whole EDSS. The EDSS must be tested to check its performance, accuracy, usefulness and reliability, both from the user's and (AI) technology/computer scientist's point of view. If these is any wrong feature in any development stage, such as model's integration, models' implementation, selection of models, database, problem analysis etc. the developers must come back in the update th required components. When the evaluation phase is all right, the EDSS is ready to be applied to the environment. The great contribution of artificial intelligence to EDSS the integration of several methods complementing the classical statistical models/simulation , statistical analysis, linear models, etc. and numerical models (control algorithms, optimization techniques etc.) .

This cooperation makes the resulting systems more reliable and powerful in coping with real world environment systems. Date interpretation has been a principal area of research in (AI) technology since the very beginning. The most demanding problem in the environmental assessment context. Knowledge representation permits the definition of the different types of data that the existing methods adapt to the process. There is also a lot of work to clean, repair and transform the huge available quantities of raw data. Apart from this, the availability of meta-information or background knowledge is required to guide the process. Data mining is multi-disciplinary: It covers expert systems, data based technology, statistics, data visualization and unsupervised machine learning. These techniques operate at the level of data and background information, where numerous and often incompatible new commensurate pieces of information from disparate sources have to be brought together (K, Fedra, 1994).

So, it seems that in the future, (AI) technology with the increasing maturity in particular those related to knowledge and engineering, new dimensions can be assisted to users in environmental decision making are available. For example, many environmental systems are characterized both by incomplete models and by limited data. Hence, in the future, (AI) technology will be applied to predict climate change to reduce crop or fruit etc. food agriculture challenge by climate change bad influence.

- Will (AI) technology influence new kinds of leisure industry development ?

To understand how the manufacturing business must adapt to prosper in the technology, we need to understand how (AI) technology will change us to shape our daily habits to satisfy our expectation of products to how we shop and even the immediate of the entire process. For example, taxi services are in the crosshairs as on demand transportation services like, available of the touch of a smart phone button expand. In fact, Yellow lab, US country , san Francisco city's largest taxi company is filing for bankruptcy as the industry starts to change faster than almost anyone expected. However, at this point, its more than an app that is changing, some our taxi passengers renting taxi transportation to catch consumption behavior.

(AI) technology will influence digital economy for taxi passenger's individual customer experience, offering a growing renting taxi to catch of service and feedback opportunities when any one taxi passenger who chooses to use mobile phone app online tool to prepaid to rent any taxi more easily.

Also in the long term, (AI) technology can influence vehicles drive themselves of behavior. Already, companies like Google and GM are working on projects to bring fleets of autonomous vehicles to cities at the path of a button.

Moreover, this on-demand service model is beginning to appear across a much broader range of markets. For example , Amazon company is investing in its own fleet of trucks, planes and even drone at the same time as it pushes for same-day delivery of products. As some point, vehicles will be autonomous too. So, it seems that (AI) technique will influence any transportations choose to use digital autonomous driving technology in the future . For Amazon company case, it is not stopping of logistics. It is also aiming to automatically manage the supply of consumer home products with its recently launched Amazon replenishment service, Dash. Dash is a digital service that enables that connected derive to automatically order physical products from Amazon when supplies are running low. So, it seems (AI) technology will be applied to logistic function by digital technology method introduction in the future.

Hence autonomous vehicles will optimize industry supply chains and logistics operations through increased efficiency and flexibility. In fact, fully automated and lean supply chains will keep reduce load sizes and inventory by leveraging smart distribution technologies and smaller autonomous vehicles by machine man assistance. If Amazon continues to grow market share for online sales by reducing effort required by the consumer to place an order, when also contributing the almost immediate

delivery of products to the doorstep. So, it will further fuel the trend toward on-demand derive. As Amazon company fuels the on-demand economy, consumers will expect immediacy in more parts of the digital economy. On top of speed, consumers increasing expect more personalization options.
So, (AI) technology will influence digital manufacturing, such as Amazon publishing to monitor every aspect of every process in real -time and communicating to self-optimized deep learning robotics, new methods of high volume and high customization will become possible. Then, as products merge into product platforms and even services, manufacturers have the opportunity to provide components and platforms used by smaller players. So, (AI) technology will influence manufacturing industry to choose automated SMI lines, robots installed, automation engineers.

Another future (AI) technology development can be applied to space science aspect, such as Automation engineering space in manufacturing process to achieve digital manufacturing benefits to any businesses in the future. Such as reducing cost, shortening manufacturing time, raising efficiency, shortening delivery products to client individual time. How can artificial intelligence give the need and advanced fast and evaluation methods benefits for space exploration? When US NASA (space exploration organization) achieves any space exploration missions, it will answer this question:
When is it useful to have a machine use (AI) technology to achieve a decision? After all, after millions of years of space exploration and rough 10,000 years of civilization, humans are usually quite good at making decisions in complex uncertain environments. Through, Johns Hoplains University's Applied Physical Lab. Research in (AI) technology enabled systems, which has identified three general use cases for (AI) technology to explore space mission:
First, for some tasks (AI) technology is more cost effectiveness than human. Second, (AI) technology is better suited than humans at solving some, but not all problems. Third, (AI) technology allows NASA organization's space exploration mission to develop machines that ate capable of responding faster than when a human is in the decision loop (D. Scheidt, 2012, A. Castano et. al. 2008).

So, the use of (AI) technology to enable science by observing the pace of rapidly evolving phenomena was demonstrated. It is more effectively coordinating and (AI) technology utilizing to earn economic benefits to use for space exploration mission.

However, (AI) technology also have current risk for space exploration. Today (AI) technology is immature and requires further development to reach its potential. For instance, the (AI) technology algorithms that detected the dust derive could not have identified whether the Martain weather represented a threat to the cover. Also it can not yet use instrument input to determine what, where and how to autonomously make the next space science measurement. An equally important factor limiting (AI)'s deployment is that lacks the methodology and technology to effectively test (AI) technology. So, the challenge will testing (AI) enabled system is how (AI) performance can be measured. It would be NASA organization's difficulty to find (AI) technology to develop to carry on researching any space exploration missions in the future. However, (AI) technology will be a good economic benefit choice for space exploration mission in the future.

- What is artificial intelligence potential
benefits and ethical considerations?

The ability of (AI) technology systems to transform vast amounts of complex information into insight has the potential to help solve manufacturing or service challenges for human needs. However, to reap the societal benefits of (AI) systems, humans will need to trust then and make sure that which follow the same ethical principles, moral values, professional codes and social norms that we humans would follow in the same scenario, research and educational efforts as well as carefully designed regulation in order to achieve the most effort of economic benefits goals. For example, international business machines corporation (IBM) is actively engaged both competitors , in global discussions about how to make (AI) ethical and as beneficial as possible for people as social economic benefits.
(AI) is usually defined as the " capability of a computer program to perform tasks or reasoning processes " that human usually associate to intelligence in a human being. Often, it has to do with the ability to make a good decision, even when there is uncertainty, too much information to handle. As an example, play chess or complex card games of entertainment activities is believed to need some form of intelligence in a human being, as well as choosing the best medical facilities in a difficult medical case, or creating something new, such as mathematical theorem or even some form of act, or even driving automatic machine man (self driving vehicle) replacing human driving in the middle of a crowded city.
(AI) needs depends on what we consider being intelligence in the behavior of a human being act a certain point in time. If human belief about human

intelligence changes and we don't believe any longer that a certain task requires intelligence, then a computer program performing that task is no longer part of (AI), it becomes just another boring computer program. So, it means that (AI) technology will replace some old computer programs, if human can invent new generation of (AI) software for any functions or activities to satisfy human needs.

As IBM, it argues intelligence. This means that we aim to build systems that enhance and scale human expertise and skills rather than replacing them. We therefore focus on practical applications of (AI) capabilities that assist people in performing well-defined tasks of needs by exploiting and wide range of (AI)-based services. We also use the term " cognitive computing" it is mean a comprehensive net of capabilities based on technology. It comprises the fields of machine learning, reasoning and decision technologies, language, speech and vision recognition and processing technologies, high performance and high efficient functions for any industries or individual consumers needs. For example, robotics, which are usually very good at doing what which are supposed to in any environment, much have public shopping center, factory etc. places which need simply services from the robot (machine man), such as cleans the floor of our houses to the robot that can work together with humans in production chains, passing through the warehouse, robots can take care of the tasks of an entire warehouse and the companion robots like Nao, Pepper, Aibo and Giraff, who can entertain use, talk to use and help elderly people to stay connected to their friends, relatives and doctors.

Google company is building automatic machine (self-driving cars) and has acquired more than 10 robotics companies. Facebook had opened whole new research facility only on (AI) research. Apply computer has developed Siri. Microsoft computer company has built a similar personalized assistant. Google has Deep mind, a UK company whose long term aim is to build general (AI) and has already great potential to win game to the world champion and IBM is investing a huge amount of resources in applying its Watson cognitive computing system to the medical domains to finance and to personalized education. In Europe, IBM is establishing new centers in Munich and Milan focused in the application of cognitive computer capabilities to the internet of things and healthcare respectively.

For example, automatic machine man (self-driving cars) are all about (AI), which used to be able to see what happens in the street (signals ,lanes, other cars, pedestrians, traffic lights, which need to able predict what other cars and pedestrians will do, and who need to be able to cope with unforeseen situations. Since, most car accidents are due to human fault, it is estimated that the adoption of self-driving cars will save about half of the lives that are usually last in car accidents.

IBM Watson company has to understand spoken language, make sense of massive amount to text , respond correctly to questions in many categories, as well as assess its own confidence in responding to such questions. In the future, (AI) technology can own question/answering capabilities that would be very useful, for example, in assisting a doctor when trying to some to the correct diagnosis for a patient and to propose the best therapy .

Intelligent machines can also rely on huge amounts of data to be used to learn how to make better decisions. This data comes from all of us over the years Facebook users have uploaded more than 250 billion pictures and every day who upload about 350 million more. Every second, we submit 40,000 google search queries. So, (AI) technology will be connected through the web from appliances to traffic lights from cars to watches. Other tasks that are very easy for humans are physical and manipulation tasks, such as walking , running, picking up an object to make its shape and location, restricted environment. But (AI) machine man technology still not able to have the general physical and manipulation capabilities even of a 6 year old.

So, it brings this question: Why do (AI) scientists need to concern ethics? Because (AI) technology is complex, information into insight has the potential to reveal long held secrets and help solve some of the world's most difficult problems. (AI) systems can potentially be used to help discover insights to treat disease, predict the whether, and manage the global economy. So, ethic issues is important to and (AI) scientists . If any one new (AI) technology research investigation could success, it will be a secret to and the (AI) scientists can not permit to their loyalty to any competitors to damage the fair (AI) technology products trading market. The country (countries) (AI) technology scientists need to concern ethic issues, who need to keep secrets for their countries economic or/and social benefits. This is moral issues to any countries/country loyalty is whose countries intangible assets. They can not sell (AI) loyalty to any their countries to assist whose economic benefits immorally.

- How can (AI) technology influence to global
health care economy development?

According to (AI) lecturer analysis, when combined key clinical health

(AI) application can potentially create $150 billion in annual savings for the US healthcare economy by 2026 year. (AI) technology is re-winning modern conception of healthcare delivery. It enables machines to sense, comprehend, act and learn. So which can perform administrative and clinical healthcare functions (Accenture, 2017).

It will help health care service organizations to reduce health care cost, will improve and raise service quality and access. So, (AI) health market size will be predicted growth. (AI) applications in health care include robot-assisted surgery, virtual nursing assistant, administrative workflow assistant, fraud detection, error reduction connected machines, clinical trial participant identifier, preliminary diagnosis, automated image diagnosis and cybersecurity.

What kind of benefits (AI) technology can contribute to healthcare service? (AI) technology can deliver what many health care organizations need, such as financial and operational of labor costs, digital expectations from patient consumers how to use (AI) technology to solve interoperability challenges in any healthcare organizations. Also (AI) technology can be applied to wellness an d lifestyle management, diagnostics, delivers financially but also way of organizational and workflow improvement. So, (AI) technology will be continue to become most prevalent and adoption to healthcare organizations , which must need to enhance structure to be position to take full advantages of new (AI) technological capabilities. (AI) technology can change the nature of work and employment is rapidly changing to make the best use of both humans and (AI) talent in healthcare industry in the future. For example, (AI) technology offers a way to fill in gaps and the rising labor shortage in healthcare. According to Accenture analysis, the physicians shortage is increasing. However, (AI) technology will manufacture healthcare machine men to replace physicians in future one day(2017). Hence, (AI) technology will be invented to raise health care service staffs work efficiency and performance in any hospitals or clinics in the future.

In conclusion, (AI) technology will raise efficiency for any service or manufacturing industries in the future, although, it is possible that it will also rise low skillful workers unemployment numbers. But, the most important influence to human technological innovation will be risen and it will influence human life will be changed to be better, e.g. self drive cars, health care physician machine men, machine man cleaners etc. intelligent machine men will be manufactured to serve for our daily life. Furthermore,

(AI) technological products will influence countries trading, some low technological development countries manufacturing businessmen can choose to buy any (AI) products to raise whose productivity and efficiency and reducing cost to achieve economic cost saving result. Also, GDP of trading growth income will increase to the (AI) products sale countries. Hence, it will be beneficial to economic development to both developed and developing countries both in the future as well as (AI) scientists time and money spending will be valued to continue to invest (AI) technology development for human life and economy benefits for long term.

In conclusion (AI) technology will raise macro economy growth and it can create many (AI) jobs , but it also raise the low level technological worker unemployment change. In the future, (AI) technology can be applied to digital technology to attempt to invent any new undiscovered (AI) and digital technology. So, it needs any scientists to continue to research how digital and (AI) technology can be mixed to satisfy human's future undiscovered needs.

Must Developed And Developing Countries Need Artificial Intelligent To Replace Human Job

Must developed and developing countries need artificial intelligent development? If one developed country, e.g. US, UK , Japan , Singapore it does not continue to develop artificial intelligence, robotic, then what disadvantges or weaknesses , it will encounter to compare when it chooses to continue to develop this artificial intelligent technology in society. If one developing country, e.g. China, Korea, Taiwan, it does not continue to develop artificial intelligence, robotic, then what disadantages or weaknesses, it will also encounter to compare when it chooses to continue to develop this artificial intelligent technology in in society. I shall explan the reasons why the results may cause to either the developed country, or the developing country as below:

● How AI help developing countries to communication and agriculture and learning and medical delivery development

Why can AI help developing countries ? Drones that pick inaccessible crops and mobile phones that give medical advice are two of the ways AI can transform life in the developing world. Artificial intelligence (AI) may improve the lives of the world's poor, the technology needed to revolutionise inefficient, ineffective food and healthcare systems in developing countries is well. For example, in low-income areas, agriculture and healthcare are two critical ecosystems that we can apply AI to immediately; this is not the far future, or even in five years.

Artificial intelligence (AI) has seeped into the daily lives of people in the developed world. From virtual assistants to recommendation engines, AI is in the news, our homes and offices. There is a lot of potential in terms of AI usage, especially in humanitarian areas. The impact could have a multiplier effect in developing countries, where resources are limited.

Emergency Response to developing countries' earthquake natural damage suddence occurrence predicting

AI and machine learning are still finding importance in emerging markets, but certain applications have emerged and are now widely used. For instance, predictive models for disaster relief enable first responders to automatically analyze large-scale behavior and movement through multiple sources of data including social media platforms, web forums, news sources, etc. Based on collected data, responders can scale reconstruction efforts and distribute supplies in a timely manner.

Why and how AI can assist farmers to predict when the earthquake occurs suddenly in order to avoid or reduce the natural damage to their agriculture productive number loss. For example, In 2015, when a major earthquake hit Nepal, more than 8 million people were affected. During the aftermath, drones were used to map and assess the destruction and speed up the rescue mission. The town of Sankhu, situated about 20 kilometers northeast of Kathmandu, was among the highly affected locations. In May 2018, my company Fusemachines and GeoSpatial Systems partnered with Sankhu's city officials to use drones and artificial intelligence in an effort to automatically estimate the reconstruction need. After processing data accumulated from a drone-powered aerial mapping of the region, the team fed this data to advanced machine learning algorithms. Combining drone imagery, digital mapping and machine learning, the team configured region modeling and infrastructure development with higher accuracy. Another organization known as One Concern, a California-based startup, has created a predictive AI program called Seismic Concern to accurately predict seism and is also working on solutions for wildfires, floods and hurricanes.

Smart AI Agriculture

Another application of AI in developing countries is smart agriculture. Farmers monitor crops more effectively and make better predictions on planting, weeding and harvesting using AI tools. It can also be used to analyze one plant at a time and add pesticides only to infected plants and trees instead of spraying pesticides across large swaths of crops. One California-based tech company is an example of this use of AI. So, the developing countries farmers in rural parts of India are also using AI to increase yields through better access to information about the farming season than they would normally have. Technology-enabled process automation offers the agribusiness industry the chance for remarkable growth -- not only in developed countries but around the world. There's a unique opportunity to increase yields, cut down labor costs and improve people's health.

Medicine Delivery to developing countries‘ patients urgent need

Companies are also leveraging AI to improve access to health care in some of the most remote areas of the world. In Rwanda, for example, Zipline is using drones to deliver medical supplies and blood to hospitals and clinics that are difficult to access by car. This has dramatically impacted people living in remote parts of the country because they are able to get medical help when needed. The drone system in Rwanda has also helped reduce waste of blood by 95%, as noted by Zipline. One Concern has created an AI program called Seismic Concern that accurately predicts seismic events and is also working on solutions for floods, wildfires and hurricanes. The medical field may actually benefit the most from emerging technologies in developing countries.

Assistance to reduce teaching work workload or psychological pressure to teachers in developing countries' schools

Another vital area benefiting from innovative technologies like AI is education. Advanced technologies can enhance how we learn, teach and perform tasks. In most developing countries, schools lack experienced teachers and resources to enhance students' knowledge. As a result, many students still have to walk long distances to get to the nearest school, which has created education gaps, especially in rural areas. AI tools such as personalized learning assistants can simplify learning by making tutoring services and learning materials accessible to all students, wherever they are. Machines can be automated to help students learn basic concepts without a tutor, which companies like Carnegie Learning are working on. This would allow students to learn at any time from anywhere. With AI, education is made easy and accessible to more people.

The initial usage of AI in developing countries has been at a micro level -- solving small, specific problems in a defined industry. As machine learning advances and there is a higher utilization of AI, we will see more complex issues being targeted and resolved. When duly adopted, AI can positively impact future developing countries people everyday lives not just in disaster intervention, education, health care and agriculture but can also help in mitigating poverty, malnutrition and pollution. Especially, in developing nations, to leverage AI's true potential and create a snowball effect. Startups are defining a holistic and humanitarian approach to building more sophisticated, AI-ready societies. Stakeholders in the AI landscape should understand the strengths and nuances of the developing world as well as the limitations of AI and create localized solutions and applications.

Why does smart phone help developing countries communication ?
Internet Seen as Positive Influence on Education but Negative on Morality in Emerging and Developing Nations. Internet access differs substantially across the 32 emerging and developing countries polled, with the lowest rates of internet use in South Asian and sub-Saharan African nations. Within countries, computer owners, young people, the well-educated, the wealthy and those with English language ability are much more likely to access the internet than their counterparts. To access the internet, people increasingly use smartphones rather than more cumbersome fixed landline connections and computers. Around the world, both smartphones and basic-feature phones alike are used for sending messages and taking pictures.

In fact, many developing countries young people, students are popular to use smart phones for internet usage aim, instead of communication. Moreover, many developing countries working people are also popular to use smart phones for any working usage in their working time , even non working time any time. So, smart phones (AI) phones will be important communication or leisure tools to developing countries people in the future. Unless, it is one day, scientists can develop another new communication tool to replace smart phones. So, artificial intelligence will be important to influence developing countries people , how to improve or bring positive learning attitudes to students in their daily learnnng lifes. as well as how to raise developing countries people, how to raise working people efficiency or improve performace in their daily working lifes. So, AI may bring positive learning or working attitudes to developing countries working people and students both.

The Positive Impact of Mass Media in Developing Countries
Radio, newspapers, television, Internet, social media, etc., all of these are

forms of mass media. Each of these outlets has the capability of bringing information to thousands of people with one device. While in some communities it is easy to take advantage of these communication outlets such as television and Internet access, not everyone has access to such outlets. Radio is one of the most common forms of mass media in developing countries because it's affordable and uses less electricity than many other forms of mass media, but only approximately 75 percent of people in developing countries have access to a radio, and roughly 77 percent of people in rural areas have access to electricity.

For developing countries that have implemented forms of mass media in their communities, there have been numerous positive outcomes are influenced to impact developing countries mass media by artificial intelligence as below:

When AI is participated to developing countries mass media, it can influence any radio, television audiences raise more attention to each other through social media platforms such as Facebook and Twitter and create, organize and initiate street protests and campaigns. Furthermore, having access to social media in developing countries, people are able to connect to those that they usually wouldn't have the chance to talk to. Moreover, AI Provides educational opportunities- In many countries, the division between local and national languages as well as issues of literacy can make communication difficult. With the use of mass media, a bridge can be built between these two gaps. In India, there is a radio station that provides information in local languages and respects local culture and traditions. One of the main ways is to create public awareness of what is going on with businesses and government officials. The media plays an important role in giving people the opportunity to act against injustice, oppression and misdeeds that they otherwise wouldn't know about. Information on available healthcare, a mass radio broadcast was sent out encouraging parents to seek treatment at local healthcare facilities for their sick children. With this mass outreach on healthcare, the encouragement of people to take their children to healthcare facilities saved thousands of lives. This easy way of encouraging others and bringing awareness about certain diseases was made possible through a simple radio broadcast. Finally, when AI is particiapted to media, it may bring many social issues to life that otherwise would remain unknown to many people. In developing countries and communities like Burkina Faso, when the radio broadcast was released about malaria, diarrhea and pneumonia, people were educated and moved to action and knew to take their children to healthcare facilities for preventative care. As it is seen, having access to different media outlets is vital for those in developing countries. Here are three ways that those in developing countries can implement mass media to help their people and communities.

When AI is participated to any internet radio or internet newspaper mass online listening or reading channel. It can provide online radios or newspapers in public places- By providing online radios and newspapers in public areas it gives community members to access news, information and emergency warnings. Even though radios can be on the cheaper side, there are still many people that can't afford to have a radio in their home. By providing one in a local place, not only would it better educate the community members but also it will bring the community together. So, it can make media outlets a two-way platform- Creating a two-way platform between the community and those who are behind the radio stations, newspapers or broadcasts makes the community feel involved and that their voices are being heard. An organization called Soul City in sub-Saharan Africa is showing how well two-way platforms work by engaging their listeners and having them contribute thoughts and ideas about complex issues. Because developing countries radio listening audiences or newspaper readers are popular to accept computer online radio listening channel or online newspaper reading channel to replace traditional paper newspapers or radio machines. So, AI may raise their listening news or reading news leisure feeling from online mass media channel in the future.

In conclusion, when developed countries continue to develop AI, it may bring positive advantages to bring raising productivies, or efficiencies, but it may also raise unemployment ratio to any low skill or low knowledge jobs in ther societies. However, human future society will need to change to be better to raise our living standard. But AI is one kind the best choice tool to achieve this aim in our future, so I agree developed countries continue to develop or research AI to be the super -human machine.

Reference

A. Castano et. al. " Automatic detection of dust devils and clouds at Mars" Machine vision and applications, Oct. 2008, vol. 19, no 5-6, pp. 467-482.

Accenture, " Why artificial intelligence is the future of growth"(2017) <http://www.accenture.com/us-en/insight-a rtificial-intelligence-future-growth>.

D. Schedidt , Unmanned Air Vehicle Command And Control, Handbook Of Unmanned Air Vehicles, Springer-Verlag, 2014. Facebook (AI) Research Available at https://research.facebook.com/ai, research at google, machine intelligence available at http://research.google.com/pubs/machineintellige nce.html; micro soft research-machine learning and artificial intelligence available at http://research.microsoft.com/en-us/research- areas/machine-learning-ai.aspx.

International Federation Of Robotics, 2016. IFR press release world robotics report. IFR, org . 29 Sept. Accessed Feb. 01, 2017. http://www.ifr.org/news/ifr-press-release/world-robitics report -2016-8321.

K, Fedra , "GIS and environmental modelling" in environmental modelling with GIS, edited by M.F. Goodchild.B.O. Parks and L.T. Steyaert, Oxford University press, pp. 35-50, 1994.

Keynes, J.M. (1933). Economic possibilities for our grandchildren (1930). Essays in persuasion, pp.358-73.

Mckinsey & Company (2013, May). Disruptive technologies: Advices that will transform life, business and the global economy , USA.

Ministry of economy, trade and industry, Japan, 2015, Japan's robot strategy. Ministry of economy, trade and industry.

Ray Kurzweil , The age of spiritual machines (1999) is cited numerously through this chapter: Kurzweilai.net http://www.kurzweilai.net

Rich, Elaine & Knight, Kevin, Artificial Intelligence Second Edition, 1991, New York; Mc-Graw-Hill.

www.ingramcontent.com/pod-product-compliance
Ingram Content Group UK Ltd.
Pitfield, Milton Keynes, MK11 3LW, UK
UKHW022026190726
13853UKWH00005B/2126

9 798888 834978